THE ART OF
THE DATA
CENTER

THE ART OF THE DATA CENTER

DOUGLAS ALGER

Upper Saddle River, NJ • Boston • Indianapolis • San Francisco

New York • Toronto • Montreal • London • Munich • Paris • Madrid

Capetown • Sydney • Tokyo • Singapore • Mexico City

The publisher offers excellent discounts on this book when ordered in quantity for bulk purchases or special sales, which may include electronic versions and/or custom covers and content particular to your business, training goals, marketing focus, and branding interests. For more information, please contact:

U.S. Corporate and Government Sales
(800) 382-3419
corpsales@pearsontechgroup.com

For sales outside the United States, please contact:

International Sales
international@pearsoned.com

Visit us on the Web: informit.com/ph

Library of Congress Cataloging-in-Publication data is on file.

Images of the Data Centers of Affordable Internet Services Online (Chapter 2), Bahnhof (Chapter 3), Barcelona Computing Center (Chapter 4), Calcul Québec (Chapter 5), Digital Realty Trust (Chapter 8), eBay (Chapter 9), Green House Data (Chapter 11), Intel (Chapter 13), IO (Chapter 14), NetApp (Chapter 15), Syracuse University (Chapter 16), Terremark (Chapter 17) and Yahoo! (Chapter 18) provided courtesy of the respective organizations.

Image of boiler room piping and closeup image of server cabinets within ACT's Data Center (Chapter 1) are provided courtesy of KJWW Engineering Consultants. Other images provided courtesy of Neumann Monson Architects.

Image of the building exterior and image of the concrete areaway of Cisco's Data Center (Chapter 6) by Douglas Alger. Image of the rooftop solar panel array by Andy Broer. Other images provided courtesy of Cisco; photography by Cyclone Interactive.

Image of the building exterior of Citi's Data Center (Chapter 7) provided courtesy of Citi. Other images by Christian Richters Photography.

Images of Facebook's Data Center (Chapter 10) by Alan Brandt Photography.

Images of IBM's Data Center (Chapter 12) provided courtesy of IBM Corporation, all rights reserved.

ISBN-13: 978-1-58714-296-3
ISBN-10: 1587142961
Text printed in the United States on recycled paper at Courier in Westford, Massachusetts.
First printing September 2012

ASSOCIATE PUBLISHER
Dave Dusthimer

EXECUTIVE EDITOR
Mary Beth Ray

SENIOR DEVELOPMENT EDITOR
Christopher Cleveland

MANAGING EDITOR
Sandra Schroeder

PROJECT EDITOR
Seth Kerney

PROOFREADERS
Leslie Joseph
Kathy Ruiz

PUBLISHING COORDINATOR
Vanessa Evans

BOOK DESIGNER
Gary Adair

COMPOSITOR
Studio Galou, LLC.

To Andy Broer, for thinking a reporter could do
Data Center work, and to Melynda, my reason why.

Contents

CHAPTER 10: **Facebook**

CHAPTER 11: **Green House Data**

CHAPTER 12: **IBM**

CHAPTER 13: **Intel**

CHAPTER 14: **IO**

CHAPTER 15: **NetApp**

CHAPTER 16: **Syracuse University**

CHAPTER 17: **Terremark**

CHAPTER 18: **Yahoo!**

Preface

Welcome to the engine rooms of the Internet.

Filled with rows of sophisticated computing equipment, massive air conditioners and elaborate electrical systems, Data Centers power the Internet, foster productivity, and drive the global economy. They're also flat out cool—ultramodern technology chambers with petaflops of processing and megawatts of electrical capacity.

I began working in Data Centers more than 15 years ago, first stocking supplies and inventorying hardware, and eventually designing and managing dozens of these specialized computing environments for Cisco. I also visited hundreds of other Data Centers during those years, taking tours and chatting with their designers and managers whenever possible. Data Center folks are all trying to wrestle the same set of physics to the ground, and I'm always curious to see what elegant (or maybe not so elegant) solutions people have implemented.

The idea for *The Art of the Data Center* orginated in 2009 while I was working on a different book, *Grow a Greener Data Center*. I was writing about geothermal cooling and wanted to provide examples of Data Centers constructed underground and discovered Bahnhof's co-location facility in Stockholm. Housed in a former nuclear bunker, it was dubbed "The James Bond Villain Data Center" by several technology websites thanks to unique features such as man-made waterfalls and a glass-walled conference room that looms over its data hall. I smiled at the cinematic touches such as dramatic lighting and artificial fog and wished I knew more about it.

Why did they build the Data Center to look like a super-villain's headquarters? How much did those features cost? How did they get standby generators into that underground space? Wait—is that a fish tank in one picture?

None of those details were relevant for my book on green Data Center design, so I moved on. The idea stayed with me, though. Find the most compelling Data Centers, explore their innovations and ask the people who built them to share their insights and lessons learned.

And so, a few years later, here we are. Bahnhof's Data Center finally gets its due in Chapter 3, as do 17 other server rooms that are also notable for their unique features and groundbreaking technologies.

WHO SHOULD READ THIS BOOK

The Art of the Data Center is for anyone intrigued by architecture, sustainable design, computing environments or technology. Although IT, Facilities, and Data Center professionals will be most familiar with some of the topics that are discussed, a background in those fields is not required. You don't have to be a civil engineer to appreciate San Francisco's Golden Gate Bridge and you don't need to be a Data Center person to marvel at these impressive facilities.

HOW THIS BOOK IS ORGANIZED

The Data Centers profiled in this book are displayed in alphabetical order, typically by the name of the organization that operates them.

Acknowledgments

Several Data Center professionals generously shared their time and wisdom for this book. Thank you to Don Atwood of Intel; Sergi Girona of the Barcelona Supercomputing Center; Jon Karlung of Bahnhof.; John Killey and Jerry Walsh of Citi; John Manville of Cisco; Shawn Mills of Green House Data; Chris Molloy of IBM; Phil Nail of Affordable Internet Services Online; Dean Nelson of eBay; Christina Page, Nick Holt, Paul Bonaro and Bob Lyte of Yahoo!; Marc Parizeau of Calcul Québec; Jay Park of Facebook; Chris Sedore of Syracuse University; Mark Skiff of NetApp; George Slessman of IO; Jim Smith of Digital Realty Trust; Ben Stewart of Terremark; Tom Struve and Lon Andersen of ACT, Inc.

Thank you also to their colleagues and associates who scheduled interviews, obtained images and clarified infrastructure details for each Data Center profile, patiently fielding my e-mails for "just one more thing." These included Xavier Gonzales of Terremark; Scott Gomer, Nancy Owen and Steve Kayser of ACT; Sara Ibáñez Leciñena and Renata Giménez Binder of the Barcelona Supercomputing Center; Alex Kirschner of The OutCast Agency; Elizabeth Kubycheck, Lourdes Pagan and Lisa Krueger of IO; Mike Lewis and Monica Penrose of eBay; Bruce McConnel and Todd Traver of IBM; Debbie McIntyre, Tina O'Mara and June Szymanski of Syracuse University; Rich Miller and Lauren Williams of Digital Realty Trust; Kristine Raabe of Intel; Denise Schmitz of Neumann Monson Architects; Janis Tarter of Citigroup; Amy Thon of KJWW Engineering Consultants; Kristian Thorin of Bahnhof; and Dyani Vanderhorst of Voce Communications.

About the Author

DOUGLAS ALGER is a newspaper reporter turned Data Center guy who has worked for more than 15 years in Data Center operations, physical design, architecture, project management, and more. He hosts the *Data Center Deconstructed* blog and has written two other books, *Build the Best Data Center Facility for Your Business* and *Grow a Greener Data Center*.

Doug is an IT Architect at Cisco. He previously was a writer and editor in the News & Publications office of Syracuse University and a full-time stringer for the *Los Angeles Times*, where he was part of the team that won a Pulitzer Prize for its coverage of the Northridge Earthquake. Doug has a bachelor's degree in journalism from San Jose State University.

FIGURE 1-1   ACT's Data Center in Iowa City, Iowa, was the first in the United States to be certified LEED-Platinum. Image provided courtesy of Neumann Monson Architects.

CHAPTER 1
ACT

ORGANIZATION: ACT, Inc.	
LOCATION: Iowa City, Iowa	
ONLINE: March 2008	
NOTABLE FEATURES: Closed-loop geothermal cooling, HVAC dry coolers, tornado-resistant structure, hot and cold aisles. Active-active configuration with a second Data Center 5 miles (8 km) away, linked by ACT's own dark fiber. LEED-Platinum certified.	
TIME TO DESIGN AND BUILD: 13 months	
SIZE: 6,700 sq. ft. (622.5 sq. m) total, with 4,000 sq. ft. (371.6 sq. m) of hosting space.	
POWER: Two .9 MW feeds; IT usable capacity of 270 kW	
TIER: III	
CABINET LOCATIONS: 150	
POWER DENSITY: 6 kW average per cabinet, 11 kW maximum	
INFRASTRUCTURE DELIVERY: Structured cabling above cabinets. Electrical conduits and air cooling delivered under a 36-in. (91.4 cm) deep raised floor.	
STRUCTURAL LOADING: 300 lb. per sq. ft. (1,464.7 kg per sq. m)	
FIRE SUPPRESSION SYSTEM: Double pre-action wet sprinklers, FM200 gaseous fire suppressant. VESDA detection system.	

Leave it to a testing organization to achieve the highest grade for its Data Center.

ACT, Inc., the nonprofit organization best known for the college entrance exam that bears its name, aced the U.S. Green Building Council's environmental building assessment system with the Data Center at its Iowa City headquarters. It's the first Data Center in the United States (and the first building of any kind in Iowa) to receive LEED-Platinum certification.

Helping earn that high mark is a chalkboard-wide list of renewable or recycled materials employed at the site including aspen fiber ceiling panels, cork flooring, cotton-wall insulation, and even a second-hand raised floor system.

Extra credit should be awarded for how the server environment is cooled. The site features a geothermal field consisting of vertical bore holes and a closed-loop piping system below ground that is filled with coolant and, chilled by the surrounding earth, functions as a heat exchanger. Above-ground dry coolers are employed as well, both as a redundant measure for the geothermal solution and in their own right when external temperatures are low enough that outside air can help cool the Data Center.

Aside from its green features, the ACT Data Center is designed to withstand a tornado with wind speeds up to 250 mph (402.3 kph), including wind-driven projectiles, and operates in conjunction with a second Data Center 5 miles (8 km) away.

Pay close attention class, as Tom Struve, assistant vice president of Central Services, and Lon Andersen, vice president of Information Technology, discuss how they sharpened their pencils, studied the details of their project, and exceeded the curve with their Data Center.

The Interview

What role does this Data Center serve for ACT?

Tom: We realized the need to establish a second Data Center to ensure the uninterrupted technology services to ACT Corporation and clients. This serves that important role in terms of having the redundancy and resiliency in the system. Just like every organization, technology is just such a huge, integral, important component of ACT as it is with other modern organizations that we just have to have the right infrastructure, resilient infrastructure, and be able to provide those services on an uninterrupted basis, internally and externally.

Lon: An initial thought process was, because of how critical the delivery through technology was to ACT, ACT and the board (ACT's board of directors) really recognized we need something heavily for disaster recovery and how we would do that. So, I think following on with that theme is, as you're seeing the trend in the industry going away from traditional disaster recovery, the plans that I have right now are starting to migrate away from 'I've got my data someplace now how do I build other servers and how do I recover' to an active-active situation where, to Tom's point, even if one Data Center goes away the other centers may run a little degradated but the service never goes away at that point in time.

So, from the concept of where they were to where we're now conceptually trying to build across the two centers is how do we get that active-active mode to where we're sharing workload across two different sites.

The fact that you knew that this was going to be part of a Data Center pair operating in an active-active manner, how did that influence the design?

Tom: One of the early decision points, as we were putting together our vision and gameplan for this, was to come to grips with are we going to utilize the traditional disaster recovery site location? What approach were we going to take in terms of DR? Went through that process, looked at alternatives, the cost-benefits, of those traditional approaches. Really as we—to cut a long story short—decided that the best overall model for us, all things considered, was to establish an active-active model and we have our Data Centers 5 miles (8 km) apart. Some people in the DR scene would just shudder at that, 'Oh, man. It should be 25 miles (40.2 km). It should be in different regions of the country to avoid seismic activity, to avoid electrical grid issues' and on and on. It's all a matter of, as we all know, how far do you take this?

LEED Certification

Leadership in Energy and Environmental Design (LEED) is a rating system for the design, construction, and operation of green buildings. Facilities can achieve ratings of certified, silver, gold, or platinum based on criteria within six categories: sustainable sites, water efficiency, energy and atmosphere, materials and resources, indoor environmental quality, and innovation and design.

What we elected to do was establish it on a separate property that we owned within the same city. One of the driving factors was that I was able to negotiate with the city of Iowa City to allow ACT to install our own fiber between the two sites. Then that starts getting in to the practical aspects that all start tying together from an operational standpoint, from a disaster recovery standpoint, by having those tied together over dark fiber.

Also, obviously, being able to have an active-active situation it's not a matter of having to go to some foreign location, try to bring the thing up, try to bring the data with you, try to reroute communications to it. It's just seamless. And if you look at it from a disaster recovery standpoint the onerous task of trying to get staff to a different location to staff it and so forth, there's that aspect. And then as we look at it from a day-to-day operation, yeah we could have established it maybe 25 miles (40.2 km) away from Iowa City. Well that, just on a day-to-day operations, impacts Lon's staff and we're not a huge global enterprise where we have thousands of IT staff. So we boiled all that together and the value of having that direct fiber connection was just huge from what that allows us to achieve from an IT perspective and also from a cost perspective. Communication costs for the bandwidth that's required anymore, even with bandwidth expenses coming down, is still really significant.

Lon: The primary thing there from a technology standpoint is it opens up all kinds of doors that aren't there when you're beyond this dark fiber limitation. In fact, when I would go to different executive briefings on future technologies—IBM happens to have one, they typically do it around their storage and they start talking about replications—they always have to back up and stop and rethink their thought process because they're not accustomed to companies having that dark fiber and that bandwidth.

Essentially, to us it all looks like just one Data Center. And the machines could just as well be sitting right alongside each other on the same floor. So for the engineers it makes a whole lot easier scenario to start envisioning and working through as to how do you make this thing work and tie together.

FIGURE 1-2   ACT's Iowa City Data Center features Tier III infrastructure and is linked to another ACT Data Center 5 miles (8 km) away. Image provided courtesy of Neumann Monson Architects.

What design parameters did you have in place at the start of the project?

Tom: As we set our project goals, we decided Tier III however we also said it's going to be tornado—you want to have it be tornado-proof; the engineers are quick to point out that FEMA uses the term of 'near-absolute protection.'

In our location, seismic zone is not an issue. Tornado is, from a geographic location and separation standpoint really probably our largest or one of our largest risks, separate from electrical zones. So that's why we said we are going to mitigate that risk by designing it to the near-absolute tornado protection.

What tier is the Data Center that this one is paired with?

> **Tom:** This Data Center is a Tier III and then Tier I on the other side.

I assume that that Tier I site was your primary Data Center, prior to this Data Center coming online. So, from a redundancy perspective you took a big step up with the addition of this Data Center.

> **Tom:** Yes. Historically, ACT has gone from outsourcing to pretty quickly being responsible for a lot of its own data and processing. Across the board all of our technology infrastructure had a huge project just to upgrade everything and this was one element of that.

It seems you did that in a big way. You've got the first LEED-Platinum certified Data Center in the United States and the first LEED-Platinum building in the state of Iowa. You obviously weren't following the pack when designing the room. You went from outsourced and Tier I to Tier III, LEED-Platinum. What made you decide to build the Data Center to those standards?

> **Tom:** Yeah. The Tier III was, to me, a no-brainer. I guess that's easy to say, but given our overall vision and where we were and where we saw our future going we just had to have this resilient infrastructure and that was part of it.
>
> The LEED aspect of it (came about) as we were doing initial almost like pre-schematic design stuff. Our process is, we have a board of directors. We needed to secure board of director approval for a project of this nature so I had to assemble just a basic outline, enough to get a budget number put together and secure board approval before we would really get serious about the project. Put together a team, we decided we wanted to pursue the design/build of the project, adopt that model if the project was approved.

We were certainly aware of LEED. The architect/engineers on the project had a LEED background. We talked about it. Frankly, at the initial stages we said, 'Boy, Data Center and LEED, it's almost kind of a non-sequitor. That doesn't necessarily follow.' We did recognize and thought we would want to follow that kind of a design framework but at that point we didn't establish a high-level LEED goal.

It went to the board and we have a very progressive board and they said 'Yeah— LEED, yeah! And if we're going to bother to do this we think we ought to set a lofty goal and go for a high level LEED certification on this.' It was great to get the board approval so that we could launch into this thing. On the other hand, we sat down with the team and said 'And… they've set this goal for us.'

You talk about one of the challenges of the project. First it was just getting over the shock of the board setting what one could view as an insurmountable goal. Back at the time the board approved this, we could discover four LEED-Silver certified Data Centers but most of them were actually contained within a larger building, which frankly allows you to achieve a LEED certification easier than, at least it was thought at the time, a Data Center project.

That really got us started. We quickly got over that and it became a huge motivation. Everyone on the team, fortunately, was like, 'Tell us it can't be done and that's a challenge.' It just took off from there.

A perception in the building industry—beyond just the Data Center industry but the building industry in general—is that building a green facility is notably more expensive than building a conventional one. Did you find that to be the case with this project?

Tom: We really did not. Going in to this, the idea was just to have a very utilitarian Data Center project. We put together a modest/frugal budget for that. We had that as one of our overall guiding base of the design elements.

Where there were instances where we added costs into the project to work within the LEED framework, we feel in every instance that it definitely added value to the project. Did it add cost? Yeah, it did. But it was not significant. And that was achieving platinum, also.

What are some of the features of the facility that helped you achieve the LEED-Platinum rating?

Tom: What it really came down to was just a huge attention to detail. On the one hand, when you walk up to the facility, when you walk in to the facility, in many respects you wouldn't even think 'Oh, gee, this is some special building.' Which is in some respects the beauty of it, also, given it's a Data Center. First and foremost we had to achieve the Tier III. It had to be resilient. We used the line 'a sustainable design from an IT operational standpoint.' However, we were also designing it within the LEED environmental sustainable design and construction process.

So, to answer your question, one of the things that really stands out is the use of the geothermal in a Data Center. It just was not used prior for Data Center projects, wasn't considered to be compatible with Data Center projects in that, as we all know, Data Centers are constantly rejecting heat. A geothermal field would just become saturated and quickly just not become functional. So it typically was just not considered.

I just have to give huge credit to every member of our team and KJWW Engineering brought to the table quite a bit of geothermal and other innovative technologies. Even before we were challenged by the board we had identified geothermal as something that we were very interested in pursuing and then they (KJWW) had been looking for an opportunity in a Data Center project; they had some ideas about how they might be able to make that work. That's probably one of the features.

We can go through a long list of things. To incorporate, for instance, reclaimed materials into a new Data Center project. It's like, 'How the heck do you do that?' And you want to be a Tier III.

When you go through the list, to me it's just kind of like 'Oh, gee, is that it?' So, we reclaimed the floor system from a prior project. As you look at rapidly renewable materials as a requirement, how do you incorporate rapidly renewable materials into a Data Center project? We used aspen fiber ceiling tiles. There are cork flooring and cotton insulation instead of fiberglass. Just things like that. Again, you walk in you don't really see those things, you don't notice them— 'Gee, there are ceiling tiles. Gee, there's a raised floor system that looks the same as everyone else's.' Yes it does. However, if you dig in to the details then 'Oh, gee, that's where that stuff came from.'

Other things where we faced some challenges or opportunities, LEED framework is to provide daylighting into staff spaces. Here we were with a Data Center project that needed to be tornado resistant, all the usual security concerns and all those kind of things. So that was an interesting challenge. What we ended up doing—again, when you walk up you don't really notice it—so there's a curtain wall on the exterior of the building, however we established a separate interior vessel that was actually the tornado resistant portion of the building.

While we incorporated tornado resistant glass, you cannot have at least at this point (in time)—I'm sure there's probably bullet-resistant stuff, but we were on a budget. So we came up with that design, not really a compromise it was just a design solution.

That's one where I would say if you were just building a non-LEED building it just would have been a concrete exterior wall. We put some additional funding, not significant, in to the project for that curtain wall. However, it really adds value. I mean, wow, when you walk into the building and the staff lab space and conference area it's nice to have the windows and to get light and be able to look out. Those are elements that are part of that.

And then from the site and so forth we have restored natural prairie vegetation, non-irrigable, that kind of thing. Again, it's just there. Do you think it looks odd and it's something really special? Not really.

It's just details, details, details and not losing sight of the overall vision. And for us it was that dual goal.

FIGURE 1-3   Tornado-resistant glass allows daylight into parts of the building regularly occupied by people. Image provided courtesy of Neumann Monson Architects.

What about how your geothermal system was designed allowed it be used effectively for your Data Center?

Tom: It probably comes down to two things. The primary thing is that we used the dry coolers and the free cooling during the winter season to circulate the abundance of cooler air to reject the heat. We take a percentage of that and circulate it through the geothermal field to basically rejuvenate it. That's the biggest thing.

And then, we have a different distance between the bores, factoring in the larger amount of heat and the longer duration of the period to avoid that saturation while we're operating.

Just like many of the other things, once you see the answer it just seems so simple. A lot of times it's an elegant solution and simple that is the best. And it works.

Some Data Center operators prefer to keep their Data Centers quite cool. Others using air economization technology employ warmer settings to maximize its benefits. With your use of geothermal cooling and dry coolers, what temperatures do you maintain your Data Center hardware at?

Tom: We're at 72 degrees Fahrenheit (22.2 Celsius) and 50 percent humidity.

We're not doing that (exploring warmer temperatures) at present. There are some additional refinements and measures like that that we recognize that we could easily put in place, we just weren't at the point where we needed that. We'll spot check what temperatures are and so forth but we don't have integral rack sensors and those kinds of things.

You obviously wanted this Data Center to score well on the LEED scale and the system can be specific about what design elements it awards points for. While LEED has been embraced by the Data Center industry more than any other environmental building assessment system, there is some hesitation that features it awards points for such as daylighting and providing shower facilities and bicycle storage lockers don't reflect how green a Data Center truly is. Was there any point at which you felt like you had to make a decision between earning more LEED points versus good Data Center design?

Tom: From the standpoint of there being tradeoffs or compromising the Data Center or the Tier III, no. We did not. Certainly we were faced with a large number of options and decisions where we had to keep looking at what's the balance here. We wanted to stay within the green framework but couldn't lose sight of the Tier III.

For instance, a green roof is commonly associated with a LEED building. We talked about that, could have done it. As we looked at what it would really take to achieve that and to really have a good ongoing green roof and so forth we felt there were some potential compromises with roof penetrations and just some different structure things that way. We looked at the options and really we were able to still be within the spirit and framework of LEED by instead putting on an Energy Star roof system. It has a double roofing system: as far as the tornado resistant structure we have a conventional roof, a couple inches (about 5 centimeters) of concrete slab over the top of that and then a single-ply membrane roof on top of that, which is the Energy Star rating.

As you say, yes we provided the shower facilities, the various other kind of things. It didn't compromise the functionality of the building.

It's a good question, Doug. It's right on target. As you know, LEED is constantly evolving and refining and I know there have been efforts to establish a designation for Data Centers. Personally I think that makes a lot of sense.

Certainly that was a challenge taking the LEED framework as it existed at that point in time and applying it to a Data Center. I would imagine that as the framework gets developed it'll be better. I don't know if you would say easier in the sense of using the framework that we had. It's just amazing what just a few years does.

At the time we were doing this, in terms of the materials that were available, that were certified appropriately, all the different sources for construction materials—we have recycled content in the steel and recycled content in the concrete and those kind of things—it was more difficult then to come up with those things than I think even it is just today not that many years later. I guess the point is, on the one hand I think the framework will be evolving and becoming more specific, which I think definitely it needs to be. At the same time, then, I would imagine that would then get more stringent from a Data Center standpoint. On the other hand, then, there's a lot of materials and technology that are now coming on-stream that one could get to make use of.

Among your re-use items you mention the floor system. Did you have that in another facility or did you go shopping for a raised floor system from someone else?

Tom: Yeah, we went shopping.

Where do you find a gently-used raised floor system for a Data Center?

Tom: At the time there was still a lot of stuff on the open market from the dot-com bust. And there are sources for used furniture, used raised floors, those kind of things.

What we did do was to specify and apply new surface material to it. So from an appearance standpoint, the tile material is new. It looks new and so forth. But the bulk of it is not the little surface it's the actual structural portion of the floor tile.

FIGURE 1-4   Structured cabling is routed overhead. Electrical conduits and cooling are provided below a raised floor. Image provided courtesy of Neumann Monson Architects.

You routed your structured cabling overhead and your power and cooling below a raised floor. Did anything drive that particular configuration? A growing number of Data Center designs now eliminate any raised floor.

Tom: We did kick around some different ideas. However, all things considered we felt that was still the best fit for us. Talking about the wisdom of stuff that we learned, one of the things is taking a look at all of the best practices out there and deciding and having a good understanding of what they are and where to best apply them and then where to maybe reinvent them. Some of the things we felt comfortable that they would best satisfy our needs currently and then going forward.

I've been in some Data Centers that don't have the raised floor thing and we just felt from a cooling efficiency value, from a cost standpoint, that the raised floor with the return plenum represented an optimal cost value and efficiency standpoint.

It seemed to me that—it could be a misconception I have—the ones that we visited and read about, not having the raised floor was really just a lot more cost-driven than anything else. They were able to achieve the cooling and the utility cabling infrastructure around it fine, but I really felt that there were compromises drawn that overall it just, bottom line, wasn't the best value all things considered.

What did you have to do to make the facility tornado-resistant?

Tom: It was really everything. Certainly the wall design, the roof design. The doors needed to be (a certain way). They do have certification rating standards for tornado, FEMA compliant things. So, from a structural standpoint, all of those elements. As we talked about, then, just from some other practical standpoints not necessarily achieving the tornado rating but being practical to ensure that the facility would continue operating is different than just having a structure standing. In that regard, from an HVAC (heating, ventilation, and air conditioning) standpoint, especially since we had the tornado portion of the building versus the other portion that we just talked about with the windows and so forth, the HVAC system has to be divided into two pressure vessels so that when a tornado would hit that the Data Center portion is protected. We do that through automated controls and sensors or if we're aware that we're in to a warning area we can also remotely or at the Data Center put it in that mode.

And then we put the generator inside the building. The sole reason was to protect it in the event of a tornado type event. It's nice from a vandalism point of view, too, but it's really the tornado thing that drove that. Again, the building could be standing but most likely in a tornado event power to the building you have to assume would be interrupted and so we need that generator to be functional. So it's within the building. Then you have the obvious problems of trying to get a massive amount of air into that generator space for cooling primarily and exhausting it. And so, on the air intakes and exhaust there's structural (barrier)—the best way to describe it is an array of steel tubes that would prevent a tornado-driven 2-by-4 or whatever to be able to penetrate in and damage the generator.

FIGURE 1-5   ACT placed the Data Center's standby generators inside the building to safeguard them from tornadoes. Image provided courtesy of Neumann Monson Architects.

What were the biggest challenges or surprises that came up during the project?

Tom: It's good to have a little bit of time probably separating from when we went through it. At the time you're in it you just do it. In some respects there weren't any huge challenges. It was really just breaking it down element by element and just working through the options, looking at the LEED framework and identifying options that we could incorporate.

We were pleasantly surprised by the synergies that ended up happening between the LEED design and achieving the Tier III. For instance, the geothermal is just a great synergy there. It has the energy efficiency and so forth. And the way we use that is in our climate the geothermal field is most energy efficient in the summertime and then we have dry coolers, out in the HVAC courtyard which as they say provide essentially 'free cooling.' All it requires is just the pump to be running out there, so we rely on them as our primary heat rejection source in the wintertime. Well, as part of the Tier III you have the N+1 redundancy of the CRAC (computer room air conditioner) units within the Data Center, however we also wanted to have redundancy and protection in terms of the rest of the system.

That's one thing that has always bothered me as I walk up to these Data Centers is you have all these condensing units outside, up on the roof or out in the courtyard or whatever, and in terms of potential risk from a tornado event or vandalism or even a car running into the things, that kind of stuff. That's always I thought a risk that's not really a lot of times appropriately addressed. Sometimes they're placed within the building and then you have a huge challenge, which can be overcome, of getting sufficient airflow in there for them to operate.

So with the geothermal everything is under the ground and the pumps are all within the tornado-protected vessel. Worst case we feel that in the event of a tornado we might lose some of those exterior condensing units but the geothermal is standalone, self-sufficient and can go. Conversely, if we have some problem with the geothermal we feel that needs addressing—you get a leak in one of the loops or something—if you need to take that offline then no problem we just go over to the other side. So that's a nice synergy, I think.

There's the energy-efficiency aspect to both of them, but you put them both together and from a seasonal energy efficiency standpoint and then from a resiliency standpoint in terms of the Data Center operation I think it's pretty cool how that works together.

Do you think the geothermal system and the other design elements that helped you achieve LEED-Platinum certification are universal solutions? Are they things that anyone building a Data Center could do now and should do now, or are some of them very specific to what you were trying to accomplish and where your facility is located?

Tom: I think the geothermal and combining that with the dry coolers is definitely a climate-related solution. If your Data Center is in Texas, it really wouldn't be a model that would fit. Above a certain latitude, then good to go. There are some things dependent that way.

Otherwise I would say the rest of it would be just pretty universally applicable, adaptable.

If you could go back and design this Data Center all over again what, if anything, would you do differently?

Tom: To date, nothing has come up. Pretty surprising.

Lon: One of the things that hasn't been mentioned is there is already pre-planning on expansion of this that got engineered and thought about before we went ahead. Even to that standpoint, if the capacity got beyond where we needed it we already had that thought into and laid out from an architectural standpoint, and pre-planning how that next piece of expansion would go. And I'm not sure that facilities typically do that very well.

Tom: We'll see how it develops, only time will tell. From my standpoint, our future roadmap would be to establish a similar Tier III facility on campus to replace the Tier I Data Center, which is contained within an office building and constrained.

What suggestions would you offer to someone else embarking on a Data Center project?

Lon: What I found when I first came in, I don't think the technical engineers were thinking about green and sustainability of what was there at that point in time. So the concept of really doing virtualization of servers, hot and cold aisles inside the center, perhaps how we do backups, what we would do those to, and how that story would be—that's the biggest thing that if I were to look at it I would say that design or that thought process needs to be ongoing and developed as the building is being constructed.

Do you have a target level for how much virtualization you employ in the Data Center?

Lon: Not a particular target level at this time. I can tell you the intent is to reduce this year (the number of physical servers) by about 50 percent and we will reduce further as we go on. We're going to reduce down from about 450 physical servers to in the neighborhood of 200.

That will come down to a point of, like most places, a percentage of utilization and that saturation of where you're actually providing decent core services versus how much you're trying to put within a particular device.

FIGURE 1-6   ACT is reducing the quantity of servers in its Data Center through virtualization. Image provided courtesy of KJWW Engineering Consultants.

Any other Data Center project strategies that you can recommend?

Tom: Establishing clear goals for the project. It's one of the obvious, simple things but man you better know what they are and keep grounding it toward that. The other thing that I constantly say is assembling the right team to achieve the goals. Like we all know, it just comes down to the people involved and working as a team on a project like this. Understanding what your goals are and then choosing the right team members that bring the right experience and the right kind of mindset to the project is just so important.

And I think that being motivated, certainly at least on this project, being motivated by having an apparently very difficult—we say almost insurmountable—task. Being open-minded and creative.

And just that details, details, details, while at the same time keeping a clear grasp of the overall goals and vision. In terms of the (LEED) Platinum, certainly, boy, it just really gets involved in the details of the thing. Like I said earlier, too, understanding best practices sufficiently to be comfortable making decisions regarding which of those to incorporate and which of those to reinvent.

Also a really key thing at least on this project was owner decision making. Ultimately this is the owner's project. You have to be knowledgeable and intimately involved. If you think you can just hire a bunch of consultants and say 'Hey, here's what I want. I want LEED-Platinum and I want whatever tier and these kind of things,' that's just not going to happen. You're not going to be satisfied overall with the project and it's not going to achieve what you need it to in all respects if you're not really involved. And you have to be knowledgeable about the subject matter. You need to make the tough decisions in a very timely manner and as an owner you need to accept full responsibility for the risks associated with non-traditional approaches. And in doing so, the owner really sets the tone by making those decisions.

If you get into a situation where you're setting up for a bunch of finger-pointing later if something doesn't work then that just causes everyone to be defensive and to fall back in to that old deal of just using the safe, tried and true best practices. To me, my bias is it's not the place for decisions by an owner committee. Someone needs to be empowered with the authority and the responsibility to make those decisions and just to make them.

We would to keep this thing moving and just a whole array with the LEED-Platinum framework and since we were in somewhat uncharted territory we would talk about things, bring them up, get them vetted and then I would just make a decision. I know sometimes they would say 'Don't you want to think about that?' but we've all investigated, all the information there is to know is here, so boom let's go this direction. We need to keep this moving. Boy, you can just get so bogged down in something like this that you just have to be willing to stand up and make decisions and move on.

"Ultimately this is the owner's project. You have to be knowledgeable and intimately involved. If you think you can just hire a bunch of consultants and say 'Hey here's what I want.'… that's just not going to happen. You're not going to be satisfied overall with the project and it's not going to achieve what you need it to in all respects if you're not really involved."

What do you think were the toughest decisions for this project, or that someone else in a similar project might find the toughest to make a call on?

Tom: I suppose because the project was successful, both from the LEED standpoint and the daily operational perspective—it's just performing great—in hindsight they don't seem like there were any hugely difficult ones. Certainly committing to the geothermal design, which was at that point not really proven. The others were just evaluating the options, the pros and cons, and understanding the dual goals and going for it.

A team dynamic that really worked—in terms of achieving it, it's more the people involved and setting the tone—is setting egos aside. And they did. As we were working through all these different options and alternatives you could have seen it stepping on toes of different disciplines. But everyone just really worked together towards the common vision and were just really open and creative and willing to sit and listen and consider different ways to do it and then talk about how maybe mechanical and controls and electrical had to come together on some of these things. How best to do that as we tried to incorporate the flexible, modular approach into things.

I'm happy with how we have done there. That requires cross-discipline approaches. I think sometimes you just get some of these egos. It can enter in. You get someone people in and they feel it has to be their way. That's easier said than done to get past that.

FIGURE 1-7   Chilled water piping for ACT's Iowa City Data Center. Image provided courtesy of KJWW Engineering Consultants.

FIGURE 2-1 Affordable Internet Services Online's Data Center operates entirely on solar power. Images provided courtesy of AISO.

CHAPTER 2
Affordable Internet Services Online (AISO)

ORGANIZATION: Affordable Internet Services Online (AISO)	
LOCATION: Romoland, California	
ONLINE: April 2005	
NOTABLE FEATURES: Solar power used as primary power source. Air conditioners use atmospheric energy process to produce cold air. Solar tube lighting and a rainwater collection system.	
TIME TO DESIGN AND BUILD: 6 months	
SIZE: 2,000 sq. ft. (185.8 sq. m) total, with 400 sq. ft. (37.2 sq. m) of hosting space	
POWER CAPACITY: 110 kW from on-site solar array	
TIER: III	
CABINET LOCATIONS: 15	
INFRASTRUCTURE DELIVERY: Power, cooling, and cabling infrastructure are provided overhead	
STRUCTURAL LOADING: Undetermined	
FIRE SUPPRESSION SYSTEM: Aerosol	

Solar power is an impractical source of energy for a Data Center. It's only available for a limited number of hours each day. It's prone to interference by the weather. Beyond those limitations, solar generates a miniscule amount of power relative to what a server environment consumes. It certainly can't serve as the primary source of power for a Data Center.

Or can it?

Affordable Internet Services Online (AISO) offers what is believed to be the world's only fully solar-powered hosting company. Located in Romoland, California, about 70 miles (112.7 km) southeast of Los Angeles, the Data Center and accompanying office space run entirely on solar power by ruthlessly stretching each watt produced by an array of 120 solar panels.

The building's white exterior and foliage-covered roof reduce how hard the cooling system must work, for instance. Seven mirrored tubes bring natural light into the facility during the day, while energy-efficient LED lighting is used at night. Tiny wind turbines installed within the building's air ducts even harvest energy from the passing air, charging batteries to run AISO's office computers. The site also includes a 10,000-gallon (37,854.1 liter) rainwater collection system, allowing it to operate without drawing upon the municipal water supply.

The two technologies that bring the most energy savings, though, are virtualization—AISO has a 60:1 ratio of virtual to physical servers—and an extremely efficient air conditioning system. The Data Center's 5-ton Coolerado air conditioners use the same latent cooling process, known as the Maisotsenko cycle, that transfers heat to a thunderstorm and makes the surrounding cooler area. According to the manufacturer, the units consume up to 90 percent less energy than conventional air conditioners.

Despite the Data Center's relatively small size, it serves more than 15,000 clients, ranging from Krispy Kreme Doughnuts to the Jacques Cousteau Foundation to the San Diego Convention Center, and its green technologies save an estimated 150,000 lb. (68,038.9 kg) of carbon dioxide per year.

Phil Nail, AISO's founder and chief technical officer, talks about the company's solar-powered Data Center.

The Interview

Solar is not typically used as a primary power source for a Data Center because it can't generate the massive amount of energy demanded by most server environments and because it's not an always-on power source. What prompted you to use solar power and how did you overcome those limitations?

We went solar because of the fact of where we are. In Southern California we get a lot of sun, we don't really get wind here. It's the best thing to do. Really, it's the right thing to do because any time you can use renewable energy you're better off.

We took this step back in 2001 (with a previous server environment) before the green movement. We kind of pioneered running the Data Center this way. It was challenging going solar because there were a lot of things we had to consider. We had to reduce our power consumption and be very conscientious of what equipment we use in our Data Center.

For us it was the right thing to do and the only thing to do. We just had to do it and we had to figure it out and we had to make it work for us.

How are you storing the energy that you collect?

We have large backup units that actually hold all of the energy and store it. The thing is with most Data Centers, now with the green movement that is out there, most of them just try to buy green credits to make it look good.

"We had to reduce our power consumption and be very conscientious of what equipment we use in our Data Center."

28

So, you think they should directly incorporate alternative energy in their Data Center designs instead?

No, not just that. I just think they need to be trying to green their Data Center as much as possible and do everything they can possibly do and not whitewash it—or greenwash it you would say—by doing the energy credits. A lot of them will say 'Hey, we're green, we're running green servers, we're running all this green stuff.' But you have to really drill down and read every single word that they have and finally somewhere in there'll be a couple little words that say 'Well, we buy energy credits.' And I hear this so much from clients. They say 'Yeah, these companies look really good but boy after you really start reading on it then you want to run.'

I think that small Data Centers should try to incorporate alternative energy solutions in to their designs. It would be very difficult for larger Data Centers to run completely off alternative energy due to the size of their footprint.

FIGURE 2-2
AISO's small number of servers makes it possible to run entirely on solar energy.

Was there a particular challenge that you had to overcome in order to run entirely off of solar energy? Have you done something that you think other companies can't do? If they can, why do you think most aren't?

Yeah, I think we have done something that's different than what a lot of companies have done. I think a lot of them just aren't doing it because of the cost factor. And because of the fact that they're afraid of about making that change. A lot of these companies, too, they have a lot of red tape. Just because the IT department doesn't want to do it doesn't mean all of the other divisions do, and it takes six to eight months to get anything done.

First thing we had to do was completely change the way we run our Data Center. We had to reduce the amount of power we were using which meant we had to reduce the amount of equipment we were running. We also had to change the way we cooled our Data Center. I think we have pioneered the green Data Center by doing something others would have been afraid to do.

Most Data Center operators these days want to show they have green policies in place but most just opt for purchasing green certificates. Our neighbor worked for the electric company running all the high voltage lines and oversaw the operations and he told me that there is no possible way that a company can choose to get only wind generated or solar generated power because all power coming in to the station or substation goes into a pool and then is sent out to customers who need the power. At any given moment the power company may need extra power so they check with other states and power companies and if that company has extra power available it is sent into the electric pool. That means any one of us who do not purchase green certificates still get some green power. We just do not know from who and how much.

Talk a little bit about the cost issue. I assume you mean the upfront capital cost to install a solar system. Did you find the system to be notably more expensive than a conventional power system?

Oh sure, yeah. I'm not sure what our cost was, it has been so long. But I can tell you that it definitely is very expensive to do and there are a lot of things that need to be fine-tuned after you install it. There are a lot of things that you have to figure out that you hope will work and there's a lot of trial and error.

Getting started is extremely expensive but in our case it has paid off. Most companies look at the ROI before they invest and the ROI (return on investment) in most cases can be 10 to 15 years.

"First thing we had to do was completely change the way we run our Data Center."

Any potential errors that you would alert someone to if they were looking to put a solar energy system in place to power their Data Center?

I can't think of something off the top of my head. Every installation is going to be different, depending upon what they're running, how they're running it. I don't think they're all going to be the same. You're going to have individual challenges for every single one. It all depends on cooling. There are a lot of different configurations.

With that extra cost up front, did you have a sense of your return on investment and how quickly you would make your money back due to reduced energy costs?

We didn't even take a look at that. Most companies they want to know what the ROI is before they even think about doing it. We just did it because we thought that's the right thing to do. We figured it would pay off in the long run we just didn't know how long.

What made you decide to locate your Data Center in Romoland?

We've always had the Data Center right next door to our house. We were looking for a piece of property that we could build a Data Center on and get up and walk next door and go to work.

We were looking for a nice place that had some property that was close to the cities but also out enough so that it could be very low key. Nobody would ever know that we were a Data Center, driving by.

Another way that you're leveraged solar power is through the use of solar tubing and windows. Did you have any security concerns about using them?

No security concerns at all. The solar tubes are small in diameter so no one can simply knock off the top and climb into the Data Center.

FIGURE 2-3
Solar tubing and skylights supplement the lighting in AISO's Data Center.

Tell me about your air conditioning system. I understand that the units you have installed actually work more efficiently in warmer conditions.

Our AC units work extremely well 99 percent of the year. The other 1 percent we need to run regular AC to help knock down the temperature inside. The reason is the AC units use water and do not work well when the humidity outside is high. The units we use are water cooled and can take 110 degree (43.3 Celsius) outside air and cool the air down to 65 degrees (18.3 Celsius).

They work very, very well. They've been a really good thing for us. Because they use water we have some large tanks we use to catch the precipitation when it does rain out here. We collect that water and pump it to the Coolerado switch and it in turn cools the Data Center. It only has about two moving parts, so the average power consumption is only about 200 watts, which is nothing.

We used to use a cooling system called Freus, which was water-cooled as well but it was down more than it was up. Our air conditioner guy was looking online one night and he happened to find Coolerado. We went down and saw them at a trade show and loved what we saw so decided to go for it.

FIGURE 2-4   AISO's air conditioners use an atmospheric energy process to produce cold air and are more energy efficient than conventional units.

I was amused to learn that you have tiny wind turbines in the ducting of your building. Where did you come up with the idea for that?

It just came to us. We said 'This looks like a pretty good idea. Let's just try it.' A lot of the things that we do, it just comes to us in the middle of the night or whenever, and we just go for.

The power from the turbine is used to charge small batteries (which then power employee computers). We use all thin clients for our computers in the office, so they don't use much power.

Speaking of that, please talk about how you are using virtualization technology.

Virtualization has played a major role in the running of our solar powered Data Center. First off we had to eliminate all the high energy computers, servers, and equipment. Then we decided on using NetApp for our SANs as they are the most reliable and most energy efficient. We chose the IBM servers as they were the most energy efficient servers we could go to. They are running the most energy efficient power supplies and the most energy efficient processors on the market. One hundred percent of our Data Center is virtualized, which also makes it extremely easy to manage.

We've gotten away from having physical boxes for every single thing that we do. It just wasn't efficient. We use virtualization for our local computers and we use that for all of our clients.

We started off with physical boxes and we migrated to virtual machines. We have chosen VMware to go in to our virtual infrastructure. We started off with iSCSI and that was a nightmare, because that didn't work very well. After we had 100 or so servers migrated across, we had a lot of slowdown issues so we had to get off iSCSI real quick and move into a different protocol. That was really the only challenge that we had. Other than that it has been just the best thing ever.

It's very, very easy to manage. It has made our life so much better. If a client server goes down and its 2 o'clock in the morning, we can just VPN in, get on and do a simple reboot. Bring it right back online from our cell phone. It's very easy, secure, and simple to manage.

It's so reliable. It just runs. I could never go back to physical servers again.

"I could never go back to physical servers again."

FIGURE 2-5   Use of virtualization has allowed AISO to expand its computing power in a small physical footprint.

Obviously not all Data Centers are using virtualized servers to the degree that you are. What do you think might be holding someone back from implementing virtualization?

I just think, especially companies that have a lot of equipment, you just have to jump up and do it. A lot of them are still afraid to do it. Plus, they want to do a tremendous amount of testing. The bigger the company, the longer the testing. For us, we're a small company so we can just jump out and do it and we don't have to jump through a lot of red tape.

Most Data Centers allow clients to rent racks to put in their own equipment and servers. Because of this model they can't simply go virtual.

Turning to your electrical system, your standby generator uses propane rather than the more common diesel fuel. What made you choose that system?

It's cleaner. It burns cleaner and we just felt that that was really the best way to go for us. We're in a rural setting and we didn't feel—being an environmental company the way that we are—that diesel was going to be the right choice.

It's easy (to use). You need more fuel you just call the truck, they come pump it in and you're good to go. You're not dealing with underground tanks or any of those other things you would have to deal with, with diesel.

You previously mentioned the rainwater collection system at your site. How much water does that typically collect?

We had a rain at the end of the season, and in just a few hours we had over 6,000 gallons (22,712.5 liters) of water. So it can collect it pretty quick. The cooling system uses only 50 percent of the water, so we take the remainder and keep our landscaping up.

FIGURE 2-6   AISO harvests rainwater to cool its Data Center and for landscaping. Collection tanks
can hold 10,000 gallons (37,851.1 liters) of water.

You started with the solar infrastructure and then put in other infrastructure efficiencies over time. What challenges, if any, did you have in introducing new technologies? Were there any surprises along the way?

There weren't really any surprises. I think the biggest thing for us was just explaining to clients that the virtualization was a better technology than having a physical box. That was the hardest part for us.

It took a little bit of convincing them. Now, people just love it. Best way to go.

Several of the physical infrastructure elements in your Data Center— the solar power, the solar tubing, the Coolerado air conditioners— aren't frequently used today in other Data Centers. Which of them do you think are universal solutions or which are beneficial based on your particular circumstances?

Solar tubing and LED lighting is one way for Data Centers to help lower their cost and start down the road of being more environmentally conscientious. If a Data Center is located in an area that does not have high humidity then I think that air conditioning technology would also be a good solution for them.

I don't think solar is going to be a global solution for Data Centers for the simple fact that a lot of these guys let just anybody off the street come in and rent racks and load up any kind of computer system they want. If they don't have a lot of land they're not going to be able to power it. So I don't think that's a good solution. But as far as the cooling, yeah, I think that could be a real good solution for them. If they're back on the East Coast, where it gets down to freezing it's probably not the best technology for them, but in the warmer climates I think it would be a very good technology.

If you could go back and design your Data Center again what, if anything, would you do differently?

I've looked at that quite a bit over the years and I don't think really much of anything. It just fell in to place very nicely the way that we did it. Other than maybe make it a little bigger, that's about the only thing. The design worked out really well. We're very pleased with it.

Are there any up-and-coming Data Center technologies that you envision implementing at your site in the future, to make it even more energy-efficient?

We are always in search of more eco-friendly alternatives and more ways to reduce energy. Our team is very motivated and dedicated to being the most energy efficient Data Center in the world and we will stop at nothing to do so.

There are some racks out there that we're looking at, kind of testing out. They don't stand straight up like your typical racks do, they lay down. You wouldn't need any cooling whatsoever to use them. You actually take the fans out of the servers. The racks themselves do the cooling—you close the lid on a rack and it's a self-contained system. We're taking a look at those and trying to see how they might fit here. We're not sure at this point, but it sounds like a pretty good concept.

What design advice would you offer to someone looking to build their own energy-efficient server environment?

I would recommend if they start from scratch figure out how much actual energy they need and build your alternative energy solutions around those numbers. Next I would look at how you would setup and handle the cooling and heating of your Data Center. Next, how will you provide light in your Data Center? How will you run your servers in the most energy efficient ways and how will you do this being fully redundant?

Look at the insulation that you build into the facility itself. The more energy efficient it is, the less your cooling (system) is going to have to work.

And then, try to virtualize as much as you can. The problem with a lot of the Data Centers is that they don't virtualize so they just use a tremendous amount of power.

FIGURE 3-1   The above-ground entrance to Bahnhof's Data Center in Stockholm, Sweden. Embedded 100 ft. (30 m) underground in a former nuclear bunker, the Data Center retains its wartime codename, Pionen White Mountains. Images provided courtesy of Bahnhof.

CHAPTER 3
Bahnhof

ORGANIZATION: Bahnhof	
LOCATION: Stockholm, Sweden	
ONLINE: September 2008	
NOTABLE FEATURES: Artificial daylight, greenhouses, waterfalls, and a 687 gallon (2,600 liter) saltwater fish tank. Two Maybach diesel submarine engines used for standby power.	
TIME TO DESIGN AND BUILD: 20 months	
SIZE: 10,764 sq. ft. (1,000 sq. m) total, with 5,382 sq. ft. (500 sq. m) of hosting space and 2,153 sq. ft. (200 sq. m) for back-of-house systems. Remaining space is for office and personnel areas.	
IT-USABLE CAPACITY: 800 kW	
TIER: Not stated	
CABINET LOCATIONS: 140	
POWER DENSITY: 5.7 kW average per cabinet, no specific maximum	
INFRASTRUCTURE DELIVERY: Cooling, structured cabling and electrical are delivered below a 3.3 foot (1 meter) deep raised floor.	
STRUCTURAL LOADING: 403 lb. per sq. ft. (2 tons per sq. m)	
FIRE SUPPRESSION SYSTEM: Novec 1230	

Anyone who sees Bahnhof's Data Center in Stockholm is forgiven the urge to hum the theme music of their favorite science fiction movie. That's because the Internet service provider purposefully designed its server environment to evoke the cinematic look and feel of *Silent Running*, *Logan's Run*, and any number of James Bond movies.

A circular, glass-walled conference room with an image of the moon covering its floor overlooks the server area. Multi-colored lights showcase man-made waterfalls and greenhouses. Second-hand diesel engines used in German submarines provide standby power for the facility. (A submarine sound-horn is installed near the engines and alarms in the event of a system malfunction.)

Cementing the other-worldly feel of this server environment is the fact that it resides in a former nuclear bunker about 100 ft. (30 m) below ground, sheltered behind 15.7 in. (40 cm) thick metal doors. Bahnhof has retained the site's Cold War codename, Pionen White Mountains, and a few of its trappings. 'These doors should be locked at DEFCON1' reads a placard near the entrance.

The Bahnhof Data Center is a truly one-of-a-kind facility that took shape thanks to a clear design vision, judicious use of explosives, and a strong desire to build something out of the ordinary.

Jon Karlung, founder and chairman of the board of Bahnhof, discusses the challenges of building an underground server environment and the value that his Data Center's cinematic features provide.

The Interview

What made you choose a bunker as an ideal location for a Data Center?

There were several reasons for it, but the primary one I think (is that) we had built five Data Centers and most of them were built in traditional environments—old warehouse redesigns and old office building redesigns—and we wanted to do something different.

We are geologically in a very stable area. Most parts of Sweden are built on granite. The mountain, the stone is solid rock and it's 2 billion years old. It's one of possibly the earth's oldest and most stable from a geological perspective.

There are fortresses and stuff from those days of the Cold War and I looked through most of them. I think I was in 40 different spots. Most of them were too small or scrapped or used for something else, but this facility was still there. We were very lucky to get hold of it.

If you work with computers, you realize that the threat to operational computers is not too much. The physical protection, okay, it must be there of course. It must be there, but now we have a mountain defined originally to (withstand) well not a hydrogen bomb outside the door but at least a hit somewhere in Stockholm and the computers probably survive even if people may not.

The place was very big and it was also located very central in Stockholm. Our competitors, and many Data Centers, are often located way outside the inner city urban area because they can be built in a larger complex outside for a cheaper price. But, you see, many computer consultants they live in the town. They don't want to travel far away to look at their boxes. It's nice to have them conveniently close to the city, actually. Of course it's very hard to find a great, cheap space where you can build a Data Center in this urban city but with one exception and that is these caves because nobody can use them for something else.

Sometimes they have been used as garages, but (at this site) the entrance was too narrow so it was impossible to build something like that. I would say it was a clear benefit that the space was so centrally located and that gave us an advantage against our competitors. Our clients can easily access the computers and after they have accessed it they are in the main city area.

"It's very hard to find a great, cheap space where you can build a Data Center in this urban city but with one exception and that is these caves…"

FIGURE 3-2   The Bahnhof Data Center's Network Operations Center (NOC). Artificial daylight, greenhouses, and even a saltwater aquarium have been installed to avoid the impersonal feel of many conventional Data Centers.

The second reason: of course, the physical protection was also great. As you know, when you work with a computer center, it might not be of that huge importance. Most errors in my work are basically caused by humans. Human error—that is the most frequent. Mistakes in configurations and whatever can make your environment go down. Not from some kind of big trouble with the physical protection.

But that doesn't matter because the clients they like what they see. From a marketing perspective, they'll of course appreciate that they feel secure. Even if I know that humans are more cause of problems than the physical location. They appreciate the solid feeling of the rock. The solid feeling of the rock gives us an advantage compared to a conventional center.

The third thing was a combination. It was fun to do it. It is like playing. The fun-ness of it also brought us an advantage in marketing. I mean, I speak to you now and we have had a lot of magazines and footage from different media channels covering it. And of course that has given us invaluable access from a marketing perspective. If I had to spend the amount of money on advertising it would have been impossible. Now we have all of this, if not for free, it has given us an advantage from the marketing perspective.

The style we chose, that was about the fun-ness of it. It's a French architect who has been responsible for the design, but he has been working very close to us and we have discussed ideas.

The great inspiration has been one-part James Bond and one part *Star Trek* or science fiction movies and stuff like that. That has been an inspiration source to do it like this. The only thing that is missing, I was considering a white cat with long hair, like the character in James Bond, that Blofeld guy (Ernst Stavro Blofeld), and sitting in our conference room in glass and have this cat. We have plants, but no pets right now.

FIGURE 3-3   A circular, glass-walled conference room overlooks the Bahnhof Data Center's server rows.

This room definitely makes an impression upon people when they see it. Did you have a sense when you were designing the Data Center that it would be so attention-grabbing?

Absolutely. There is something magical about caves. I don't know what it is but people are sucked in to the facility and immediately like it. Even when we were at a very early stage.

We defined it completely from the beginning.

We have blown out 4,000 cu. m (141,300 cu. ft.) of stone additionally, on what it was before, with dynamite. We were building it for almost for 2 years. The neighbors in the area were not so happy from time to time from this dynamite. Once accidentally there was an explosion and the coverage from the front door was not enough so a small piece of stone penetrated a car outside the entrance. Luckily there were no people there and nobody was harmed.

When we had it very early people were very interested in it and they wanted to come and see it and looked. Right now we have delegations from companies and universities and interesting parts. And our policy has always been to be very open about it. We invite people and we have meetings and visit the facilities— not where we have the servers, in that space, but in the other parts of the facility where you can see it very well.

How long overall did it take to design and build the Data Center?

Maybe two and a half years from the start. We hadn't built a Data Center in solid rock before and this was so different. It depends upon where you build it. If it's in a warehouse it takes a certain amount of time but this was so special. It took us about twice as long as we foresee from the start.

This was a success. It has been a commercial success and it's a success from a design point (of view), from all angles, actually. Even so, I'm not sure if I had another opportunity to build a similar Data Center again I don't know if I would do it because it was so tiresome to remove all this stone, and it was a risky project. It could have gone wrong. There could have been problems with water from the groundwater. There could have been different types of problems. It is cool and it has been a success both technically and commercially but it was a lot of work to do it.

I remember when I presented it (the proposal) to the bank, when we had some investment loans to carry some of the initial investment, and I told them that we were going to build a James Bond fortress in the mountain. This is long after the dot-com time. It might have sounded like a dot-com project.

Well, it turned out good and we had investments that are not huge. We kept a very tight budget so it was built with very little money, actually. We put in mostly our own work and found solutions ourselves to do it.

FIGURE 3-4
Solid rock surrounds the server cabinets within the Bahnhof Data Center.

Obviously, having to blast through solid rock to expand your usable space is a major challenge. Were there other challenges specific to this site or the fact that you were building it underground?

Each problem was very unique. If you have built several Data Centers in conventional spaces you know basically what problems there are and what you have to do. But with this every day was a new one.

I was worried that big huge blocks of stone might be loose and just fall down, but it was not the case. It was really solid. We had some at the entrance we modified something and when we blew up the space after that we added cement just to fixate some of the rocks at the entrance.

I was talking about that before, it was built in the urban city area. People were sleeping and living very close by. It was not a business-to-business area. There was a church above us. I was worrying that (someone from) the church might call me and say 'Well, we have to tell you that the church has fallen to pieces' and that would not be so good. That was my nightmare, but it didn't happen.

We actually had measuring equipment placed on the buildings outside just to see if there were any troubles caused by the dynamite, but it turned out alright and we didn't encounter any such problems.

The area where the Data Center is located, about 30 meters (98.4 feet) above us, we have these old, 18th-century wooden houses. So it's a big contrast, we have this fortress in the mountain and then you have these small wooden houses. It's a cultural park, a preserved area for older, traditional Swedish houses and then we have this big church also. We have this contrast with the high high tech, science fiction facility and the old environment outside.

I imagine it was difficult just bringing some of the traditional Data Center infrastructure technology below ground, even once you had the space cleared out the way you wanted it.

Yes. We lowered the floor 2 meters (6.6 feet) almost, to make the room have better airflow. I would say the actual computers they are based on traditional level floor cooling where they blow up cooling from the floor and into the cabinets. I know there are different technologies today, but our clients are mostly co-location customers. They come with different boxes of all types and they want access to all types.

It's very hard to build individual coolness in individual cabinets unless you know exactly what type of computers or configurations people are using. When you're doing open co-location space it must be very flexible. We have clients even with old power models, God forbid, but that is the case. And the client is always right. Then it has shown the most convenient way to do it is to have this level floor cooling model.

In all other aspects it's a conventional Data Center from a technology perspective. We have great redundancy. The network is coming in from three different places. The electrical power is also coming in from different places. The unique stuff is the atmosphere and the protection it gets from the mountain.

At the early stage we discussed the use of some kind of geothermal cooling: you drill into the mountain and bring up coolness from the ground. This turned out to be insufficient, we have too much energy. We investigated that but I was told we would have had to drill under several hundreds of homes and it would have been of effect for a limited time span. Sooner or later we would eventually warm up the entire mountain and then (the geothermal cooling) would have no effect. So we decided to use the outside air cooling instead. One advantage in Sweden is that the climate is colder, so we can very often use the outdoor temperatures in the cooling system. We use conventional cooling also but using free cooling from the outside air.

FIGURE 3-5
The underground Data Center incorporates outside air cooling rather than geothermal cooling, to avoid warming the mountain that surrounds it.

Did you have any particular challenges around ventilation and using outside air, with the Data Center being embedded in a mountain rather than in a conventional space?

There was no problem in that. It was built to have air in it in the beginning because it was built for people. There is a ventilation shaft going up, on top of the mountain where we bring in the ventilation for breathing. It's very clean air. It's fresh air in most parts of Stockholm, but it is exceptionally good because it's very high up also. We have very good air inside there.

Right now there are 15 people working there. It's our NOC, basically, the network operations center for our Internet telecom operator. We have been there in an operational sense since it opened in 2008. We have no problems.

There are plants there, also. We had to bring some organic feel into it. If you are forcing people to sit in the mountain you must have something that humans like. And that is plants and we have a big fish tank, about 2,500 liters (660.4 gallons) I believe, with saltwater fish. We tried to simulate daylight, stuff like that. It's very much built for people.

Did you know from the beginning that you wanted to have those sort of features in a facility or did that come later?

Definitely. That was initially planned. They were in the budget from the beginning. It was a strategic decision very early. We decided that this should be a nice James Bond fortress and if you have a James Bond fortress you should have a fish tank.

We originally were planning to have piranha—you know, the little fishes that eat meat. But I was told that they are so boring. They just stand still and are not so colorful. So we decided for saltwater fish and colorful instead. And, the plants, I think it was a science fiction movie *Silent Running*, something from the early '70s, where we had these space stations with greenhouses floating around in outer space. This was the original idea. Everything was defined with this in mind. It was not added on later. It was the idea to have all this from the beginning.

FIGURE 3-6   Artificial waterfalls within the Bahnhof Data Center.

It's impossible to argue with the logic that if you're going to have a James Bond villain lair you should try to include fish tanks with piranha in them. That's certainly consistent. You mentioned the raised floor system for the delivery of cooling. Is the Data Center's power and cabling infrastructure delivered under the floor as well?

Yes, that is under the floor. That is why we lowered the floor so much, to give us additional space. I know that you can have it above, but aesthetically we didn't want to have too much stuff (visible). It should be clean and look science fiction-properly. That is why we decided to have them under the floor. It is a higher (deeper) space than normally so this gives good airflow flowing in. I know sometimes you get problems with the cables under (a raised floor) because they can hinder the airflow, but this didn't happen. The raised floor is definitely higher than in our conventional Data Centers.

If you could go back and design the facility all over again, is there anything that you would do differently?

Maybe blow out more space. Because now we have all of the cabinets are almost gone (occupied) now. We should have made it bigger. That was the mistake. It was a matter of cost, also.

Second, maybe even add even more (features). I designed with the plants and stuff like that, but we scrapped other ideas. With the ventilation shaft there was a possibility to build an elevator, and I was considering to have something like a Batman elevator (with Bat-poles) going in to the cave from the top of the mountain, but it was too expensive. Given the chance again I would definitely add the Batman elevator to the facility.

We were also considering a small railway from the entrance down to the center, but it was too complicated. Given the chance again I would add something more like that. And my recommendation for guys building computer centers is (to understand) that people like this kind of stuff. Even if you don't have a cave you should definitely consider adding stuff that gives some kind of human touch or a feeling or atmosphere for the facility because computer centers can be so boring.

Many of our customers, it's included in our offering, they can bring their own clients and can have presentations (at the site). It's a great facility to have a presentation if you have some kind of new website or project to present. The clients appreciate having meetings in this kind of environment. That enhances their experience and gives them great value for placing their servers and applications here.

"I presented to the bank...and I told them that we were going to build a James Bond fortress in the mountain."

FIGURE 3-7   Two Maybach diesel submarine engines, complete with accompanying sound-horn,
                    provide standby power for the Data Center.

You've anticipated my next question somewhat. Not everyone would entertain the idea of putting a greenhouse or these other features in their Data Center. For the amenities that you have installed, do you think these are universal in that anyone who puts them in to their Data Center would see a benefit or are they useful at your site solely because you decided to have a theme?

Let's face it. Data Centers have been built by technicians for technicians but sometimes we have forgotten about the human touch and to give some style on something. I think you have to add that.

I don't say that you should have to build a fortress in this special style in a mountain that we have done. But if you have a conventional center you can always enhance your experience by playing around with stuff and doing it differently. Something that gives it a unique feeling. That is often neglected. People spend a lot of money on traditional marketing, but just by giving these small items you can bring a lot of extra value. And many of the clients appreciate it, too. From that point of view it's definitely worth it to invest and give that. Especially if you want people to work in the Data Center. People are more productive and happy if their environments are nice than if you are working in a boring space.

Do you have plans for any future Data Center buildouts—for any other Bond villain lairs if you will?

Yes. We are working on a concept with modular Data Centers. The idea sprang from that fact that if you build in a mountain you realize that the mountain it is very hard to expand in space. Once the space is finished you have to do something else. So, I would like to build Data Centers in modules where you can have module after module after module when you need more space.

With those modules, are you also going to put in any interesting features?

Absolutely. Absolutely. I'm considering building a space theme. Imagine a space station on Mars or something like that, with modular tents and very scaled design. It should be defined.

If you consider the Swedish products like the Absolut vodka bottle. We can always say that the bottle is a bottle. But if you add some design and add some concept with it it enhances the experience. It's the same. If I say 'We are going to build modules' people will believe it's containers, but it's not containers. They will be designed differently and they will for sure give the fun factor we are looking for.

I have gotten a lot of publicity for this project. A mountain is a mountain, so maybe that is hard to top in terms of the atmosphere. But we will give our best to do it.

Any final advice that you would offer to others who work on Data Center design projects in the future?

I think you should give the human factor a great thought. Computer centers should be built for humans and for their clients. Most often you focus a lot on the technological aspects but you forget about the humans who are going to work there. Also, giving this design you add an experience for the client. That is very often forgotten in these type of projects. Bring a human touch to the computer center, that's my advice.

FIGURE 3-8   The Bahnhof Data Center's electrical room.

FIGURE 3-9
The reception
area at the
Bahnhof Data
Center.

57

3: Bahnhof

FIGURE 3-10
Greenery is planted in the Network Operations Center (NOC) to make the environment more comfortable for employees to work in.

FIGURE 3-11
The Bahnhof Data Center's fire suppression system features a gaseous suppressant.

FIGURE 4-1   The Barcelona Supercomputing Center resides in the Torre Girona Chapel. Images

CHAPTER 4
Barcelona Supercomputing Center

ESSENTIAL DETAILS

ORGANIZATION:	Barcelona Supercomputing Center - Centro Nacional de Supercomputación
LOCATION:	Barcelona, Spain
ONLINE:	April 2005
NOTABLE FEATURES:	Server environment is located in 1920s chapel and houses the MareNostrum supercomputer
TIME TO DESIGN AND BUILD:	7 months
SIZE:	Overall chapel floor space undetermined. Hosting area is 1,722 sq. ft. (160 sq. m)
POWER:	1.4 MW used by the entire facility, with about 850 kW consumed by computing hardware
TIER:	0
CABINET LOCATIONS:	48
POWER DENSITY:	Varies by cabinet, up to 22 kW maximum per cabinet maximum
INFRASTRUCTURE DELIVERY:	Electrical conduits, cooling, and cabling all delivered under raised floor
STRUCTURAL LOADING:	512 lb. per sq. ft. (2500 kg per sq. m)
FIRE SUPPRESSION SYSTEM:	Water mist system

When Spanish government officials needed to find a building that could be quickly modified to house the MareNostrum supercomputer they had what some might call divine inspiration. They would convert Barcelona's Torre Girona chapel into a Data Center.

The deconsecrated building had sufficient space to house the supercomputer yet lacked the physical infrastructure to support what was then the fifth fastest supercomputer in the world. As of this writing MareNostrum can perform more than 94 trillion operations per second and includes more than 10,000 processors. It is used for intensive computing tasks such as human genome research and cosmological simulations that replicate the development of the universe.

The challenge for the designers and builders was to upgrade the 1920s building to support the ultra-modern supercomputer while leaving the chapel's distinctive architecture fully intact. The result of their careful work is a facility that is frequently described as one of the most beautiful Data Centers in the world.

Dr. Sergi Girona, operations director for the Barcelona Supercomputing Center, discusses the challenges associated with building the server environment.

The Interview

What drove the decision to locate your supercomputing center in the chapel?

In 2004 the Spanish government had the opportunity to buy MareNostrum, the supercomputer. The reason that Spain was able to do so is because a large supercomputing research group from the Technical University of Catalonia was working, since 1980, with very good cooperation with IBM. This offered the Spanish government the chance to get them the system. But then the deal was to have the system installed in four months very close to this research group, that is, in the Technical University. So, as you can understand, a new computer room setup in four months requires an existing building, but an existing building with some special facilities. At this point of time there were only very limited spaces available and one of them was the chapel, because it was a clear floor plan of more than 120 square meters (1,292 square feet) with no columns; a height of more than 5 meters (16.4 feet). So that was one of the possibilities, and the best one in fact.

So you needed to install the supercomputer in just four months. How long did you have to design and build the Data Center to house it?

This comes with the story. The agreement between the Spanish government and IBM was signed on March 10th, 2004. The objective for IBM was showing the system in November 2004, at the next supercomputing conference, and so this four month requirement was in place. On March 11th, we had this horrible terrorist attack in Madrid that, along with the deaths and all the disaster, motivated a change of the governments in Catalonia and in Spain. This meant that we were delayed for the construction of the computer room for three months. We used this three month period for designing the facility and for discussion, not beginning any construction, just making decisions, analysis, and processing.

Then after a few months they made it clear that we needed to start building up the facilities, so we started building in July and the facility was completely set up on October 12th. Because of this delay we were not able to have the system installed in MareNostrum in October to make the Top500, so we pre-installed part of the system in Madrid. IBM was providing the Spanish government with facilities that could host part of the system. Not the system in full production, of course, but a sufficient size of the systems to run the Linpack test.

So in reality, we started the design of the system in April 2004 until June, with construction spanning from July to October. This construction include the computer room itself, the site facilities with the control switches and fire detectors and alarms, and also the electrical transformers, because we are connected to a medium voltage ring so we have to transform this to normal voltage.

Even with that outside delay that's still a relatively short amount of time to bring all of that together.

Absolutely correct. And it happens to be also in the middle of summer vacation here in Spain. You may know that in Spain, and normally this is true in the south of Europe, because of the heat it is always difficult to have normal people working. It's almost given that everybody is on vacation. You must have any material you need in storage before starting, or you will not get any material at all.

This is obviously not your average building to construct a Data Center in. What special restrictions or challenges did you have to deal with as part of building a server environment within the chapel?

The first one is that we didn't want to change the structure of the chapel. So that means that the chapel has the existing walls and we didn't change any walls.

Second, a chapel is intended for people to get in but not for machinery to get in. So we have a very strict limitation on the size of equipment that can get in to the chapel. We are only using one door that all the material in the chapel is going through because all of the other doors are limited to people, so no big material can get in.

Another important condition is that chapels here in Spain and in Europe, I learned, use the chimneys of the nearby kitchen for heating inside. That means that the floor is not thick enough for having very heavy components on top. So we had to eliminate the chimneys on the basement of the chapel and then start building the facility on top of that.

And another important one: the chapel does not have a roof that is thick or strong enough for having the chillers on top. So we had to install the chillers underground next to the chapel. For people from the United States this is a very weird solution, because they consider that if a tornado is coming then you can cover it and there is no destruction. But in Spain we don't have any tornadoes and it's more difficult to get fresh air in these basements. So that was also another challenging situation.

So were there any modifications to the building itself? It sounds like you very much tried to leave it in its pre-existing state.

The only modifications we made in the chapel were three or four channels connecting from the main hall of the chapel to the corridor where we have installed facilities, and one big channel connecting to the outside for the chillers. This is absolutely not visible because it is underground.

If someone else was trying to build a Data Center in such a special location, where they wanted to impact their surroundings as little as possible, what advice do you have for them?

To schedule properly with all the people working on the facility. Because you can discover very last-minute that they are thinking of working in parallel and this is not possible. Because everyone is thinking of his field but not in the others' field.

As an example, they were thinking of installing the beams and the glass of the computer room at the same time that we were installing the channels for the cabling. But of course you have only one space for moving the forklifts, and this is the space of the channels. So you have to schedule that properly on your own, and not to rely on the engineers that are working independently by areas of the project.

We have a glass box inside the chapel, ok? This construction is governed by an architect. And then you have the facility inside which is governed by the engineer. Normally they are friends, but they don't share lunch. You know what I mean? They talk to each other but they don't speak the same language. So, they have different compromises and different points of view that they don't share at all. Someone has to consider that part of the work.

FIGURE 4-2   The supercomputing center resides in a large glass box, providing maximum visibility of the surrounding chapel.

Speaking of the glass box, why did you enclose the Data Center in that way?

With the building completely finished the architect told us that it is simply furniture inside the house, inside the chapel, because we don't want to modify anything on the chapel itself. If you are installing some walls inside the chapel, you will destroy the image completely. If it is glass, on the other hand, everything is completely visible on the other side, so the chapel is always there.

But there is also another reason. In Spain we installed the computers, called PCs (PC for portable computer). We installed those and we said that this place is called a pecera, because it's the place of the PCs. But in Spanish, *pecera* is the translation of 'fish tank.' So we have a very big fish tank for the computer.

Normally computer rooms have windows. Not those that are reserved in the U.S., but here normally you have windows to look inside. So we have a very big fish tank for our computer room.

It helps at the same time for visibility and branding. Having walls that hide the chapel would not be a good solution. You have seen the walls of the chapel it is not a good solution because they are having columns on those walls that we have to void for the cooling of the system.

What degree of infrastructure redundancy does the supercomputing center have?

We have some redundancy. This is a computer center which is for scientists in Spain, so we don't have any restriction on services. We don't have any severe service level agreement with our users. We decided to maintain limited redundancy in all the concepts.

For example, we only maintain on the UPS (uninterruptible power supply) and a generator the file systems and the networking to the outside. So in case of failure we simply lose all the computing capacity. We made the decision based on our needs and on the overall total cost of ownership of the system with a different solution.

Your power, cooling and cabling infrastructure are all delivered under a raised floor, yes?

Yes. Every one of those racks is using 22 kW. At that point of time the cooling was by air, so we decided to have a 97 cm. (38.2 in.) elevation for the first floor and all the facilities and all the services went on this first floor.

"Having walls that hide the chapel would not be a good solution."

We have the distribution of the water pipe for the chilled water and this is connecting up to 12 CRAC (computer room air conditioning) units for a total capacity of 1.1 MW cooling capacity. We change the temperature of the chilled water depending on winter and summer time. Normally in winter we operate with warmer water and in summer we operate with colder water.

On the first floor we also have the channeling for the power and the networking, with different levels for different channels and for different concepts. One level for the power, a second level for the copper Ethernet, and another level for the fiber. We try to keep what's called the cold aisles clean of any channel so all the channels are below the hot aisles.

We have these compute racks and the floor was designed to be able to resist up to 2,500 kg per sq. m (512 lb. per sq. ft.). This is standard today but it was not at that time. So what happened is that we decide to have the entire floor with this capacity and we failed on the fluid dynamic analysis, on the amount of air that was going through the tiles with holes.

So we substituted those tiles with open ones, and those tiles are not capable of handling this weight but give more air to the environment. Following this direction, I designed hardware that we placed in front of the rack to force all the air that is coming from the first floor to go directly to the rack. It's like a chimney but it forces the cold air to go directly inside the rack.

So we don't have cold aisles anymore, because the cold aisle is limited by this device. And all the computer room is now a hot computer room. So the average temperature in the computer room is today 32 Celsius (89.6 Fahrenheit). We used to have 34 Celsius (93.2 Fahrenheit) but we changed it to 32 because of the heat exchange to the exterior of the chapel. In the summer time people visiting us complained about the heat that we were transferring to the outside.

To my knowledge, we were one of the very first computer rooms becoming a hot computer room instead of a cold computer room. We produce cold air to 18 Celsius (64.4 Fahrenheit) but all the cold air is limited to the computer rack so it's going there directly. But not by a closed cold aisle, but the aisle is completely attached to the device of the computer.

What made you decide to run the Data Center at a warmer temperature?

Efficiency. My problem was the delta-T of the CRAC units was not very high: it was 3 to 4 Celsius (5.4 to 7.2 Fahrenheit) in total. Now I have a delta-T which is above 12 Celsius (21.6 Fahrenheit) and this means that the CRAC unit is working at a convenient performance for this machinery. It has been designed to work in this environment and we maintain it. If you operate a computer room in cold, then the cold air is getting back to the CRAC unit. Then it's not having enough delta-T so it's not giving all the performance that it can deliver. You are using those CRAC units less efficiently.

So with these devices and operating in warm temperatures we manage to have all the fans of the computers working at the minimum speed. And we also manage to have the fans of all the CRACs working at a very low speed. Very low speed for this is about 70 or 60 rpm. If you are experienced with that you will know that a fan working at 80 percent of capacity is using 50 percent of the energy. That really was affecting my bill. In fact, one of the things that we detected after doing all those modifications is that our electricity bill was decreased by 10 percent. And I can tell you that our electricity bill on a yearly basis is about a million euros. So a 10 percent discount is some money.

So the problem is that everyone has their own point of view but you have to design that specifically. The point is that air conditioners are normally working to adapt to changes, but we don't have any change on the system. The system is in full production all day long. We have a heater completely working all day long, 24 hours a day, which is changing temperature from 18 to 32 every day, every moment. We are not changing the conditions of the computer room as in a normal facility. It is fixed and very stable.

I assume you don't have a lot of turnover of hardware. Are there regular upgrades to the supercomputer and associated hardware or do you maintain the same set of equipment over a long period of time?

Normally we don't change the systems in less than 6 months. So in 6 months maybe another rack is coming in and an old one is going out. Shorter term we don't do anything. This is a computer room that is specific for supercomputing, other systems are located in different facilities.

FIGURE 4-3   The MareNostrum supercomputer performs 94 trillion operations per second and includes more than 10,000 processors.

What type of fire suppression system do you employ?

I was completely against using any gas for two reasons. One, for humans inside the computer room, although the number of people that can get inside is very limited because it's visible from the outside, so nobody is normally inside.

The other reason is legislation. It's changing continuously here in Europe with regards to which is the gas you can use for fire extinguishing. So we went with mist of water. We use very small drops of water at high velocity for extinguishing any fire.

I was visiting them (the manufacturer) in a facility they have for testing and I was impressed by the results. They were showing me an environment where a PC was discharged with this water mist twice a day and the computer room is still operational.

And the other more impressive one, they start a fire with gasoline inside a tank and it took three minutes with normal water to extinguish the fire, and it was extinguished because the gasoline was consumed. But they start the same test with the water mist and they stop the fire in 15 seconds. And they showed me that they can restart the fire because the gasoline was still there. So it was able to extinguish the fire with the fuel still available, so it was very fine by me.

Also, if it has been fired, recharging is not so expensive. This is an advantage against the gases, which are very expensive to recharge. So this is just normal water with some treatment. There is a cost but it is one-tenth the cost of the gas for being reloaded to the facility.

If you could go back and redesign the Data Center all over again, are there any design approaches that you would do differently?

With the technology today, yes. With the technology today, of course. For example, we are changing the facility so we will have the capacity to cool the racks by air or by the rear doors. So we will be having these two possibilities in the same facility.

What else would I change? Not really a lot of other things.

You're referring to liquid-cooled rear doors?

Correct. We have a limitation that we can only have 48 racks in the computer room. This is because of the space required for the hot aisles. Otherwise it's too dense, and it's too hot there. If we want to have an additional row (this is an additional eight racks) the only way we can have that is if those racks are water-cooled. And this can be achieved with the rear doors.

So we are updating the facility to be able to have most of the racks with this rear door cooling. And then we will be extending the capacity of the total computer room in terms of power and cooling capacity.

Are you bringing in more power or is this merely allowing you to make more use of electrical capacity that you already have?

I will be adding more capacity and using more capacity. Right now we are using 1.3 or 1.4 MW in total. I'm expecting to use a total of 2 MW. But I will be adding more capacity to still have some backup capacity, so we will be installing a total capacity of around 4 MW. But I'm planning to use a maximum of 2, 2.1 MW.

And the same goes for the cooling. We will be using the same we have but extending it for redundancy, and we are planning to expand the total capacity. So instead of having racks up to 22 kW we are looking for racks that can have up to 28 kW.

In a way you are getting to go back and redesign. A lot of the physical infrastructure is in place already, but you're once again trying to work inside this building that you don't want to impact. Has that influenced how you approach the upgrade?

Yes, absolutely. First of all, I will be thinking very carefully for the scheduling and the planning for all of the piping and all the analysis, and decommissioning the old system and installing the new system. That has to be really planned and scheduled. But of course any new system must be coming with an option for having the rear-door heat exchanger, because otherwise I cannot host a lot of them in my computer room. That will be a requirement for all the new computers in this computer room. Including the disks, because the disks I have right now are using 5 kW but the new disks we are just installing are using 15 kW. That's already a lot of heat that you can get out of a rack.

The original chapel obviously didn't have sufficient electrical capacity to operate a supercomputer. What sort of capacity did you install?

The chapel didn't have any power capacity at all. We installed it in this big hall, this big bunker we have next to the chapel. It was created by us in 2004. We installed transformers with enough capacity for the computer room, not for the chapel. The chapel originally had some lighting, but not very powerful. We installed three transformers with enough capacity. This is connected to the medium voltage ring of the university and we can get a consumption of 3 MW and we are going to be extending this to 4 MW.

What structural loading capability does the chapel have? Obviously it wasn't originally designed with any thought to supporting computer hardware.

Except for the area where there were chimneys in the ground of the chapel, which we covered completely, all the rest of the chapel is on the ground level. The weight of the chapel is on the ground, persistent and therefore no problem. The first floor can hold 2,500 kilograms per square meter (512 lb. per sq. ft.).

Did you have to take any special measures to reinforce the area where the supercomputer resides or was the original infrastructure adequate?

No, that was adequate already. Outside of removing these chimneys everything else was adequate. So we have continued construction on this ground level floor.

Looking back on the project, were there any surprises that came up along the way?

Not really, no. Just normal problems. Things that everybody knows but nobody knows how to fix.

For example, the humidification problem. We have the CRAC units, 12 of them, humidifying and humidifying continuously because of the change of temperatures. But if you are humidifying, it's very expensive. It's three times the cost on the power that the CRAC unit is using. If you are not humidifying you are saving a lot of money. And you can humidify very simply.

I don't know if you live in the mountains or you live in the coast area, but in the mountains for getting humidity what people do is just have a bag of water on top of the radiator. This heats the water to the temperature that the water evaporates and creates the nice humidity. So we have humidity problems in the computer room and we are fixing it from time to time with bags of water and saving a lot of money. Because this is just what you learn from nature. Humidification in nature comes from the sea and with the sun that's getting the water to the environment.

Your supercomputing center has been described in several publications and web sites as one of the prettiest Data Centers ever built. During the design phase, how much attention was given to the look of the facility? Did you consciously focus on aesthetics or did its striking appearance just happen to come from the design?

It's most likely the second one.

It really comes from the fact that we are installed inside the chapel and we don't want to change the chapel. We want to maintain the chapel visible. It's not the computer room that is nice itself, it's the sum of the computer room and the chapel and the fact that we are not changing any of the chapel and we are getting the computer, the capacity of running in full operation, in this environment.

Of course we designed the computer room for efficiency. So if you have a look at the pictures you will notice that all the beams of the computer room are mostly located outside of the computer room not inside and this is to not influence the fluid dynamics of the room.

We designed this to be 5 meters (16.4 feet) high instead of 3 or 4, because we want to have better fluid dynamics. This gives us the possibility of matching the size of the complete box with the size of the chapel, in terms of having the top of the computer room at the same level as the upper floor of the chapel. And that's given a dimension and a conjunction of the two bodies, the chapel and the computer room, which is very good in terms of visibility and environment. It happens to be that this solution fits efficiency for the computer room and at the same time the visibility.

It sounds like after the decision was made to build this in the chapel the design pieces came together as you worked around the constraints of the building. You didn't necessarily intend for this to be a showpiece, but by virtue of putting it in the chapel it became that.

That's correct. When people realized that this is inside the chapel, the architect had a challenge because he wanted not to destroy the chapel, but to show all the vantages of the chapel. For the engineer developing the air conditioning it was a challenge because in the design everything was very efficient, although inside the chapel, not so much.

We wanted to have this visible from every place in the chapel, so we designed everything very clean in spaces. All the underground is visible from outside. So you must have all the channels properly installed and labeled and everything has to be very carefully placed.

You should know that we have visits every day into the chapel by universities, schools, politicians; everyone comes here to visit us because of the chapel. This is very good because then we can show what we are doing with the computer and what the scientists are doing with this facility.

FIGURE 4-4   The height of the supercomputing center's glass walls were chosen to optimize airflow and align with the physical dimensions of the chapel.

FIGURE 5-1 Calcul Québec's Data Center resides in a concrete silo that originally housed a particle accelerator. Images provided courtesy of Calcul Québec.

CHAPTER 5
Calcul Québec (Compute Québec)

ORGANIZATION: Calcul Québec (Compute Québec)	
LOCATION: Québec City, Québec, Canada	
ONLINE: August 2009	
NOTABLE FEATURES: Server environment is located in circular building that previously housed a Van de Graaff generator	
TIME TO DESIGN AND BUILD: 29 months	
SIZE: 2,340 sq. ft. (217.4 sq. m)	
POWER: 1.2 MW	
TIER: 0	
CABINET LOCATIONS: 56	
INFRASTRUCTURE DELIVERY: Power and cabling infrastructure are provided overhead. Cooling is distributed through a ring-shaped, cold plenum, with hardware exhaust vented into a cylindrical, hot core.	
STRUCTURAL LOADING: 940 lb. per sq. ft. (4,589.5 kg per sq. m)	
FIRE SUPPRESSION SYSTEM: Double-action dry pipe sprinkler system	

Data Centers are typically all about squares and rectangles. Hardware and cabinets, power distribution units and air handlers, floor tiles and server rows: there's not a curve among them.

What if those boxy shapes and their 90-degree angles were placed in a circular space, though? Can a Data Center's square pegs fit gracefully—and perform well—in a round hole?

Oui.

On the campus of Universite' Laval in Québec City, Canada, research consortium Calcul Québec has converted a cylindrical building that originally housed a Van de Graaff particle accelerator into a Data Center. The silo now contains the group's Colossus supercomputer, whose users perform research in a range of scientific disciplines.

Three levels have been constructed in the 2,340 sq ft. (217.4 sq. m.) silo to house computing hardware. Server cabinets are arranged in outward-facing circles: the outer ring acts as a cold air plenum while hardware exhaust is vented into a hot core at the center. Grated floors allow air to pass through, drawn downward by a bank of 3.3 ft. (1 m.) wide fans capable of moving 120,000 cfm (3,398 cmm) of air.

Marc Parizeau, professor of computer engineering at Université Laval and deputy director of Calcul Québec, discusses what it's like to do computing in the round.

The Interview

Please tell me the history of the silo building that houses your supercomputer.

The building was built in 1965. It was a research center in nuclear physics and it had a Van de Graaff particle accelerator.

We had to make some relatively minor changes. At first I thought that it was big changes, but in fact demolishers are very efficient at what they're doing.

The silo was housing the accelerator itself. And it was accelerating particles vertically into a room underneath the silo and then the particles were deflected at 90 degrees horizontally into a larger room which was called the target room. This is where the physicists would make their experiments.

At first we wanted to put the Data Center in that target room, which has a very high ceiling—it's an 18 ft. (5.5 m.) ceiling, a 3,000 sq. ft. (278.7 sq. m.) room. And there was this silo that nobody knew what to do about. We had the idea of putting the computer inside the silo but at first it was just a crazy idea. We didn't know how to proceed.

So we started designing a room into the target room, which is a large rectangular room in the basement. It's not underneath the silo but it's just beside it. We had the regular issues about trying to configure the room for contained cold and hot aisles and putting the CRAC (computer room air conditioning) units inside and having everything fit into the room. We had an objective of allowing up to 60 cabinets in the room and it was not quite large enough. And then we started to think about the silo again. We had a team of engineers and we started to brainstorm about what we could do and after a while the second option became the first option because we could put a larger machine inside the silo and have a better Data Center, more efficient.

To come back to your question, what needed to be changed: inside the silo, it was mainly open. There was the accelerator but essentially there was a concrete slab on the ground floor. We needed to remove that concrete slab. There was also a mezzanine that was built inside the silo. And the mezzanine was originally designed to support the accelerator housing because the accelerator itself is under a metal shell and when it operates this shell is filled with inert gas so that the accelerator that works essentially with static electricity so that the large electrical charge that accumulates in the accelerator does not spark everywhere. It was contained inside a metal shell and inside the air was removed and it was filled with an inert gas—helium I think.

The mezzanine was there to support this metal shell that was on top of the accelerator. When the physicists needed to do maintenance inside the accelerator they had to lift this shell which weighed several tons and they used to put this shell on this concrete slab mezzanine. So we needed to remove that. That was it.

"We had the idea of putting the computer inside the silo but at first it was just a crazy idea."

How long did it take for you to come up with a design and then to make the necessary conversions?

The design took about a year. At first we were thinking about the target room that I spoke of, that was in January 2007. A year later the engineers and architects were doing the detailed plans and specifications. The first four months were spent working on the Data Center inside the target room and afterwards we shifted toward the silo design and that took another eight months before we settled on all of the small details that needed to be done to have it working.

When did the facility formally open as a Data Center?

The servers started to be delivered in June 2009. The power was put on the machines in early August and it was definitely accepted in November 2009, just in time for the Top500 (supercomputer) list announcement.

The Colossus supercomputer within the silo occupies 56 cabinets that are ringed around three levels?

The design was made for up to 56 cabinets but the current supercomputer that we have is much more dense than what we expected at first. At first we designed the site to be able to host 1U servers because we didn't know what we would get. The worst case was a machine with 1U servers.

The machine we got was using blades and so the machine was much denser than we anticipated. It occupies 20 cabinets right now on two levels. We have three possible levels; there is one that is completely empty.

This facility supports a supercomputer rather than being a production Data Center, but is it equipped with any standby infrastructure?

Yes. We have partial redundancy. We don't have any redundant power for the compute nodes but all of the file systems and the network switches are under UPS (uninterruptible power supply). At first we didn't have a backup generator but we will have one soon because the university is building a new Data Center right beside us. So they will be providing a generator very soon. The basic infrastructure of the machine will be protected by a UPS and generator, but not the compute nodes. The idea is that we are not doing any production work—it's only research—so if there is an event then the worst case is that we lose the currently running simulations and the researchers have to start them again when the power comes back.

The only thing that we need to protect is the file system. So that if there is a power outage we don't lose anything in the file system because file systems don't like power outages, especially large parallel ones with thousands of disks. There are always disks that suffer when the power goes out.

Tell me about the cooling configuration of the Data Center. Your server cabinets are laid out on three levels of the silo, facing outward so they are surrounded by a cold air plenum and there is a hot core in the middle, while the Data Center's mechanical components are in the sub-basement.

There is a cold plenum on the outside of the machine. It's an annular, ring-shaped cold aisle. The cold air comes from the basement, goes up into this vertical cold plenum, which has a ring shape. The air is drawn by the compute nodes, the file server, every piece of equipment draws air from this cold air plenum and throws out the hot air in the center cylindrical hot aisle. And then there are six large variable drives, industrial blowers, that pull the hot air down into a square room that has cooling coils on three sides. These are walls of cooling coils, custom-designed, about 12 ft. (3.7 m.) wide by 8 ft. (2.4 m.) high. Very efficient coils, four layers. They could absorb up to 1.5 MW of heat. So the blowers they force the air to go through the cooling coils and then the air comes out—first the air goes through filters of course before going through the cooling coils—and then it exits on the peripheral cold aisle and goes back up again.

I always get the question of why we were pulling the hot air down and pushing the cold air up. If we wanted to benefit from the natural convection of the hot air upward we would have to put the cooling system on top. So then we would have the water on top. It would be more difficult for the maintenance because we would have to climb all the way up to do the maintenance, change filters and all that. And also, we wouldn't want the water to be on top of the servers. And the convection effect is negligible compared to the blowing capacity that we have.

Each blower can pull up to 20,000 cfm (566.3 cmm) each, so we have 120,000 cfm (3,398 cmm) of blowing capacity. These blowers are very efficient because they are very large and they're variable drives.

FIGURE 5-2   Variable drive blowers move air through Calcul Québec's Data Center at low velocity, consuming little power.

I understand you're recycling some of your heat to help warm the buildings on your campus.

On the Laval campus they have two water loops. There's a chilled water loop and a hot water loop. The chilled water loop is connected to all of the air conditioning units all over campus and the hot water loop is connected to all buildings. The hot water loop is used to heat the campus in winter. During winter what we want to do is we want to use the chilled water from the campus facility, which is very efficient because they use outside air to make the chilled water. They send us chilled water at about 4 degrees Celsius (39.2 Fahrenheit). We heat up the water to about 25 degrees Celsius (77 Fahrenheit) and we return it to them and they are able to pump the heat in the chilled water return and transfer that heat into the hot water loop. So in effect we are heating the campus building during winter. This is what we want to do because in winter producing the chilled water is very cheap compared to producing the hot water. It's about five times more expensive to produce the hot water than the chilled water. So during winter we want to recycle all of the heat, to pump this heat into the hot water loop of the campus heating system.

Of course during the summertime it can get quite hot in Québec City. So during the hottest months, July and August, well then we do the same. We don't have much choice. Mostly we use the chilled water produced by the campuswide facilities and of course then we cannot recycle any of the heat, so the heat is put in the cooling towers and it goes back to the atmosphere.

The university needs to heat the buildings about eight months per year. During four months the temperature goes below zero, but there are four other months where we still need to heat the campus. During the coldest months of the winter the university can recycle maybe up to 90 percent of the heat during winter. Of course during summer they are not able to recycle anything. So on average they can recycle between 50 and 55 percent on a yearly basis of that heat.

We also have another cooling system, a free air cooling system in the silo. We are able to draw up to 12,500 cfm (354 cmm) of outside air to cool the machine. In practice this system can almost cool the whole machine. During winter when it's below 4 degrees Celsius (39.2 degrees Fahrenheit) outside we can cool about 80 percent of the machine using outside air. But during winter we don't want to do that because it's cheaper for the university, it's better to recycle the heat for heating the campus because producing chilled water is cheap and producing hot water is very expensive, so the university prefers to do that. But in between, during fall and spring, then there is a computer-controlled system that decides whether we should recycle the heat or use the free air cooling system.

For instance, this year they are renovating the building which is adjacent to the silo. For the cooling system we are connected to the pipes that bring us the chilled water. The university will use the same pipes for the new Data Center that I spoke of before. They needed to disconnect us for a few days so that they could connect the new Data Center, so during three days in February we operated on the free air cooling system. At first we operated 100 percent of the machine but then the temperature was rising in to the silo and the system was not enough to keep it within reasonable levels. So we had to shut down part of the machine. We could have shut down only 10 percent of the machine but we shut down 20 percent. We didn't want to take any chances of having problems. We ran 80 percent of Colossus on free air cooling for three days. That was very practical. We didn't have to completely halt the machine while we were making some piping modifications.

What operational temperature do you maintain your supercomputer's hardware at?

Currently the temperature in the cold aisle is regulated at about 18 degrees Celsius (64.4 degrees Fahrenheit), which is probably too low. We could operate much higher than that, but this is the temperature that was set and we haven't changed it. In the hot cylindrical core it depends on the applications that are running but it can go up to 35 degrees Celsius (95 degrees Fahrenheit). The highest temperature I have seen is 35 degrees Celsius (95 degrees Fahrenheit), when the machine is very loaded it can go all the way up there. Otherwise it's around 31, 32 degrees (87.8, 89.6 Fahrenheit) on the hot side. The temperature that is regulated is in the cold aisle.

There is something that is specific, very particular about our design. We are regulating the differential pressure between the cold and hot aisles. This is the secret sauce of our design. As far as I know nobody is doing that in any Data Center because when you have several aisles, even if you can contain your aisles, it's very difficult to control the differential pressure between the cold and hot aisles. But since we have only one cold aisle and only one hot aisle, because these aisles are vertical, it's very easy to control. We just put the differential pressure sensor between the cold side and the hot side.

And we have very low air velocity. This is the second ingredient of our secret sauce. It's having very low air velocity. So then the cold aisle is really a plenum. The velocity is below 2.4 m. (7.9 ft.) per second, which is quite low. And that would be if we would fill the silo to capacity, then it would go to that figure but it's probably in the area of 1 meter (3.3 ft.) per second. So you can barely feel the air move inside the cold aisle. Essentially, it's a real plenum. So we measure the relative pressure between the two aisles and if the servers accelerate their fans to draw more air because they're running hot then we just accelerate our fans to provide all of the air that they need.

The problem in Data Centers is when the air velocity goes to 5 meters (16.4 ft.) per second or above. Then you get differences in pressure in the aisles. Maybe at one end of the aisle the pressure will not be equal in the whole aisle. Some servers will have less air than others, so they will start to accelerate their fans because they are running hot. They don't have the air that they need. So in our design, by regulating the differential air pressure and by keeping the air velocity very low— and why is it low? It's simply because the cross-section of the floor is very large. In our cold aisle we have 32 sq. m. (344.4 sq. ft.) of hole. The flooring is grating flooring, which is open 90 percent. Not like regular tiles in Data Centers with raised flooring, where the tiles are perforated but the percentage of the surface is quite low and the percentage of the surface that is perforated is even lower.

What's the weight bearing capability of that floor grating? In a conventional raised floor perforated tiles often support less weight than solid tiles and, as you say, your flooring has a greater percentage of openings.

When we designed the silo we had a structural engineer. He asked me what I needed and I told him that I needed to be able to have up to 20 racks per floor and I needed to have these racks anywhere on the floor. He made his computations and he arrived at a figure of 940 lb. per sq. ft. (4,589.5 kg per sq. m.) of load capacity on the floor. This is way above the standard Data Center. Regular Data Centers are either 150 lb. per sq. ft. (732.4 ft. per sq. m.) or when their floors are very strong they are 250 lb. per sq. ft. (1220.6 ft. per sq. m.). The grating is very thick; it's very high and it's very strong. It's supported by beams underneath and the beams were sized accordingly.

We didn't want the floor to move because we needed to contain the cold aisle from the hot aisle. I didn't want the floor to bend. It's so strong that we didn't have any issues with that.

Any other interesting design elements in your Data Center that people should be aware of?

The most important thing is that we are using large, variable drive industrial blowers. The blowers have a diameter of 1 m. (3.3 ft.) so they turn very slowly. I don't recall their power consumption but they consume almost no power if you compare that to the blowers that you will find in servers or even blades that have more efficient blowers. These are order of magnitude more efficient and they are variable drive. So, we blow the amount of air that the server needs. Because we have a very large cross-section so that this air can go through and we keep the air velocity very low. Beneath 2.4 m. (7.9 ft.) per second in the worst case. That's if the blowers were running at full speed, 120,000 cfm (3,398 cmm) through 32 sq. m. (344.4 sq. ft.), then we would get about 2.4 m. (7.9 ft.) per second. And we have pressure differential sensors to measure the amount of air that is going through the servers and we just replace the air that the server needs. And because the air velocity is so low the pressure is uniform within the cold aisle. The problem with air velocity is when it goes too high the pressure inside the cold aisle is no longer uniform, then there is friction. Friction produces turbulence and turbulence produces differences in pressure. This is the root of all cooling problems in Data Centers, is turbulence.

FIGURE 5-3
Hardware exhaust vents into a hot core and then is drawn down through the floor grating to cooling coils on the ground floor.

The other factor about our design is that the racks are arranged in a circle. That's another interesting detail. Usually in Data Centers when you have problems of turbulence, of differences in pressure or differences in temperature because of pressure or because you need to move the air through very long distances, they are at the end of rows. Sometimes in Data Centers the air will be very cold on one side and at the other end of the aisle, the end opposite to the CRAC units, then maybe there will be hot spots. And the hot spots are caused by turbulence and turbulence is caused by friction and by corners, also. In a circular arrangement like ours there are no corners.

I'm curious, how are the noise levels in your Data Center? With the airflow moving slowly, I assume the mechanical system is relatively quiet.

When we designed the site, around the area where the blowers are installed we installed on the walls sound-absorbing material because we were afraid that these blowers would make a lot of sound. And they do make some sound but they make much less sound than the servers themselves. It is noisy, but it's the noise of the blowers of the blade systems. The blowers of equipment that we got are relatively noisy. So, it's not quiet inside. If you need to work there for long times it's better to wear ear protection gear.

Were there any surprises that came up during the conversion of the silo building into a Data Center?

We anticipated that we would have problems demolishing stuff. I told you about the mezzanine and the concrete slab floor that needed to be removed. This is a concrete slab floor, 2 ft. (.6 m.) thick, armored very strongly. The silo itself has 2 ft. (.6 m.) thick walls of armored concrete. It was a nuclear grade installation so it was made very, very strong. In the basement the walls are 3 ft. (.9 m.) thick, armored. We needed to cut some openings in there. We thought that would be an issue but in fact all of the demolition and cutting out some openings in to the silo and to the walls in the basement it took less than a month. And we needed to remove also the metal enclosure of the accelerator. This thing was maybe 25 or 30 ft. (7.6 or 9.1 m.) high and it's a metal enclosure that was 2 in. (5 cm.) thick. We thought it would be a big deal to put that into pieces but in the end it was very easy.

During the construction there were delays. Essentially it was the subcontractor that prepared all of the metalwork for the floors. So the beams, the grating, that took a lot of time. It took several months of delay because the subcontractor did not do his job very well. He was late. So that was the explanation for the delays. It took about 4 months more to build than what was expected. We expected about 4 or 5 months and it took maybe 8 months.

FIGURE 5-4   The housing for the Van de Graaff particle accelerator was sliced into rings to facilitate its removal. Shown here, the accelerator base rests on the floor.

Surprises? No. We didn't have a lot of cost overruns. We had a few but not too much. The biggest one is that at first for the fire protection system, we thought we could use water from the adjacent building. When they made tests they realized that there was not enough pressure. So we had to cross the street to get the water for the fire sprinklers. That was a small surprise that cost about $100,000 to drill through the street. On the campus we have the problem that the water pressure that we get from the city is barely enough. It depends on when you make the test, sometimes the pressure is enough and sometimes it isn't. When we made our test it wasn't. So we had to take measures.

We didn't have any problems with the design. The design works well and we didn't have any surprises there.

The shape of your building is obviously unique and influenced the design of your Data Center, but are there any general design strategies that you think others can take away from this project? Anything that you have applied to the building of your next Data Center, for instance?

The new Data Center uses some of the ideas that we used. They measure differential pressure between cold and hot aisles, but they use a rectangular room. It's on two levels, so there is one level with the server cabinets and another level for the cooling system. They re-use a similar design but it was not in a silo.

One thing I can mention, when we were designing the silo we had a problem—how to access the different levels inside the silo? At first we wanted to have a freight elevator. The problem is where to put it. We didn't want to put it inside. We tried to put it outside. Then we had problems because it would have cost us about a half a million dollars more and we didn't have that money, so we couldn't. In the end we needed to, so we put stairs. The design of the stairs that we put inside the silo needed to be optimized. We wanted to take as less space as possible for the stairs, to keep the space for the servers.

It took us about four months to optimize the design of the staircases because the building codes required us to have two fire exits on each level. So there are two intertwined staircases that are round. That was a part of the design that was—it looks kind of boring designing stairs but in that case it was quite a challenge.

How do you bring server cabinets and hardware in to the various levels of the silo?

Inside the silo there was on the roof, built in to the silo, a movable crane. It was a very sophisticated crane that was used to lift the housing of the accelerator, for maintenance. This housing weighs several tons. There was this moving crane attached to the roof of the silo. So we used that for building. If we didn't have this crane inside the silo it would have been much more difficult to build, to demolish what needed to be demolished and to build everything inside the silo.

The crane, it could move in two axes—one longitudinal, in a straight axis, and it could also rotate around the silo. It could move from one side to the other and it could also rotate, so you could bring the crane at any position. And of course it can go up and down. So it had three degrees of freedom.

If the building people if they did not have this crane for the construction, it would have been very difficult for them because they used it a lot to lift stuff and for the demolition. Like the mezzanine, for instance, they removed it in one piece. They cut it from the wall and they cut the columns that supported the mezzanine and they removed the floor of the mezzanine in a single piece using this crane. It was quite impressive to look at that when they were doing it.

There is an opening also inside the silo. And this opening was existing in the original silo. It was the opening through which the accelerator was brought inside the silo. This opening was originally filled with concrete blocks. So it was kind of closed but it was just concrete blocks that we removed and we put in a very large window. In fact, the window has the height of the three levels where there are servers. When the machine was delivered this window was not there. It was left out. We put it at the end. So, the cabinets were delivered, and put in each level through this window with the crane. In fact, with a truck with a platform

FIGURE 5-5   The silo's crane, originally installed to lift the housing of the particle accelerator to enable maintenance, used during demolition and construction of the Data Center. Here the crane removes a concrete column.

lift. Anyway, if we need to bring more racks then we use the crane that is still attached to the roof of the silo and we remove some sections in the center part of the grating floor. We remove sections and we can lift the racks on the second and third floor using the crane. The crane has a 25 ton capacity so we can lift any rack with any content.

It would not be an easy operation, this is not something you would want to do every day. If you bring 10 more racks it will take maybe a day to lift them one by one—an hour or maybe 30 minutes each.

If I were to re-do this design, it would be better to put a freight elevator. We tried that but we didn't have enough budget to pay for that because the construction budget was limited and we didn't want to have overruns. Even if we had the budget we had another problem because on campus there is this committee that overlooks all construction projects. At first we tried to submit to them a proposition of adding a structure outside the silo, a rectangular structure that

FIGURE 5-6   The original appearance of the silo building, before its conversion into a Data Center.

would house a freight elevator and some outside stairs and they rejected it. So even if we had the budget they didn't want us to modify the silo because it's kind of a landmark on the campus so we weren't allowed to make modifications outside the silo. We looked at the possibility of putting a freight elevator inside the silo, but we still would have needed some stairs. So adding the freight elevator would have used even more space, and then there were security issues, building codes.

FIGURE 5-7   The metal structure of the three data floors, as seen during the early stage of construction.

FIGURE 5-8   Power and cabling infrastructure are delivered overhead to cabinet locations
on three floors.

FIGURE 6-1   The Cisco Data Center in Allen, Texas, is linked with a second facility 15 mi. (24.1 km) away, allowing it to instantly failover to one another if necessary. Image by Douglas Alger.

CHAPTER 6
Cisco

ORGANIZATION: Cisco
LOCATION: Allen, Texas
ONLINE: April 2011
NOTABLE FEATURES: Linked to a second Data Center in the same metro area. Enclosed cabinets with chimneys. Airside economizer. Rotary UPS. Rooftop solar panels. LED lighting. Lagoon to capture rainwater for irrigation. Building reinforced to withstand 175 mph (281.6 kph) winds. LEED-Gold certified.
TIME TO DESIGN AND BUILD: 22 months
SIZE: 162,000 sq. ft. (15,050.3 sq. m) total, with 27,700 sq. ft. (2,573.4 sq. m) of hosting space.
POWER: Two redundant 10 MW feeds; IT usable capacity of 5.25 MW.
TIER: III
CABINET LOCATIONS: 754
POWER DENSITY: 6.5 kW average per cabinet, 20 kW maximum
INFRASTRUCTURE DELIVERY: Structured cabling, electrical conduits and air cooling delivered overhead
STRUCTURAL LOADING: 250 lb. per sq. ft. (1,220.6 kg per sq. m)
FIRE SUPPRESSION SYSTEM: Pre-action dry pipe sprinklers, with VESDA smoke detection

What's better than a highly-available, energy efficient Data Center that hosts cloud computing resources for your company? Two of them, of course.

When Cisco opened its Data Center in Allen, Texas, in 2011, the facility came with several features common to a modern server environment. Enclosed cabinets with chimneys isolate hardware exhaust from incoming chilled air, an airside economizer uses outside air for cooling more than 50 percent of the time, and a rotary UPS provides ride-through power in lieu of conventional batteries. Additional features including a 100 kW solar panel array, LED lighting, and a lagoon that collects rainwater to irrigate indigenous, drought-resistant landscaping helped the Data Center achieve LEED-Gold certification.

Perhaps most interesting about the Data Center isn't its physical infrastructure design, though, but how it is linked to a second Data Center 15 miles (24.1 km) away. The Tier III sites serve as active-active mirrors of one another, providing immediate failover capability in the event that either suffers an outage. When data is updated at one Data Center the changes are instantly synchronized at the companion facility. Cisco calls this approach a Metro Virtual Data Center and the company is consolidating much of its Data Center resources into a smaller portfolio that includes three MVDC pairs around the world.

John Manville, senior vice president of Global Infrastructure Services for Cisco, discusses the MVDC model and how the Allen facility was designed to take advantage of the networking company's technology.

The Interview

What is Cisco's overall Data Center strategy? What is the company's goals for its Data Center portfolio?

Two things. One is we need to address the business requirements as they pertain to Data Centers. Number two, showcase Cisco technologies that are relevant to the Data Center and generally raise the awareness and the mindshare that Cisco has with prospective or current customers out there.

What are those business requirements?

There are three main pillars that we wanted to address, that are the Data Center outcomes from some of the business requirements.

One is we have to get the right capacity in the right places in the country, and actually globally as well, and use that capacity in the right way. So we need to optimize the use of it and possibly we need to build or partner with people to give us Data Center space and—probably increasingly in the future—other resources in the Data Center.

Number two is we need to increase the reliability of Cisco's IT environment in general so that (if) there's a catastrophe in one area, a natural disaster wouldn't significantly influence Cisco's business.

And number three is we needed to change how we provided technology infrastructure services to Cisco. This basically means moving to a services based organization and using a lot of automation, understanding our costs really well, driving down the cost, benchmarking many different aspects of how we provide services.

Within that strategy, what functions does this Data Center in Allen, Texas, serve for Cisco?

At a high level they, in conjunction with our Richardson, Texas, Data Center, increase the reliability because for the necessary applications we can operate in much more of an active-active way. So we definitely increase availability and reliability of the services that we provide both internally and to external customers, because Cisco.com for example is serviced in large part out from those Data Centers.

LEED Certification

Leadership in Energy and Environmental Design (LEED) is a rating system for the design, construction, and operation of green buildings. Facilities can achieve ratings of certified, silver, gold, or platinum based on criteria within six categories: sustainable sites, water efficiency, energy and atmosphere, materials and resources, indoor environmental quality, and innovation and design.

We're raising the tier level of the Data Center so just by itself moving these applications and these business processes into a Data Center with a higher tier level, even doing that increases the availability of the applications.

We are using a lot of Cisco technology and several of the pieces of technology have new innovations and other features in them that address some of the capacity and some of the reliability and actually probably some of the way that we offer our services. Some of the new acquisitions from Cisco that we're using down there in our cloud, for example, specifically address how we provide services. So I think all three main areas of what we were trying to do with the Data Center strategy are tangibly implemented in Allen and with its partner Data Center just down the road.

FIGURE 6-2   One of the two data halls within Cisco's Allen Data Center. Image provided courtesy of Cisco. Photography by Cyclone Interactive.

You mention Cisco moving to a services model. How did the mission of this Data Center influence its design?

We did have discussions about whether we should have lower tier Data Centers—we built two Data Centers reasonably close to each other, maybe 15 miles (24.1 km) away from each other, and then used some active-active technology to distribute the applications between them—whether we needed to build a Tier III plus Data Center, which the Allen Data Center is, because it would probably have been cheaper to do that (build to a lower tier).

We decided that in the end it did not make sense to do that because not all applications are architected to operate in an active-active manner even though sometimes that's what the users of those applications and business processes actually need. There were many examples of mostly legacy but even newer applications that we felt should be housed in a Tier III plus Data Center. There is a cost difference between a Tier II and a Tier III plus Data Center but when we looked at the increase we felt that since there were these applications that couldn't make use of active-active capability, that still needed some higher level of foundation and an increased level of reliability, so we would go with making it a Tier III-plus Data Center. That's one thing.

We also needed to make this a multi-tenant Data Center. There are some business units at Cisco that wanted their own cage or wanted almost like a mini co-lo inside that Data Center. Our goal is to provide infrastructure services but at the moment there are valid reasons why some business units only need Data Center space, where we provide them network, power, and cooling.

So there's multi-tenancy and it's environmentally friendly. We made several design decisions, many design decisions actually, to make it as environmentally friendly as we can. We've got Gold LEED certification for that Data Center, several other things that we've done like using rotary UPSs for example.

As far as the technology that's being put in the Data Center it's obviously a newer version of some of the old legacy Data Centers that we have and we've used a lot of the features of mostly Cisco but other partners as well. Technology that gives us better reliability or is better easily managed or we can automate it better. One example of this is we've built out one instance of our private cloud called CITEIS (Cisco IT Elastic Infrastructure Services) is based down there. And that is highly automated provisioning of infrastructure services.

Did you have to incorporate any particular design features to accommodate the different operational policies of the tenants within the Data Center?

From a Data Center space point of view we did design the corridors and access capabilities to it and entry doors and things like that so that we could provision off, reasonably easily, certain parts of the Data Center while giving access to the right people and allowing them to have different maintenance windows, different freeze periods, and different access control mechanisms.

What prompted Cisco to locate the Data Center in Allen, Texas?

We already had a Tier III Data Center that was reasonably new—the Richardson Data Center—in that location. When we made the decision that we wanted a pair of Data Centers the decision sort of made itself.

Really the question is, is it a bad location for a Data Center? I don't think it's a bad location, I think it's pretty good from a natural disaster point of view. It doesn't have earthquakes. It does have tornadoes sometimes but you can harden the buildings for that. The power down there is cheap. It's a little bit hot during the summer so we can't use free air cooling all of the time but even there our estimates are we can use it 56 percent of the time. So it's not a bad location at all. In fact, it's relatively good. And also by the way it's in the middle of the U.S., which means that if there are any latency issues it's equidistant from major population centers in the U.S. so I think that's an advantage.

If we were building from a greenfield site we may have made other choices but given some of the business realities in terms of we already had a Data Center down there we weren't obviously going to move that one, this was the right business decision. The location is maybe not the ideal location but it's a very good location.

FIGURE 6-3   Adjustable louvers allow outside air to be brought into the Data Center. Image by
                    Douglas Alger.

FIGURE 6-4   Thirteen air handlers feed cool air into a common plenum above the server rows. Airside
                    economization allows the facility to be cooled by outside air more than half of the time.
                    Image provided courtesy of Cisco. Photography by Cyclone Interactive.

You mentioned this Data Center being connected to another one in the area. Can you talk about Cisco's Metro Virtual Data Center concept and how that's designed?

The idea of this MVDC or Metro Virtual Data Center is that from an application point of view these two Data Centers look as though they are one Data Center. However, if there is an issue in one of those whole Data Centers then the application can recover reasonably transparently if not transparently and still provide these services that either the application or business process is meant to be providing.

There are technologies that we are using—some from Cisco some from some of our partners, like Oracle especially on the database side, that let us do this. There are certain requirements on the application as well though, obviously that the application is architected to support MVDC. But a lot of the underlying infrastructure and middleware environments also have to support this and provide the foundation to enable the applications and the databases to be serviced from either Data Center.

Basically, it's a way to provide almost continuous operation if there was an outage of one of the Data Centers. It is quite expensive to do this from an infrastructure and middleware point of view so not all of our applications use this capability. We've been through a criticality rating exercise with all of our business processes and applications, rated them and then worked out which ones should be riding on MVDC and which ones need not be riding on MVDC and then obviously made those decisions and we're well down the path to move the ones that we think should be on MVDC to MVDC.

"The idea of this MVDC or Metro Virtual Data Center is that from an application point of view these two Data Centers look as though they are one Data Center."

With Allen and Richardson, Texas, being only about 15 miles (24.1 km) apart, is there any concern that both Data Centers could be hit by a single disaster event?

There is a chance that both will be taken out by a natural or other type of disaster. We think it's very small, however. But there is a chance and therefore we have a disaster recovery site about 1,600 miles (2,575 km) away. It's a non-production Data Center so when there's not a disaster all our development and other non-production use cases go on in this Data Center. It's in RTP (Research Triangle Park) in North Carolina and if there was a disaster that took out both of those Data Centers in the Dallas area then we have the capability of bringing up the business critical applications in our RTP facility, in our DR facility.

The physical distances among the three Data Center locations were determined in part by the pre-existing location of Cisco's campuses in Richardson and RTP. Generically, if someone was looking to implement this model, with two linked Data Centers in a metro area and a DR facility outside of the area, what are the recommended distances to have among the three facilities?

The main technology issue is about how far the pair of Data Centers can be apart from each other given that in most cases you need dark fiber and probably diverse dark fiber between the two Data Centers. It's not really the physical distance it's the distance of the fiber between them.

My recommendation is to get them as far apart as you can given that you want to stay within around about 60 miles (96.6 km) from a fiber distance. The reason why that it has to be of that order from a fiber distance point of view, is because if you are going to use synchronous write technology on the storage it's important not to introduce too much latency into the application and most applications will work with a fiber distance of 60 mi. (96.6 km). Some of them start having issues after that.

How did Cisco approach the design of the mechanical system? Texas isn't the first place people think of for using outside air cooling, but the Data Center incorporates air economization and uses outside air more than half of the time.

For environmental and for cost reasons we wanted to use as little power as possible in this Data Center. One way of doing this is to use outside air to cool the Data Center when the outside air is an appropriately low temperature. And that's just what we've done.

We have a lot of air intake so are able to take outside air when it's sufficiently cool outside. I was pretty surprised, actually, how large the percentage of time is that we think we can take outside air from in the Texas region to cool the Data Center. We did raise the inlet temperature in the Data Center as well so that definitely helped. If it's less than 72 degrees (22.2 degrees Celsius) or so outside we can start taking air in from the outside rather than actually using a specific chiller to actually do that and using power, so I think that's a great result for us. It saves us money and as I said it helps the environment as well.

One of the design points obviously is to keep the hot air totally separated from the cooler air and that's been implemented down there. In that facility we use chimneys on top of the cabinets and that works really well. There's very little if any crossover between the cold air going straight into the hot air intakes and we've done a lot of testing to make sure that the cabinet temperatures are appropriate. We've optimized the inlet temperature into the cabinets so that the equipment stays within the range of what the equipment maker feels that those equipment can withstand and keep it within the warranty and maintenance limits of the device. So we did some optimization there.

FIGURE 6-5   Enclosed cabinets with vertical exhaust ducts isolate hot and cold airflow, providing
increased cooling efficiency. Image provided courtesy of Cisco. Photography by Cyclone
Interactive.

How does Cisco deal with the fact that some of its own hardware models vent exhaust to the side rather than following that front-to-back pattern that is preferred for Data Centers with hot- and cold-aisles?

There are a few answers to that. One is, we continually work with our BUs (business units) and the BUs are pretty aware of this. There are just some specific physical limitations when you start getting large switches, with cooling front to back. We haven't been able to solve that issue.

Number two is we have come up with some pretty inventive cabinet designs where even though it is side to side airflow for cooling we can still use a chimney design.

The third thing is that we obviously realize that there are going to be some equipment that just won't fit into one of these cabinets. For that—and it's not just Cisco equipment, in fact it's primarily not Cisco equipment—we do have to understand that some equipment, maybe some storage equipment is the most common, is going to be out on the floor and it's going to be pretty difficult for us to put a chimney on top of their proprietary cabinet. In that case we keep those out on the floor. We position them in the most optimal place but the actual environment is cool out on the floor because we're using chimneys and that gets cooled in a more traditional way.

This Data Center uses Cisco's Unified Computing System, which integrates networking, storage, and server functionality. How did the anticipated use of that technology influence the design of the facility?

The major influence was on the cabling. We are using far fewer copper cables in the facility than we have done ever before. We also have optimized and changed actually the type of fiber we use so that it can support 10G now and in the future up to 100G. Even if we hadn't used Cisco's innovations in terms of converged fiber channel and Ethernet and some other ones as well it would have still have been a valid design decision to put far less copper cables in and a much, much higher percentage of fiber connectivity.

There are two schools of thought these days around whether or not to use a raised floor in a Data Center. What prompted forgoing it in this facility?

With the higher power densities that cabinets are capable of supporting these days, under floor forced air cooling is becoming less and less the right choice. It's becoming harder and harder to cool these cabinets using under floor cooling. Given that and some weight limitations in some of the equipment and some costs actually—putting in a raised floor is quite costly—we've made the decision in this facility and in any future ones that we may build to not have a raised floor. Have the cabling and the cooling and the power provided overhead. And we've come up with some, again using our engineers, we've come up with some ways all of those technologies can be provided overhead and co-exist and I think it's worked out really well.

This was the first Cisco Data Center to use a rotary UPS instead of a conventional battery-based UPS system. What were the drivers behind that choice?

It was environmental. Dealing with the lead and the acid from the batteries would have been more impactful to the environment, so we decided to go with a rotary UPS. And for the size of this Data Center it will allow us to get the PUE slightly lower by using rotary UPS.

Any concerns about the shorter ride through time provided by a rotary UPS rather than what you can get from a bank of batteries?

Not really. I feel as though there are a couple of failsafe mechanisms on those rotary UPSs. One of them is that in the end if the diesel generator is having trouble starting, there is actually a clutch that kick starts the generator. We did some testing of this and we think this is a valid way to go now. I think this will soon become relatively mainstream, to use rotary UPSs.

FIGURE 6-6 Cisco employed a rotary UPS rather than a conventional battery UPS system for ride through power. Image provided courtesy of Cisco. Photography by Cyclone Interactive.

We have talked about several elements of this Data Center's design: the MVDC concept, chimney cabinets, air economization, the Unified Computing System technology. Do you think the solutions are specific to the function or geographic location of this Data Center or are they universal and can be applied to most facilities?

I think each Data Center has some tradeoffs about which technology you should use or which ones you shouldn't. In fact, we make tradeoffs when we build Data Centers, not every Data Center is the same. However, I think some of the techniques and technologies that we've spoken about should be at least considered. People implementing Data Centers should make a choice and be aware of the choices that they're making around some of these subjects. I'm certainly not saying that everybody has to or should follow the same design that we have. There are some specific business reasons why we wanted this design. But all of these decision points should be considered about what power density you need, should you use outside air for cooling, and various other things. At least a discussion should be had about that and an optimized decision made.

I don't think there's a cookie cutter Data Center that's going to fit everybody but I do think there are various almost a la carte options that you should consider when building a Data Center and some of these we've spoken about.

If you could go back and design the Data Center again, what if anything would you do differently?

I would revisit the decision to have chimneys and lay on the table again whether we should use chimneys or whether we should use warm air aisle containment. I think that's a different decision. They both get to the same point, which is keeping hot air and cold air away from each other, but I do think it's valid to revisit that decision.

As you say, both solutions get to the same point. What would make you consider warm air aisle containment over the enclosed cabinets with chimneys?

I think you can get better separation. I think you can handle higher density of heat inside a cabinet using hot air aisle containment. As long as you don't go overboard on how you design the containment mechanism, I think it'll probably be cheaper to implement that. You do need to make sure that the hot aisle containment mechanism is flexible enough to allow you to expand or contract the equipment and the number of cabinets you have in there. I don't think it's a slam dunk but I do think it's a better design. Each implementation is slightly different and depending upon the business requirements it could go either way.

Are there any other lessons from this project that you plan to take forward into other builds?

The slab decision, I think that was a great decision. I think the density of power distribution. I think we would spend more time making sure that we don't leave any stranded power in the Data Center. We may make the power distribution mechanism even more flexible than it is in the Allen Data Center.

What advice would you offer to someone taking on a Data Center project?

Make sure that the right levels of management are involved in quite low level details about how the Data Center is built, because some of those details have major ramifications in the future and realistically you're going to be in this Data Center for 10 to 15 years. So, a lot of the design decisions have long-term ramifications.

Also, there are always trade-offs regarding cost. My advice would be to make sure that you really understand what is driving the cost of the Data Center and that you feel that whatever decision you are making and the cost associated with that provides the necessary value back to the business for the amount of money you're spending. Understanding the cost of some of those decisions is very important.

A Data Center's design will obviously vary based on its location and the facility's mission, but generally do you think this facility represents the baseline of how Cisco will build its Data Centers going forward?

Yeah, I do. We'll tweak things. There's new technology that comes down. More flexibility about power distribution, for example, is another one but I think in general yes I'm pretty happy with the design decisions made here.

We may make slightly different decisions depending upon the business needs and other things in the future, but I'm very happy with this Data Center. I think some of the decisions we made were great, working out very well, were the right ones to enable us to provide the necessary services to Cisco and some of our customers. So, yes, I think it will serve as the baseline and will be tweaked from that.

Let me offer you the final word. Is there anything else you would like to highlight for people about this facility?

Please come and visit it. We have a tour in a hall around the outside of all the Data Center. We can show you a lot of the design decisions that we've made now, that we've been talking about. We can show you them actually working and discuss the pros and cons of them. I would certainly have liked to have seen a Data Center like this before we made the decisions about how to build ours because at least then you can learn from other people's mistakes or other things other people have done right. I would welcome any people, any readers of this book to come visit the Data Center.

FIGURE 6-7   A 100 kW rooftop solar panel array provides enough energy to power the office area for personnel who support the Data Center. Image by Andrew Broer.

FIGURE 6-8   The Data Center features non-chemical condenser water treatment and an on-site rainwater retention system for site irrigation. Image provided courtesy of Cisco. Photography by Cyclone Interactive.

FIGURE 6-9   Four 20,000 gallon (75,708.2 liter) tanks of generator fuel, four 15,000 gallon
(56,781.2 liter) tanks of chilled water, and one 355,000 gallon (1,343,821.2 liter)
tank of domestic makeup water reside behind the Data Center. Image provided courtesy
of Cisco. Photography by Cyclone Interactive.

FIGURE 6-10   Server rows in the second data hall are separated by cage walls. Image provided
courtesy of Cisco. Photography by Cyclone Interactive.

FIGURE 7-1   Citi's Data Center in Frankfurt, Germany, was the first in the world to be certified LEED-Platinum. Image by Christian Richters Photography.

CHAPTER 7
Citi

ORGANIZATION: Citi	
LOCATION: Frankfurt, Germany	
ONLINE: May 2008	
NOTABLE FEATURES: Green roof and green wall features. Reverse osmosis water treatment for cooling. Harvested rainwater used for irrigation. Rotary UPS. First Data Center certified LEED-Platinum.	
TIME TO DESIGN AND BUILD: 20 months	
SIZE: 228,000 sq. ft. (21,181.9 sq. m) total, with 100,000 sq. ft. (9,290 sq. m) of hosting space	
POWER: 14.4 MW from two separate feeds	
TIER: III	
CABINET LOCATIONS: Information unavailable	
INFRASTRUCTURE DELIVERY: Structured cabling is provided overhead. Power and cooling are delivered under a 31.5 in. (80 cm) raised floor.	
STRUCTURAL LOADING: 250 lb. per sq. ft. (1,220.6 kg per sq. m)	
FIRE SUPPRESSION SYSTEM: Pre-action sprinklers	

Much as car designers strive to find the sweet spot between acceleration and fuel economy, fun and practicality, Data Center designers often seek a happy medium between high availability and green optimization.

That's because the two qualities are traditionally at odds with one another in Data Center design: higher availability means extra layers of standby infrastructure, which in turn mean more material used and more electrical conversion losses.

Citi found a way to achieve both with its Data Center in Frankfurt, Germany. The facility, which is the financial services company's main computing center for Europe, Middle East, and Africa (EMEA), is the first ever Data Center to achieve LEED-Platinum certification. It also contains sufficient physical infrastructure redundancy to satisfy the stringent uptime demands of a financial institution, with a Tier IV equivalent electrical system and Tier III equivalent mechanical system.

John Killey, head of Citi Realty Services for EMEA, and Jerry Walsh, head of Design and Construction, Citi Realty Services for EMEA, discuss how they were able to make sustainability and availability contribute to one another within the design of their Data Center.

The Interview

What prompted you to locate this Data Center in Frankfurt, Germany?

John: We went through a very detailed site assessment process that looked to a number of factors and at the end of the day those factors pointed to Frankfurt being the optimum location to construct.

To give you some feeling for what those factors were, they included obviously risk in terms of the nature of both sovereign risk and physical risk. The second one was availability of power supplies. The third one was availability of network connectivity both nationally and internationally, so international network gateways.

Next was the right sort of construction infrastructure that could actually build what we were looking for, both technically and also practically. And then also our ability to support it ongoing in terms of the right level of infrastructure support both in terms of the market and also from the Citi perspective.

Put all those into an equation and you come up with a number of solutions; one of those is Frankfurt. And we decided to go with Frankfurt because we could then find availability of the sites and so forth that allowed us to do what we needed to do.

How long did it take to design and build the Data Center?

Jerry: (It was) quite a fast track program. We started the whole process in 2006. We had earmarked a locality by mid-2006, but then of course we had to go through quite a process of approval to acquire the site, et cetera. I can say to you that really the design process started in September of 2006 and then we went and had our bid documentation for design, et cetera, by February 2007. We went out to bid in February/March 2007. We had a contractor on board and on site in May of 2007. And within nine months we had available to us 12,500 sq. ft. (1,161.3 sq. m.) of data space and by May of 2008, exactly one year later, we had the facility complete. So it was a very fast track process.

John: The selection of that site and also the country of location assisted us in meeting those sorts of timeframes.

Jerry: It did indeed, because with contractors in Germany it's different from say in the States where we also had a quite significant Data Center rollout. There the procurement of the construction part of the project is usually done under the construction management type procurement method. In Germany it's much more traditional so we had to have all our designs in place. So it was very critical for us to get the right team on board. And we did that via a special vehicle where we had a specialist, a very large international mechanical and electrical engineering company, and a dedicated construction company and they came together and formed a partnership for this particular project.

LEED Certification

Leadership in Energy and Environmental Design (LEED) is a rating system for the design, construction and operation of green buildings. Facilities can achieve ratings of certified, silver, gold, or platinum based on criteria within six categories: sustainable sites, water efficiency, energy and atmosphere, materials and resources, indoor environmental quality, and innovation and design.

Also in Germany we had the advantage that a lot of the major elements in construction they're very used to pre-cast elements and doing a lot of pre-fabrication work off-site. And that certainly helped us deliver this project as well. Again, Germany helped us because that's the particular expertise that was available to us.

Did you know, as you went through the site selection process, you would be able to complete the project more quickly by building it in Germany than other potential locations?

John: Our knowledge of the markets, yes. We had that as part of the selection requirements because we knew the overall program we had to meet and it was one of the factors. At the end of the day it wasn't an overriding factor. What was the most important factor? It was the network connectivity. Second most important was the power availability.

Jerry: And then of course the question we had to take into account was can we deliver to our program. And we were confident we could do that because of the expertise in Germany.

But I would also have to say that we would have done it—using different procurement methods—if it was done for instance in the UK. I think we still would have met those same timelines. But it certainly was part of the decision on location.

This is the first Data Center in the world to achieve LEED-Platinum certification, so it's obviously green. Data Centers for financial institutions typically have high availability requirements, though, which means more standby infrastructure and therefore more components and electrical conversion losses. How were you able to balance those different requirements in your design?

John: How were we able to balance it? It's a very trite answer but very effectively. Because what we did is we embodied the overall sustainability requirement as a key design requirement along with availability, reliability and performance. If you build it in at that stage and you understand the impact of a sustainable solution and what it has on the overall performance of the facility actually sustainability can add to the availability, not work against it.

A good example is, if you go down the route of a free cooling solution it can actually give you enhanced availability because 80 percent of the time you're getting free cooling and for a significant portion of the time you're getting free cooling completely which means that you're totally divorcing yourself from the need for chillers and the associated equipment. So you could actually suffer multiple chiller failures to a greater level than you would in a more traditional design and still having no impact on your availability. And that's the understanding of the overall impact of sustainability.

Now, one of the things that we did do is, and again this is part of the process when we went out to look at both the design team and also the construction team, we made sure that sustainability was a contractual obligation of all those individuals from Day One. Not added on at a later stage or an optional extra, it was an integral part. So when we selected for instance construction elements, sustainability, embedded CO^2, those sorts of considerations were made alongside things like performance, cost, et cetera.

Jerry: We had written in to our contract with the main contractor that our minimum target was LEED-Gold. As you may well know, the contractor has quite a considerable contribution to make to obtaining the necessary credits to get LEED accreditation. However, it wasn't just about going for the highest LEED accreditation, it was in support of our corporate sustainability goals as well. And as John said it was absolutely embedded in the whole process of procurement, design, delivery, and construction on site. In addition to free cooling we also had reverse osmosis, where we save about 50 million liters (13.2 million gallons) of water per year. Again, there was no interruption in design, this was just part of the whole design consideration.

John: Even down to the design of the UPSs (uninterruptible power supplies), we were able to use diesel rotary UPS models, and understanding what that does in terms of reducing down the amount of cost for medium voltage units, understanding what that does in terms of reducing down the amount of copper, for instance. Reducing down the amount of construction that you require for the building because they have fit a smaller footprint. Reducing down the need for batteries with the associated issues in relationship to gas discharge and so forth. All those aspects as well as performance decisions are sustainability decisions. And so, again, that's how you can get a sustainable and green Data Center that is as effective with as good availability.

"If you build it in at that stage and you understand the impact of a sustainable solution and what it has on the overall performance of the facility actually sustainability can add to the availability, not work against it."

Now, does it at the end of the day use lots of energy? Yes, course it does. Because a Data Center will do. But things like the integrated design means that you get a much better PUE than you would likely get with a more conventional design as well as the advantageous lower environmental impact during construction, commissioning, and then operation.

FIGURE 7-2
Citi uses reverse osmosis to reduce sediment buildup in its cooling towers and saves about 13.2 million gallons (50 million liters) of water per year. Image by Christian Richters Photography.

I understand Citi was very particular about the materials used in the construction of the Data Center and their embodied energy. Can you provide some examples of how that influenced your choices?

John: We used things like recycled materials in relationship to some of the cladding systems. We used locally grown timber, naturally seasoned so that from an ongoing maintenance perspective as well there's no great issues in that respect. We also looked at things like the roof—the roof actually is a green roof on there, which again has an impact over its total lifecycle. Because that's the other key issue, you don't just look at it in the short term you look at it across its total lifecycle to see what impact it has from an energy perspective. So those are examples of that type of approach.

Did you use a particular source for defining the embodied energy values? A challenge with embodied energy is that there isn't universal agreement as to how to measure it. Also, the embodied energy of an item can differ greatly by location because what's local to one site isn't local to another and what's abundant in one location might be scarce in another.

John: You're correct, and that's why it's very important to have a partnership with a design company that understand your objectives and understand the issues in relationship to sustainability as well as having a local knowledge and a local presence.

We were fortunate in that we utilized Arup Associates. They are a multidisciplinary both architectural and M&E practice that were also based in the Frankfurt area as well as LEED accredited. They had LEED accredited professionals, they have local knowledge, and they also have a great commitment to sustainability. They have been actively engaged in the Qatar naturally–cooled football stadium, for instance. They are leaders in quite innovative sustainability designs so that did help us immensely.

Jerry: In a lot of our workshops, that expertise came across and it played a big factor. I may also say that our contractors were very committed to us attaining the highest sustainability rating we can. They were very keen also to ensure that recycled content of the materials were used as much as possible. They had to go out to their suppliers, their subcontractors, as well and ensure that message was got through the whole pipeline.

And indeed we ended up that the recycled content of the materials on the project were specified at 27 percent and local sourcing of materials we exceeded 40 percent. That was because everybody knew how important it was to Citi but also they all bought in to that goal. Again, Germany it's pretty highly regulated about waste and material, et cetera, so that information and audit was there for us as well.

You mentioned that in the design of facility you reduced the amount of materials used such as copper. Did you accomplish that entirely through building a smaller facility or were there other elements of the design that allowed you to streamline the infrastructure?

John: There were two aspects to it. The cabling aspect comes very much from the UPS design. You can put in less copper because if you're transmitting voltages around the building at medium voltage then obviously you need less copper. What we also did from a data perspective is we made sure we tried to optimize our cable runs on the data side to reduce the amount of cabling and the amount of copper we've got. It was important to integrate that in to the cabinet layouts, in the frame layouts, and so forth. So again you're making decisions with sustainability being one of the criteria that actually also improve performance in terms of optimizing the layouts for cooling effect, et cetera, et cetera.

The big message that I always try and stress is if you design sustainability in, not from Day One from Day Minus One that is, before you start the project—that actually it assists you in the overall design process in many aspects and does not hinder you. You can achieve optimization of that overall design without compromise to sustainability, performance, reliability, or cost.

Cost is a key issue because if we'd gone down the route of a more traditional UPS solution then that would have cost us more money. We did spend more money than we would normally have done on the mechanical side but that was offset by the electrical costs, lower cost from drops. And also lower construction costs because you're not building big battery rooms with all the issues that go with them. When you look at it overall it can be beneficial.

Your facility has several water efficiency measures incorporated into its design including reverse osmosis water treatment and rainwater harvesting. The Data Center industry today is focusing on energy efficiency but water usage hasn't received as much attention.

John: I would point out that Citi is the first bank to have published water reduction targets as part of a sustainable agenda.

Do you think this is an issue the Data Center industry as a whole is going to start paying more attention to in the future?

John: I do believe that water is a major issue going forward. You could argue, why is it an issue in the likes of Germany where water shortage isn't a particular issue? If you look at the U.N. environment agencies, water maps that identify where there are likely to be issues, Germany isn't going to be a problematical area for quite a long time. However, what I think you have to do is you have to look at embodied water issues much wider. We didn't look at water in that respect at that time but actually when you start to think about the impact that construction materials have, for instance, or the systems you put in, then water becomes a major issue. So I think longer term we will have to do it because it will become more and more of a challenge, particularly in relation not only to direct water usage but also to indirect water. I can't remember the figures off hand, but if you look at how many liters of water to make a cubic meter of concrete it's quite significant.

Using less concrete saves you money. Using less concrete has a lower embodied CO_2 requirement because of the reduced amount of energy and also saves water. If you understand that and the drivers that show that being economical with design from say a concrete perspective can have an impact in terms of cost, CO_2, and water. It's understanding that holistic impact that your decisions have upon the sustainable agenda overall.

FIGURE 7-3   Citi's Data Center includes a green wall and a green roof that reduce the heat load on the building and last longer than conventional materials. Image by Christian Richters Photography.

Your site incorporates a green roof and a green wall and there's a lot of landscaping across the facility that -

John: I would say there's not a lot of landscaping. Actually, the landscaping was done as part of our need to provide water settlement. There were two aspects to it. One, you have to have runoff from a roof and it has to be held before it goes out to the sewer system simply because in a major flat roof you have a lot of water coming off there and the sewer systems can't take that volume. So the landscaping was done because of that.

But of course because we've got a green roof the actual roof acts as a reservoir anyway, so it reduced down the amount of landscaping we did and it reduced down the amount of earth we had to move to create those. So again the impact of a green roof, not just from the roof perspective but what is a knock-on effect from a sustainability point of view was a consideration at the time when we made that decision. It's offset partially by the fact that you have got a slightly heavier structure to support it, but again you get longer term benefits because actually a green roof lasts longer than a conventional roof because it's not subjected to the same deterioration from a UV perspective or from a mechanical damage perspective. So again sustainability solutions give you a better performance.

There isn't a lot of landscaping there. There is some but not an enormous amount.

Were there any challenges incorporating the green wall or the green roof?

Jerry: No, definitely not. The technology was there, the design was there, it was just a matter of us adopting it. And it certainly was not an issue from either a cost or a delivery aspect. Again on cost, the roof lasts twice as long as it otherwise would because we have this covering.

Tell me about your infrastructure delivery. Do you have a raised floor or is your infrastructure provided overhead?

John: Let me be very clear. While we like to make sure that we are using technology to its greatest advantage we're also a bank and consequently we are relative conservative in terms of design. While we want to be on the leading edge we don't want to be on the bleeding edge. So when you look at what we've put in there it's all very, very conventional. It's not particularly innovative other than the fact that we've taken great care in selection and putting the whole lot together.

So, yeah, it's a conventional raised floor, it's got a suspended ceiling, the layout is relatively conventional—so if you went into that Data Center it wouldn't look a lot different at all from any of the other Data Centers we have.

I take it then that the solutions used in this Data Center are universal and can be used at any Data Center facility.

John: There are some advantages in being in a Northern European site because obviously from a climatic perspective we can harvest the climate to our advantage. You couldn't do a Data Center such as this in an equatorial site. So there is some benefit from that perspective.

Jerry: Exactly. Particularly the free cooling as somebody mentioned earlier. And indeed the green roof. It remains green because we use rainfall to irrigate during the drier periods.

John: But in terms of the technology, a lot of the way we put the technology together could be used anywhere. As long as that technology is supportable. For instance we use diesel rotary UPSs. Diesel rotary UPSs are very widespread in Europe. You very rarely see them in the U.S. And that is a function of the market penetration of the manufacturers who have tended to be and continue to be European based.

FIGURE 7-4   Implementing diesel rotary UPS systems helped Citi eliminate batteries and other building materials. Image by Christian Richters Photography.

As you look back on the project were there any surprises along the way? It sounds like a lot of what you did in the room you had decided early on, but was there anything unanticipated that came up during either the design or construction?

Jerry: That's an interesting question. I was trying to rack my brain and see if I could come up with something. We produced our concept design report and that was our bible. Any variance from that we had to go through a whole change control process. Really, looking back there were very few changes.

John: I think that was one of the reasons why we could deliver it in that time frame. Because the design had been well developed to a point where there was not a lot of need for change. We did a lot of value engineering and so forth as part of the design process. It meant that the suppliers themselves—and it's very important when you're doing a lot of off-site fabrication you can't change your mind once you get to the site—so it was important that we got it right and we did. And actually if you look at the concept design document and took it onsite you could navigate yourself around the site very, very effectively.

Jerry: Overall by way of change orders—and this is from memory—for a job of this size we were something like 50 or 60 change orders and a lot of those were referring to locations of some doors and some things to do with the admin buildings and the ancillary spaces like storage areas rather than the central plant and the data hall. So there were no surprises, really.

John: The only thing that was a surprise, but it was a pleasant surprise, was it was a mild winter. That was the one thing that I would say, it was not a hard winter. Winters in Frankfurt can be very cold, very long, very hard. And we were very lucky that that year it wasn't.

I realize this is still a relatively young Data Center and you sound very satisfied with it, but if you could go back and design it all over again what might you try to do differently?

John: To be perfectly honest I have not given it any thought, and nothing jumps out at us. I'm sure there are now improvements and changes in terms of availability of materials but I wouldn't change the design team structure or the construction team structure. I think that worked extremely well. There's not an enormous amount we would change.

I read that 100 percent of the Data Center's construction waste was diverted from the landfill. What special steps had to be taken for that to happen?

Jerry: I think, again, we had the advantage of being in Germany. It's highly regulated anyway. Where you have waste you have to separate it on site. So we had a set of requirements setting that out. Our original task was something like 50 or 70 percent to be diverted from landfill and we got up to 100. And we got up to 100 simply because we made the commitment to maximize and we had our specifications and our documents in place and the contractual obligations there on the contractors and subcontractors.

For anyone starting a Data Center project, can you offer them some advice?

Jerry: A big advantage for us was having an integrated team. We were very conscious at the very beginning that we needed somebody who could provide the architectural, the mechanical, the electrical, the security, and indeed IT advice as well, and risk assessment—all that capability and disciplines within one firm. That was a big advantage for us. We were very clear on our coordination, very clear where the responsibility laid. We had the advantage of this particular consultant and this is the way we wanted it. They had all the necessary disciplines. I think that helped tremendously.

And also as I mentioned before, having the concept design report and having that as our bible that was very, very critical. Because for us much of the early design, the concepts and requirements, were put together here in London and we worked with our consultants here in London and then of course we had to transfer at a certain stage back to our colleagues and indeed transferring design over to Germany as well. The same firms, the same groups involved but we then had the language to contend with as well. Because all bid documentation, drawings, et cetera, then had to be in German. But having an integrated design team was a great advantage.

John: I would reiterate that. That is the biggest benefit I think. It was a team and we were able to integrate then our requirements including the sustainability from Day One, which I think also was a very key point.

Are there any final lessons that you would like readers to take away from this project?

John: From a personal point of view, I think the lesson is integrating the team, integrating the sustainability alongside the other requirements of a Data Center performance—reliability, availability—and that you can achieve each of those and each of those are mutually enhancing rather than working against each other. That's the message I would get. If you approach it right and early enough you can get benefits in all of those areas and it's not the detriment of one or the other.

Jerry: The only thing I would add is that it involves the entire supply chain, down to your contractors, down to your subcontractors and suppliers. They have a big role to play as well.

FIGURE 7-5   Citi's Frankfurt Data Center at night. Image provided courtesy of Citi. Photo by Steve Kay.

FIGURE 8-1   The Lakeside Technology Center in Chicago is a registered historic landmark and houses multiple Data Centers. Images provided courtesy of Digital Realty Trust.

CHAPTER 8
Digital Realty Trust

ORGANIZATION: Digital Realty Trust	
LOCATION: Chicago, Illinois	
ONLINE: First constructed from 1912 to 1914. Converted to telecom use between 1998 and 2000. Acquired by Digital Realty Trust in 2005.	
NOTABLE FEATURES: Designated historic landmark building. More power capacity than Chicago O'Hare International Airport. One of the world's largest carrier hotels. An 8.5 million gallon (32.2 million liter) brine tank for thermal storage. Includes a 20,000 sq. ft. (1,858.1 sq. m) data hall that was first in the United States to be certified LEED-Gold.	
TIME TO DESIGN AND BUILD: Varies by data hall	
SIZE: 1,133,391 sq. ft. (105,295.5 sq. m)	
POWER: 102 MW	
TIER: Varies by data hall	
CABINET LOCATIONS: Varies by data hall	
INFRASTRUCTURE DELIVERY: Varies by data hall	
STRUCTURAL LOADING: 250 lb. per sq. ft. (1,220.6 kg per sq. m)	
FIRE SUPPRESSION SYSTEM: Dual interlock pre-action system with above and below heat and smoke detection	

When design began in 1912 on the RR Donnelley Printing Plant and headquarters in Chicago, it was done with an eye toward the future.

"We are trying to make the whole building dignified and beautiful," said then company president Thomas E. Donnelley. "Something that will be beautiful not only today, but 100 years from now."

A century later, Donnelley's vision has been fulfilled in ways he never could have imagined. Today the eight story building is known as the Lakeside Technology Center and houses a collection of Data Centers operated by Digital Realty Trust. It's one of the largest carrier hotels in the world and has the most electrical capacity in the region, exceeding even O'Hare International Airport. Despite its change in function, many of the building's core characteristics as well as its distinctive gothic architecture live on.

Sturdy floors that once supported presses that printed everything from hardcover books to telephone directories to the Sears Catalog now bear the weight of storage frames and standby generators. Vertical shafts that permitted huge paper rolls to be transported between floors now convey electrical conduits, structured cabling, and cooling. Even amenities for workers such as ample ventilation and natural lighting have been incorporated into the building's modern incarnation.

Jim Smith, chief technical officer for Digital Realty Trust, discusses the evolution of the facility, what it's like to operate a Data Center at such a massive scale, and the challenges that come with doing so within a designated historic landmark.

The Interview

Let's start with some background about the Lakeside Technology Center. What can you tell me about the history of the building and how it came into the possession of Digital Realty Trust?

The site was the headquarters of the RR Donnelley Corporation and Mr. Donnelley had his office there. If you ever get a chance to go to the building, there's this incredibly beautiful library and that library housed all the first edition books that they printed.

It's got this cool industrial story. He was one of these guys who was an industrial humanist, where he was really into the workers. And so the original construction had a lot of natural lighting and ventilation because he felt like that was good for the workers. So it's got a cool Donnelley story. They built it in phases as they grew the business.

It became defunct. That part of the city was a really run-down piece of the city. If you're a big fan of the *Blues Brothers* movie, like I am, there's a scene where they come off the expressway and you can see the building in the background. And it's like something out of a *Terminator* movie. It's a wasteland, and the building's got broken windows and it's open. I freeze the frame and think, 'That's our building?' It's just all torn apart.

In the turn of the millennium a group was put together to redevelop it and they had some funding from the Carlyle Group. That initial redevelopment happened in 1998, 1999, 2000. You have to remember at that time this kind of telecom boom was going on. People weren't so much building Data Centers as they were building switch sites. We were calling them Data Centers at the time but they are as much switch POPs as anything and sure enough the initial leasing in there was a lot of telecom carriers and people were thinking in terms of telecom centers and telecom hotels. So, that original developer started the development and it's an interesting spot because it's adjacent to the McCormick Place convention center and there's a very large trigeneration plant across the street. That trigeneration plant was built in support of the convention center and the hotel complex there and it was built at a time in the energy markets where there was a lot of arbitrage between daytime and nighttime use and the convention center load profiles are really sharp. At night nothing's happening and then (during the day) they turn on the convention center and conventioneers arrive, you get this huge spike in cooling and heating demand. So the tri-gen plant was an economic story built and it has a huge thermal storage tank, a brine storage tank. It's enormous. It's the largest chilled water tank in North America. They built the plant and sized it so it could run all night. Fill the tank at low electricity rates and then in the mornings when they hit huge demand from the halls, they could either cool or heat the halls as needed. They ran a turbine on gas to generate electricity, they used the waste heat to make chilled water, and then they had these big, medium voltage chillers in there.

So, the original developer looked at that and said 'This plant is big enough to provide cooling for this building and I can avoid the capital to build my own cooling system.' So the original building and redevelopment concept had that energy plant as a big part of it.

Those guys had some success. They leased a couple floors. At this point in 2000, 2001 two or three of the floors were leased and enclosed, but there were whole floors like the fourth floor or eighth floor that were open. They were open to the elements and they weren't contained so the chilled water plant that ran through there had to act like it was exposed to the outside air. So it was a 30 percent glycol plant for freeze protection. The building wasn't in very much pretty shape, although it was pretty functional.

They got an offer they couldn't refuse from El Paso Corporation. At the time El Paso was building a fiber network inside of natural gas lines. They had raised money; they were flush with cash, so they bought out the original developer. Then as El Paso flamed out and the dot com business wrapped up—it stabilized, it had some cash flow but it wasn't really healthy.

In the time when El Paso was wrapping up, as Digital was growing we had a funny conversation with El Paso and they said 'We intend to sell you this building but we're busy getting rid of billion dollar assets. After we get rid of the billion dollar scale assets we'll call you when we're ready because we're really busy.' So we waited patiently and courted our target and over a period in early 2005 we were able to conclude the transaction and we acquired the building in June 2005.

It was something like $150 million. It was a good price for both of us. They were able to get a good rate. They lost quite a bit of money on it but at the time there was not much going on. We didn't have to 'overpay'. We got a fair price for the income that was there and lots of surplus space and assets. It was really a ball of wax. We had to spend a lot of time figuring it out.

So in 2005 we took over the building. We started some basic rehabilitation, putting in better security, just the kind of thing that a professional building owner does. El Paso was never a real estate company. As soon as they bought it they were in, generally speaking, financial trouble. So they weren't investing in the building. We started the basic investment program and started to market it for lease. At the time there was an Equinix Data Center in there, the Chicago Mercantile Exchange was in there, Qwest had a cyber center and a POP there, so it had pretty good density and it was pretty well built out. But there were still two and a half or three floors of vacant space so we knew we could do some other work with it.

FIGURE 8-2   Built in the early 1900s as a printing plant, the building's strong floors and large
vertical shafts made it an excellent candidate for conversion to hosting space.

We started by rehabbing the base building and then we went around and we
found a number of Data Center telecom spaces that had either gone bankrupt
or reverted back to the building's control and we did a lot of surplus work. So,
we would take a 500 kW, DC powered, 50 watt per foot (538.2 watts per square
meter) telco space. Generator was good, switchboard was good, cooling loop was
good, density was wrong, power was wrong. We would rip out the DC plant,
put in a UPS (uninterruptible power supply), re-engineer the cooling, give up a
bunch of space. We would bring to market a 75 watt per foot (807.3 watts per
square meter), non-raised floor Data Center space but we did it very inexpensively
so it was priced really attractive and we got great customers. We started to do
some of that where we would rehab the building and this is where we developed
our skill set, taking these kind of scary situations and doing some really, really
hard engineering and turning lemons in to lemonade.

That's a cultural trait that Digital has that's really important to us. We're a real estate company that happens to do technology property so everything we do is driven by economics and it's not easy to get internal capital and we have to make good arguments and good argumentation. We always have something a little bit imperfect to work with, especially in those early days before we were doing the big developments. That makes you a better engineer. We're really good at building and we're really good at stripping costs and finding where capacities exist and taking advantage of surplus work.

About that time our business started to grow. We started to get some reputation and the market started to recover, 2005, 2006. The surplus Data Center market had mostly been consumed, the economy was getting better, and tech was buying again. That building became a marquee spot because it had the Mercantile Exchange for trading hub, it had Equinix for peering, it had other telco. There's a lot of fiber density. It had access to power, it had good cooling.

The LEED Data Center we built, we had a client who came in and said 'I want to be in the building. I want you guys to build me a Data Center with the client capital.' It was a big energy company and they wanted to be green. They said 'We have a story to tell about sustainability and how do you think we can do that?' Remember, in 2006 The Green Grid didn't really exist or they had just started. The idea of high density was really just coming out. The ideas around containment, higher operating temperatures, free cooling with outside air— these are all relatively new, right? We were still in traditional high-availability Data Center mode. So we didn't have a lot of levers to pull like we do today. We didn't have that stuff—it wasn't in the playbook at the time, certainly not for commercial companies like us.

One of the areas we thought we could do some work with them for sustainability was LEED. None of us had built a LEED project. In fact, many people in the company had never even heard of it. But it came up as a topic and the customer loved it. They said, 'Yeah, this is what we wanted to do.'

LEED Certification

Leadership in Energy and Environmental Design (LEED) is a rating system for the design, construction, and operation of green buildings. Facilities can achieve ratings of certified, silver, gold, or platinum based on criteria within six categories: sustainable sites, water efficiency, energy and atmosphere, materials and resources, indoor environmental quality, and innovation and design.

And then we had this sinking feeling of, uh-oh, what have we done? Have we just added a lot of cost? We had no idea. We had looked at one checklist. We had no idea. So of course you hire a consultant who is going to charge you a fee for it. And what we found with LEED is it's relatively straightforward to get done. There are no big secrets to LEED; it's really just a good list of best practices. And they're not just best practices on energy they're best practices on building and water use and cleanliness and waste diversion.

In hindsight, the biggest benefit we got was not that we learned how to do LEED. It was that (for) everybody in the room on the construction and the client and the engineering side, it became clear that sustainability and efficiency were important to senior management and clients. So everybody changed the way they think. It wasn't build it cheaper. It wasn't build it faster. It wasn't build it right. All those were always there. But they said 'Hey I have some freedom and some license to figure out other things. Should I even bother looking at low flow faucets in the bathroom?' Yeah, you should look at that because sustainability's important. From my perspective that was the revolution that we created for ourselves, really for our teams and our clients: sustainability is important. And that was the first time anyone had ever said that.

If you know Data Center engineers they're very smart people. And if you unleash them on a new dimension they're good. They figure stuff out, man. Hey, how do you get a LEED point for this category? Well, you put windows in the UPS room. What? Nobody puts windows in a UPS room. Well, daylighting is an important energy conservation technique. You can make an argument about, well, is daylighting important in a non-occupied space? Well it's important when there's a technician in there, and there's a technician in there frequently and there are people doing rounds frequently and if you can keep the lights off that saves energy.

Interestingly, in that building one of the biggest headaches we have to this day is the external windows. Many of the windows are or were original and they're historic, so to replace them at the time was just this monstrous expenditure. So that's the kind of thing for Digital we've done replacements slowly but surely over time. Well at the time we couldn't afford or it didn't make sense to replace all the

"...that was the revolution that we created for ourselves, really for our teams and our clients: sustainability is important.

windows, so much of the building architectures have an inner wall that allows access to the exterior windows. We've got this kind of double pane effect just by the need to be able to get to windows. Because of their age and their materials the thermal expansion properties of the old glass are poor so they frequently break in the hot and the cold from contraction. We have a big budget to replace windows.

Well, that worked very well for daylighting because it wasn't like we were putting a single pane of glass in the UPS room. We were putting in a double set so that you had some containment. If you had a window break you had a whole other window. So, there were some architectural things that played in. And that was one of those challenges that drove us crazy. 'We've got to put in two windows? No, that's expensive! We don't want to do that.' But in the end, the form follows function idea played well into that. Where it made sense architecturally, we preserved the historical look without having to replace the exterior windows and we got daylighting in. And it wasn't a completely insane (scenario in which) there's a single pane of glass between the outside world and the UPS room.

FIGURE 8-3   Digital Realty Trust installed a second layer of windows behind the originals, providing more physical security while allowing natural light in to certain areas.

With you needing to justify the merits of a project in order to secure funding, what convinced you that this building was worthy to obtain and develop in the way that you have? How did you spot the diamond in the rough and realize where you would want to go with it?

Remember, at the time, most people were still operating in the telco metaphor. High ceilings. Heavy floor loads. It's interesting because now we own a bunch of buildings with very high ceilings and they're a huge pain in the butt. They're very expensive to build in high ceilings. In fact, as the world goes more and more to containment as containment gets acceptable, I'm shrinking the building heights a lot because with high ceilings containment becomes more expensive, too. You need more material to go to the ceiling.

So, for us it was floor loading, access to electricity, access to cooling, and then the footprint. The footprints and the floor plates in this building are about 140,000 feet (13,006.4 square meter) and they have a nice ability to be broken up. If you look at our business and people like us who do redevelopment of telecom and Data Center facilities you see a couple types that show up. There are a lot of printing facilities because of paper handling and the weight of the press and the weight of the materials. There are a lot of printing facilities that have turned in to Data Centers. There are quite a few downtown core department stores. Department stores typically have high ceilings for light and good view of the retail products. They usually have a lot of elevators for shaft space and they usually are concrete in construction because of the ceiling heights.

This building as a former printing facility it had fabulous shafts. They used to move paper vertically from the basement storage up and down to various floors, so the 350 Cermak building has something like 25 different vertical shafts. Including some that you could drop a city bus through. They're huge. They're massive shafts. That was another key piece of appeal for us.

Have you used those for cooling or are you routing physical infrastructure through them?

Routing infrastructure. The base building uses four of the shafts for common area cooling and that plant we run, but for the most part we use them for routing. It's really interesting because not every building, especially the vertical buildings, not every building can you get segmentation of the routes. So for the most part, shaft 21 will be cooling, shaft 5 will be telecom, shaft 6 will be primary power, shaft 7 standby power. We brought to clients the ability to have segregation of their services through the building. And that's an attraction for some of these big footprint builders.

It also had some other features. This was a blighted area so the city was very, very pro 'Let's give you guys what you need to get the job done.' The city did a great job. The original developer did a great job. So the building got a couple of key code variations. One of them was, in this building we can run medium voltage in metallic conduit. Generally speaking, it's a union and utility convention in the Chicagoland area that medium voltage needs to be encased in concrete. That was one thing right away everybody recognized the building's so big we're going to need to throw some medium voltage around and there's not enough physical space and that'll be too expensive. We're going to need to run it in metallic conduit. So we have a waiver for that. And that's been really critical to us for development because we have some very large medium voltage generating plants and because the building is so large we have to put in the big scale industrial equipment.

Another exception or variation we got is that we were able to take generators and day tanks and elevate them off the ground floor. Usually the general building code convention would be no diesel fuel above any occupied spaces, which really just means never off the ground floor. In this case the building has 40 or 50 generators on the first and the second floor that are stacked above each other, and that allowed the limited yard space to grow the footprint of the building. There's something like 90, 96 engines programmed for this building and about 85 installed so getting the physical space for that many engines would require this huge piece of land. So we were able to take advantage of that original variance and get interior generators without housings, with remote radiators and pretty complex air handling equipment, in on the first and the second floor. That was a bit of planning that we inherited or we purchased that really, really made the building work from a master plan perspective.

I'm intrigued by the prospect of operating and adding on to a Data Center in a building that's not only about 100 years old but also a historic landmark. What sort of restrictions does that present as you're trying to design, build, and operate spaces within the building?

The main limitations on the historic designation are around the façade. The exterior façade is the key protected piece—the shape of the building, the types of windows.

It's a very successful property for us, both from a financial perspective and a reputation and landmark. Part of our story is we'll come into a building and maybe we paid a lot for it or it needs a lot of sales to get going, but as buildings start to grow and become healthier and stabilize we divert quite a bit of the cash flow back into the building. We're making long-term investments.

FIGURE 8-4   Architectural details from the building feature symbols from the history of printing.

For example, at first this window budget was killing us. As we stabilized the building and grew it we were able to meet with the city and find a solution where we have to buy a fairly expensive window but it matches the look and feel of the historic windows. So, slowly but surely we've been replacing those. So, those are the main things.

This is one of those buildings where normally the traditional real estate parts of the building—the landscaping and the toilets and the parking lot—are very simple and then the Data Center is complex. This is a building where the Data Center is complex and the building management is complex, because of things like the maintenance of the façade. There are a bunch of little architectural features embedded in the concrete in the window sills. Sometimes those fall, so you've got to be careful from a safety perspective that that old stuff is maintained and you're not adding risk to the population, and then the look and feel of those things have to be right. So the façade is really one of the dominant pieces.

Then there are a number of historic lobbies and common areas. Those we really just have to maintain this incredible, beautiful walnut woodwork and sandstone carvings. And so those are places where we're just off limits from development. The management offices for many, many years were the original; Mr. Donnelley's corporate office was where the general manager sat. We've since leased that to customers who love it. We've built some more traditional functional office but there are sections of the building where we go, 'It is what it is.' We can't take any of that wood out. We can't reroute the electrical. We can do some wireless LAN but there's some historic office that we've leased to customers and it's going to be historic offices for the life of the building. But we knew that going in, so it wasn't a place where we said 'If we could rip out all of this office we could put in a Data Center.' That fit into our master programming as there's going to be some office there.

So, there's certainly an element of that. But those are benefits, right? Those are attractions to the building. They get a lot of press. People love to see them. In fact, this library I mentioned is common area in the building. So any of our customers in the building can check out the library for meetings and events, it's a big conference room and it's beautiful. That's a nice feature. I'm sure the property manager and the guy doing the economics would like to be doing something different with it, maybe it costs too much to clean. But from a branding and a product part of the building it's a huge positive.

One issue that has come up is, when we first did the development there was nothing down there. Well, as Chicago has grown and the economy has recovered that area has become gentrified. We have all the proper permits and licensing for all the equipment there—the generators and the equipment—but we've gotten some noise complaints from some of the local neighbors. Without being compelled to, we've had to spend extra dollars on sound mitigation just trying to be a good neighbor. That's just as a landlord one of those things—yes we have all the permits but you have got to be a good neighbor, especially if it's a nice neighborhood. So, fine, we've spent some extra money. And I'm not talking about a few hundred thousand, I'm talking about a few million dollars of noise abatement.

But other than that. The floors are incredibly thick. These buildings were built before there were pocket calculators, so everything's generally overengineered. Just cutting a hole in the floor it adds a lot of cost. So there are little things like that. The age of the building changed the construction. But from an operations perspective the paper-handling nature of the facility gives us a lot of benefit. Like I said, the shaft space, heavy floor loading. Great spots for storage of equipment and fuel. Great basement, good fiber entry because of the basement spaces. It's as much positive as negative, I think.

FIGURE 8-5   Once abandoned, the building was converted to telecommunications use beginning in 1998 and has since been fully restored.

The building obviously wasn't originally constructed with green considerations in mind. What challenges did that present when you sought to obtain LEED certification for one of its data halls?

LEED is an incredibly successful program and I think the USGBC (U.S. Green Building Council) people should be proud of the work that they've done. I think LEED gets maligned. Depending upon which faction you're in, you can always say something positive or negative about it. The thing that I like about LEED now, having done—I think we're into 35 or 40 projects—it's very flexible. It's very customer friendly.

When our Suite 610 got LEED-Gold I don't tell people that it was LEED Commercial Interiors or LEED New Construction, because I don't want to explain what all the variances are, but LEED is flexible. Commercial Interiors is specifically designed for a tenant in a building that they don't own that's doing a fitout. So it's great. In this case I happen to do the construction and I own the building but it's a multi-tenant facility. I didn't get LEED on 350 Cermak, we got LEED on Suite 610. And so that flexibility just makes the certification process different.

I'll give you an example. One of the categories of LEED is about materials and waste. Some of those features are, did you source your materials locally? So if you get concrete for a project and the concrete has to travel 2,000 miles (3,218.7 km) over road, you don't get LEED points for that. If it comes from within 100 or 200 miles (160.9 or 321.9 km) you get a point for the fact that you didn't use fossil fuels to transport your materials. Similarly, if you divert all your waste—your miscellaneous wood and rubble and fiberglass—if you separate those and send them to the appropriate recycling spaces you get more points. Well, on a commercial interiors job, it's pretty easy to get the waste diversion points because you're not knocking down a building. On a LEED for New Construction or a LEED for Redevelopment if you tear down any of the structure you get murdered on points because you're creating so much rubble. Each little category has its nuances. And someone could make the argument 'LEED CI isn't as good as LEED NC.' Well, whatever. That may or may not be true but guess what, I wasn't building a new building I was doing a commercial interiors and the USGBC people have a program for that. So in that context it's just like every other project. Across the criteria, there's where your materials come and go to, indoor air quality, fundamental commissioning, energy performance, access to transit, things like that. So A LEED CI job is just a subset of the requirements for your particular thing.

So there wasn't anything specific to 350 Cermak that hurt us. There were some benefits. Like, the access to transit piece is an important one for people.

One issue was this daylighting issue. The building is an eight story building with roughly 140,000 feet (13,006.4 square meter) per floor, so it's a big rectangle, a big rectangular volumetric space. The interior part of the building historically had a hole cut in it for light wells to get to the workers. Well, the original developer filled that in to create more floor space. So, one of the reasons we to get our daylighting credit we had to do them in the UPS rooms is because the UPS rooms happen to be on the perimeter. It would have been better to do the Data Center with daylighting because that's where more people spend time but that part of the building was interior. We didn't have any exterior windows. So that was one little difficulty.

Other challenges related to LEED? I think of the biggest ones was none of us had done LEED. And LEED has some funny quirks to it, right? You have to have your commissioning agent selected before you go into design. That's common in the Data Center business now, but commissioning usually was at the end of the project. That was one that luckily we caught it so we had someone on board.

Oftentimes we do projects in two separate phases. We usually do what we call our Powered Base building where we might do the medium voltage, the basic pipe work, and then we do our turnkey or our fit-out phase. Well, with LEED you need to submit a single permit package. That was another one where procedurally we got some good advice beforehand so we didn't make any mistakes on the delivery.

I think cost-wise we probably overpaid for our LEED consultant the first time. Now that we're very experienced what we find is we may go to a new market and meet a new architect and they'll say 'Oh, LEED. We'll do that. It'll be, say, $50,000 extra.' We now say 'We will teach you how to do LEED since you don't know how to do it and the cost will be free.' That's a negotiation point in the supply chain because we historically and typically have a lot more experience than our architect partners. And we have a LEED person internal, who works out of our Boston office. She is an architect, we hired her just out of school and said 'You run this program.' She is the keeper of all of our points and our certifications. She probably knows more about LEED for Data Centers than anyone else in the world because she's the one whose name is on the forms, who reviews the criteria and comes to me and says 'We're going to get Silver. We're going to get Gold. We're going to get Platinum. Here are the levers we need to pull to move our rank.'

I normally ask about power density and how many cabinet locations a given Data Center has to offer. I assume that varies among the various data halls within the facility.

It does, but since I was involved from the acquisitions due diligence to the master planning to the final build out I can tell you with pretty good certainty. This building—remember, most of its programming and most of its large footprint customers moved in in the 2000 to 2004 timeframe—so outside of one financial services company that owns almost a whole floor, much of the space is between 50 and 100 watts a foot (538.2 and 1,076.4 watts per square meter). There's not a lot of ceiling height here so there's a decent proportion of the suites that don't have raised floor so you're naturally limited to 75, 100 watts a foot (538.2, 1,076.4 watts per square meter).

The newer builds, Digital has built up to 200 watts a foot (2,152.8 watts per square meter). One of the clients in one of these very high density 25,000 to 30,000 foot (2,322.6 to 2,787.1 square meters), have built up to 400 watts a foot (4,305.6 watts per square meter), but I would guess the building average is probably 75 (538.2).

Do you have a default way that you provide infrastructure or does it vary from suite to suite?

Because in this case there are so many customers that built their own it's all over the map. In Digital's case we generally build a 2N UPS system. Except for the generator plant it's a Tier IV type UPS and distribution architecture, in Uptime standards. It's a double corded, concurrently maintainable system. Concurrent maintenance is the key to availability for us. We're operating at such a big scale that making our operators happy is the big part of my job. So, that 2N, double conversion UPS is a very traditional plant. It's very simple, very easy to work on.

For example, when I tell you we have a floor that's, say, four suites and 1,350 kW apiece, that's not one big 6,000 kW system. At Digital Product we try and make our pods and our suites as discrete as possible. And that's how we attract enterprise clients because the enterprise clients they feel like 'Hey, look, this UPS plant? It's mine. There's nobody else on here. I'm not sharing it. I don't have to synchronize my maintenance calendar with a hosting company. I get to do it all.' And that's a big part of our product position.

In this building, however, the building configuration (is complex). When we go to suburban Dallas—in Richardson, Texas—we build single story buildings, dedicated generators, dedicated UPS, dedicated security systems, dedicated doors to clients. In these more complex buildings you generally have to share some systems. For us (at this site), for example, the eighth floor is one common medium voltage paralleled generator plant and then the suites are broken up into discrete UPS and cooling loads.

In this entire building, Digital's infrastructure is run by the chilled water plant across the street. And that chilled water plant, we actually have a long-term, 25 year agreement with them where we went in, we re-engineered their plant, we put in the generator capacity, we re-engineered all their valving and piping, we added another riser. We were able to take a very large, robust industrial plant and make it a mission critical environment so that it's concurrently maintainable as well.

One of the cool things about that site, we have this thermal storage tank. At our current loads, we're the only people who can draw on the thermal storage tank because the thermal storage tank is for the hotel and for the convention center. So under normal operation the convention center hammers the tank, up and down, up and down. In a power outage scenario the convention center and the hotel have to evacuate. You can't have people in occupied buildings with no power. So they have to evacuate. So we're the only people who have emergency power on the thermal storage pumps. At our current loads we have something like 40 hours of thermal storage. It's just an unheard of number. We have more thermal storage than we have fuel.

That's one of those artifact features. 'Why do you guys have this?' It just was there and we showed up. And we have a great relationship with the owner. It's owned by the state. We put capital into their facility so they loved us. And we extended our contract so they loved us. We have a very good relationship with that plant.

At this site you're dealing with massive infrastructure capacities. Are there any particular challenges that come with operating at that scale?

Yes. There are benefits first. We call Cermak the vertical campus. When we have a place like Santa Clara or Richardson or Virginia or New Jersey, we have these campus environments where we build multiple buildings with multiple Data Centers and multiple customers. On a campus you get incredible economies of scale from management. You still have a chief engineer at every building, but the property manager and the tax people and the operations manager you get a lot of leverage on those folks. I imagine this funny scenario where there's a battery technician somewhere in 350 Cermak and he never leaves the building. We just send in tacos and food and sandwiches and he's just doing battery maintenance in my building forever.

We do see a lot of those advantages of scale with the maintenance guy for UPSs, for spares. In that building I happen to have one more than one UPS type, but it's only two. I have a Liebert set of spares and I have an MGE set of spares. I'm able to take that spares kit and spread it across 10, 15 MW of load. So there are a lot of efficiencies at this scale.

On the headache side, certainly on the chilled water plant it keeps people awake at night. A big common system is risky. One of the things about when we build our Turn-key Data Centers, they're usually 1125 or 2250 kW, we have dozens and dozens of those systems so if any one of them blows up and fails our fault is contained. We don't have our whole client base exposed to a common system. So any time we do things at large scale with big common systems it makes us a little bit nervous. Our competitors build bigger systems and we think that's risky and a lot of our customers agree. They like that they have these smaller, discreet things. Until we did the complete upgrade of the chiller water plant across the street that was my nightmare scenario. Something happened at the Cermak cooling plant and we have to turn most of the building off. Now that we've been able to invest more than $10 million in the infrastructure of that facility I can sleep comfortably because its reliability and its availability and its design are just like everything else we have, so it's neutral. So that's certainly one (challenge).

"On a campus you get incredible economies of scale from management. I imagine this funny scenario where there's a battery technician somewhere in 350 Cermak and he never leaves the building. We just send in tacos and food and sandwiches and he's just doing battery maintenance in my building forever."

At that scale on the power grid, you start to have higher profile and bigger impact. Typically Chicago will have utility scale outages on incredibly hot days. That's where they get hit up in Chicagoland. In that scenario, when the grid gets a little bit unstable, if we make the choice or if our customers make the choice 'Let's go off the grid, let's run on gen because things are a little haywire out there,' we have to be much more tightly coordinated with the networks when we come back on. That's a skill set and a set of phone calls and a set of procedures that are not common. And because we're a big client, Com Ed (Commonwealth Edison) loves us, we love those guys. They're one of our favorite investor-owned utilities. They're really, really good. We have very close relationships with them. We have access to senior management, we have access to operations people. That's one of those key things where, if the Fisk substation has an outage at the transmission side and all of the sudden we've got a bunch of stuff running on gen, we are on the phone at the utility level talking about what's going to happen and when we're going to restore.

There's always an environmental concern with the volume of fuel. Two hundred thousand gallons (757,082.4 liters) of fuel, you're nervous about that. Once again, some of it's customer owned some of it's owned by us. But it's a lot of fuel to keep track of from an insurance and environmental and liability perspective.

And then people. That building has more than 2,000 badge-ins and badge-outs per day. The physical flow of people—we have a huge security staff and a huge operations staff because there's so much activity in the building. A couple of our customers in there are co-location providers so their clients are coming through our security perimeter. There's a lot of physical management.

That particular building is blessed with four very large freight elevators. But the freight elevator scheduling during construction times, when we were developing the building, it was a 24-hour operation with a manager and logistics people at each elevator. And there were periods where if a contractor missed a 15 minute window he might have to wait a day to get back on the elevator.

Similar to the people control, is security. There's just a lot going on. I don't even know how many cameras are in there. Once again, that's a case where we're testing the limits of human factors. Let's presume I have a security station and there's people there—five or six or one. How many cameras can they actually cover? These are these things, we get tested at scale. Over time we've ebbed and flowed up and down. Touch wood, we haven't had any meaningful security events there but are we more exposed, are we more risky because we're at scale? I don't think so but we're not really sure. It's a different thing. There's not a lot of other people we can go to for this type of experience.

FIGURE 8-6
Employees and customers enter and exit the 1.1 million square foot Lakeside Technology Center more than 2,000 times per day.

Since obtaining the facility and doing various buildouts and upgrades, have there been any surprises that have come up?

What we found was, after the first year we thought we had a pretty good plan. We studied this thing. I feel like I would go to Chicago and I would sit in the lotus position on the fourth floor and commune with the building. 'What can you do baby? Where should I go next?' I was up and down the stairways and what about this and pipe routing and engineers and studies...' What we found was we were getting better every time. Every job we did we got smarter.

We got into a rhythm of once per year we got all the major stakeholders—me, the person running the construction group, the property manager, the construction manager on the recent jobs, and then the P&L owner for the region—and we would redo the master plan. We felt like it was wasteful because we did all this work last year, but what we were learning was 'Hey, remember on that last job when we thought we didn't have enough height for on that interior gen? Well, we fixed it by changing the order and now actually we can put gens over here.' Or 'Remember we had that prospect and they really wanted us to do this crazy stuff so they funded the engineering study to do the work and they didn't really buy from us but we have this engineering study that showed us this?' So, I think it wasn't really so much that we were surprised by any one thing as that we got better at owning the building, if that makes any sense. The more time we spent with the machine the more intimate we got with the machine and the machine ran faster.

The noise surprised us, I suppose. Everything we did was good. Every individual Data Center was well built and well planned and all that but the aggregate noise on the roof surprised us. We didn't plan to do some of that sound attenuation. Strictly speaking we could have just fought but it's just easier to be a good citizen and like I said the building is very successful, it's very profitable so we reinvested that profit in the asset. It's a fair decision.

If you could step back in time to 1998 to be part of the redevelopment of the building is there anything you would do differently to it?

I think it's a good posture in business to be a little bit skeptical of your own success. You never know if you're going to make it. When we acquired 350 Cermak we acquired it on its merits. It had cash flow. It had a value. We paid the right price for it. We were able to invest more capital and grow it. Now it's worth, whatever, hundreds and hundreds of millions of dollars.

If I could do everything over, knowing the end state of the building and the financial success—one of the interesting things that's going on in the Data Center business is there's lots of growth. There's some big mega stuff: Apple, Facebook, Yahoo!, Microsoft. Those guys don't deal with capital like we do. They're different types of companies. They have different disciplines. They have different hopes and dreams and goals and accounting treatments. If Microsoft or Google or Apple or somebody is building a 100 MW Data Center they probably wouldn't build it like we would, and so if I did something different I would've acquired the energy facility across the road, built a 50 MW trigeneration, gas-powered facility with a 50 MW utility intertie and if I had that today I would be operating a traditional Data Center with traditional chilled water with a traditional PUE but my energy source and my chilled water creation would be putting my energy and carbon performance on line with the Facebook Open Compute Project—1.05, 1.1 PUE.

That doesn't make economic sense at 10 MW in an urban environment. But at 100 MW this would be a showcase of how 100 MW Data Centers should be built. The issue that we all have, even at our scale—we've got a $10 billion balance sheet, $1 billion of revenue, hundreds and hundreds of megawatts of Data Centers—even me, I'm not going to build a 100 MW facility on Day One for almost anybody, even if a client says they'll fund it all. That's I think one of these inflection points we're at. The industry is scaling. We're growing. We're going to run up in to some limits and we're going to have to do some new more industrial things. But the economics are so intimidating that nobody's going to be that first one to do it.

But I really feel at 100 MW scale trigeneration for a Data Center is perfect because you've got baseload demand for the cooling, you've got baseload demand for the electricity. You get a nice big gas feed. Get a system tuned up. Tied in with the grid so you can take it off and maintain it just like other power plants do. Then the question becomes should Digital own that or should Com Ed own that or should a third party own that? The ownership piece I don't have solved but the engineering piece, I think large 100 MW trigeneration scale is going to be the right tech.

Not that most people are going to fall into this sort of Data Center project, both in terms of massive scale and dealing with a unique building, but are there any design principles you would recommend for someone taking on a major Data Center project?

Yeah. I am a big fan of outside air, whether you want to go direct or indirect. And if you want to incorporate outside air at large scale the volumetric dimensions of your building and land become critically important. This building is a giant cubic form so the volume of the building that doesn't touch an exterior edge is massive. And I think at scale you want to be building flat, large buildings. Or tall and narrow. You want to make sure your ratio of interior volume is matched to how much surface you can touch because you need that surface to move air through the facility.

So the question becomes, can everybody build in remote areas? And the answer should be yes and no, because we can't all go to Utah or Wenatchee or Nashville or wherever. There's still demand in urban centers. It's amazing. Why are people building Data Centers in California? It's doesn't make any sense. It's expensive. There are earthquakes. It's hard to build here. Yet it's one of our biggest markets if not our biggest market. So that's an interesting piece. Anything I could tell you on form and function and design could be blown out by market demand. I think that's the biggest takeaway.

We have a new template of a building that we call our PBB Plus, our Power Based Building Plus, where we took a form factor that matched the volume of the Data Center, the volume of air that needs to flow through it, with a physical set of dimensions in steel, that creates a kind of a Data Center unit. We can put 10 of those together. We can put 40 of them together. We can put them two stories. We can put them single story. And in each one of those we can feed them with outside air, so when we go to the business from the design team, we say 'Hey, what do you guys want to do in market x?' They go, 'We want to put 10 MW.' 'Then get me a piece of land of this dimension.' Or 'I've got a piece of land of this dimension, what can you guys do there?'

We have this pre-built playbook of the building physical structure that then we can put in a couple different facility architectures inside of it. But that building configuration becomes the driving factor. If you look at Facebook Open Compute, the Yahoo! Computing Coop, you see that. The building config is the Data Center now.

I have seen a lot of Data Center projects over the years where the server environment wasn't a primary consideration during planning of the building. It's a turning point when the Data Center design is given priority. A lot of new capabilities can be enabled.

This is one of the issues with the Data Center business. Even at some tech companies, Data Centers aren't at the forefront. They you go into a traditional enterprise where tech's just a service and it's way down the list.

We started our discussion of building configs as an economics thing. I said, 'Look, I'm sick of these complex buildings. I love them, they've made me the man I am today, but I think if we spend time and design a building right it'll be cheaper.' We had this big argument. 'No, the time to develop land and build the buildings will interfere with the economics.' We said, 'Yeah, that might be true in some cases.'

What we did was I told (Digital Realty Trust vice president) Steve Kundich—he's an architect by training and he ran this group for a long time—'Go take a blank sheet of paper and design me the perfect Data Center building, in a vacuum with no one else telling you what to do.' And then when we costed those up, sure enough we found out you know what we can actually save quite a bit on the Data Center fitout if we build the building right. And then the benefit of having it pre-designed obviously is big for us because it allows us to be more agile.

After working on several Data Center projects in which being green was a priority, I reached the conclusion that green design is fundamentally good design. Even if someone isn't compelled by the environmental merits, you're streamlining the design and operations so that things function while consuming fewer resources, which means greater efficiency and cost savings.

I once did an exercise with Liebert—we were doing an account review and they were showing us what we bought and what the roadmap was—and I said 'I would like you guys to come back to tomorrow's part of the meeting and I want you to show me your entire large frame UPS product line on a price per pound basis. They were like, 'What? In great British pounds?' I said, 'No, by weight. Like, how many pounds does each UPS weigh?' And they said, 'Well why do you want that?'

I said, 'Don't ask. I'll tell you later, but just go do it.' So they did it and what I was trying to get was, what percentage of their gross margin was from innovation and technology. I wanted to strip out the material cost. I presume it's an equal volume of steel, lead, and copper.

Sure enough, it was a completely linear relationship with price per pound. And so I said, 'I would like to buy the lightest UPS please.' It's one of those things where, guess what, the lighter models were the ones that were transformerless, etc. And maybe those don't fit and maybe they do but it was that concept you just talked about, of stripping things out. And weight, it's cost, it's shipping, it's materials, it's smelting. Weight's an important factor in these things. Lightweight stuff is more sustainable.

Let me offer you the final word. Is there anything else people should know about this site?

At the risk of inflaming the marketplace, because this is one of these image issues we have: Data Centers consume a lot of power, is that good or bad? My argument is Data Centers are huge engines of productivity increase. Data Centers using a lot of power is good for the world.

But I think the takeaway is, this building and its recent load growth is now the largest power consumer in the city of Chicago. That for us is a good milestone in that we're helping the city of Chicago transform from its former industrial base into its new industrial base built around service and technology. And financial services are a big part of that, because that's a big client base there. That I think is a good anecdote and a good milestone for the building. We passed O'Hare Airport in the last year.

I do think it's elegant, the function of this building had in the past and the one it has now. It seems very evolutionary.

From an economics perspective, like what is redevelopment, we're taking capital and materials that came from the Industrial Revolution and we're reusing them in this revolution. It's a cool, cool circle that we're in.

"…we're taking capital and materials that came from the Industrial Revolution and we're reusing them in this revolution."

FIGURE 8-7   Additional architectural details of the Lakeside Technology Center.

FIGURE 9-1 The Project Mercury Data Center in Phoenix, Arizona. Images provided courtesy of eBay.

CHAPTER 9
eBay

ESSENTIAL DETAILS

ORGANIZATION: eBay	
LOCATION: Phoenix, Arizona	
ONLINE: October 2011	
NOTABLE FEATURES: In-building data hall, containerized Data Centers on the roof. Air and liquid cooling to cabinets, outside air cooling, adjustable computing capability.	
TIME TO DESIGN AND BUILD: 22 months	
SIZE: 42,000 sq. ft. (3,901.9 sq. m) total, with 14,000 sq. ft. (1,300.6 sq. m) of hosting space in the building and rooftop containers.	
POWER: 4MW for IT initially, expandable to 6 MW for the in-room data hall and 6 MW for containers	
TIER: II	
CABINET LOCATIONS: 256 on the main floor; roof can house 10-12 containers, whose rack count can vary by configuration	
POWER DENSITY: 14 or 28 kW per cabinet	
INFRASTRUCTURE DELIVERY: Electrical conduit, structured cabling, and cooling are delivered overhead. Liquid cooling piping is routed below a 6 ft. (1.8 m) raised floor.	
STRUCTURAL LOADING: 750 lb. per sq. ft. (3,661.8 kg per sq. m)	
FIRE SUPPRESSION SYSTEM: Double action, pre-action interlocked system. VESDA detection system.	

When online marketplace eBay built its Project Mercury Data Center in Phoenix, Arizona, in 2011, the company outfitted it with the sleek, futuristic look of *Tron: Legacy*.

A computer-circuit pattern is etched on the doors, accent lights adorn the walls, and ice blue panels at the end of each server row are numbered with the movie's distinctive font. (During Project Mercury's grand opening, eBay played a 10-minute video that includes staffers in *Tron* attire wielding glowing data discs and light sabers to combat a denial of service attack.)

Beyond *Tron's* neon-lined styling, eBay apparently took to heart the movie's tagline: "The game has changed." Rather than designing the Data Center in-house or using vendors from previous projects, for instance, eBay issued a public RFP (request for proposal), inviting firms to submit competing designs. It employed a similar approach with Data Center container and hardware manufacturers. The company meanwhile streamlined its operations: standardizing hardware configurations, prioritizing applications, and creating processes to deploy fully-occupied racks and containers, allowing thousands of new servers to be installed as demand warrants.

The Data Center's physical infrastructure includes game-changers as well: including hot water cooling, rack and container accommodations, air- and water-based cooling, and a raised floor deep enough to race light cycles underneath.

Dean Nelson, Senior Director of Global Foundational Services at eBay, talks about how the company's supply chain and Data Center design have each been optimized to operate efficiently and scale rapidly.

The Interview

Project Mercury's design came about in a unique way, with eBay specifying requirements and then having design firms submit proposals. Tell me about its development.

I joined eBay in 2009 and they were right in the middle of Project Topaz, which is a Tier IV Data Center built in Salt Lake City. I took on that project kind of mid-stream, and then brought that to completion which was in May of 2010.

Tier IV, they did a lot of innovative things in there. They got to a PUE design of 1.4, so they elevated the temperatures. They've done a lot of the best practices to go back and get the best efficiency. They've gone to 400 volts, they've done a lot of things in the industry. They did a lot of best practices and it will serve our needs. But the problem is, it still had a lot of the same older approaches in it.

There were fixed UPS amounts per room. There were three 20,000 sq. ft. (1,858.1 sq. m) rooms. It was expected to have lots of space that you could spread out. And so the philosophy of 'space is cheap I should build that up and I can just spread things out as I need.' It was a lot of facilities-focused decisions in that. And what I found was everything was also based on a Tier IV expectation. So, the applications no one had really done the inventory to find out what has to be in a Tier IV Data Center and what could be in a lower tier Data Center. So that was the first thing I did was just go back and assess that. And what we found is up to 70 or 80 percent of the applications that run in our Data Center, the equipment that actually runs in the Data Center for those apps, can be in a Tier II. So we're spending a lot of money to basically do overkill on a lot of applications that are resilient already.

That was now where we said let's right-size applications. That was the first philosophy.

I work in an organization right now where all costs are included. So I own all of the Data Centers, the networks, supply chain, security, etc. My peer owns all the provisioning. He takes the cache equipment we have and he basically creates the infrastructure as a service to deploy out whatever we need for whatever app. So you profile equipment, you can now make a decision and push things out. And then my other peer is the one that does site operations and analytics. It's really looking at the health of the site and the uptime and then all the data around that and presenting all that information back.

What we found was, let's filter through these apps and from there let's figure out what we should put in the Data Center. The other part was, we don't know really what we need when we need it so we need to build a generic, modular approach. That's one of my background pieces—modularity is really important in all of this. And modularity at almost every level, to be able to scale out components as you need. And multi-tier. Since we had a Tier IV Data Center how would we augment with a multi-tier center next to it. Don't lose your investments that you've already had. Let's figure out how we could build, utilize the Tier IV to give it more runway but now take out things to free up capacity in the Tier IV and put them into adjacent Tier IIs that utilize the same power infrastructure, that utilize the same security teams, support teams and delivery channels, and all that on the same site.

After that then we started really looking at well what are we putting in the Data Center. And (there were) tons of skus, tons of configurations, lots of people making the choice about what hardware is going in there and not really standardizing. Just earlier this year we looked at how we could reduce the number of skus and have standard skus. We took 15 of the top skus— companies can have hundreds of them; we had well over 100—and we were able to get those down to two. One for was Hadoop, which required a lot of local storage, and the second one was for everything else. We got common CPUs, common memory, common bus, common network speeds—all those pieces so now we could say 'Well maybe we can do front end for search or a pool or any other kind of application could run on this equipment.'

With that, then we started to apply that to the supply chain and we started to find the sweet spot. So now we've got standard skus how do we package them? The packaging was really, for me, once we started handing off to the vendor to do a thing called rack and roll and that's where we give them the spec and the configuration they need to do. They acquire the components, they build, they rack, they cable, they image, they test, they validate and then they ship us a rack that we basically plug in the power and the network and then turn up.

When you start to look at that, the efficiencies that we get of now streamlining the supply chain process and the amount of volume we start to get because we have all the same type of hardware being ordered and then the competitive RFPs we can put out there—lots of people competing at it and we get great pricing. So that was the next piece was consolidating those skus.

Then, what we found is that the sweet spot as we started doing the calculations of running this workload at this much wattage, there are two values—and they're 14 kW and 28 kW—that we want to go after. So it's a 48U rack, it's up to 3,500 lbs. (1,587.6 kg) In our one config it's 96 servers in a rack. We've got the ability now to put in multiple failure domains from a network perspective. We've got the optimized power strips. We've got the optimized cooling. All of those components fall together that we have this unit and that unit now is what we can order from the vendors. And that 28 kW really works in to I can deliver a lot in less. I have less racks I have to do. Because of the co-los we're in, we're paying rent in a footprint based on the density. And so if I get lower density it sounds like it would be cheaper but the problem is you're getting more racks to do that same work and you're actually paying more money.

FIGURE 9-2   Greetings program. Visitors first encounter the eBay Data Center's *Tron* theme at its entrances.

So when we looked at that total cost we decided that the sweet spot here was 28 kW and 96 servers in a cabinet. Or 48 servers, for sku two, which is the Hadoop one. And then we started pushing that. Then we were designing the facilities to be able to handle any load, but really the scale is that every footprint should be able to scale up to 28 kW over time.

Then we start looking at what we're building in Phoenix. How do you build the maximum density inside of a Data Center that can scale both on the infrastructure side and then as you're doing tech refresh and rolling equipment in and out? You can replace it with footprints and double them as the business needs it.

Now all those pieces started coming together. And then we said 'I want free cooling in the Data Center. I want it in Arizona.' It's one of the hardest places for us to solve this. We put the public RFP out there for the industry to take these parameters—free cooling in Arizona year-round, modular, multi-tier Data Center solutions, and ultimate flexibility: we want to be able to have racks or even containers on the roof. And so we did this in a small footprint. We were building the building already, and we said let's build up as a Data Center adjacent to our current one on the land we have. That's where we started saying 3,500 lbs. (1,587.6 kg), with containers and everything else. We need 1 million lbs. (453.6 mt.) of steel in the building. We're basically building a 10-story building in 3 stories.

But once we had all of those parameters together, we really figured out the optimum way from a cost standpoint to build a multi-tier center. Because we've got the Tier IV next door to it.

The challenge out to the industry, this is what really worked with the public RFP process. The design and consulting engineers out there, the architecture firms, the engineering firms, they love this. Because it wasn't a company like eBay coming out and saying this is how you have to build the Data Center. It was 'Here's our business problem, here are the components that we really need you to design to. Now you tell us how to design the Data Center.' And that worked. That worked really well. We had some great innovation and the guys really thought about it. It took away a lot of the constraints they had in the past and came at it from a problem statement.

And what we came back with, we finally chose EDI as the winner and they brought in Winterstreet Architects and AHA Consulting Engineers and between those three they had a really flexible, simple, efficient, and modular design. And then when they brought that back in we saw the concept and said 'Ok, now we've got to blow that up a little bit because our demand just doubled. Here's the footprint which you have to play with. You've got a little more space. What's the max you can fit in there? What can I fit in that building? What's the optimum capacity I should put in? And then I want to grow it in 2 MW chunks over time.'

What we ended up with, in 14,000 sq. ft. (1,300.6 sq. m), was the ability to scale from 4 MW to 12 MW of IT capacity. If you start to divide that out with the amount of footprint in 14,000 sq. ft. (1,300.6 sq. m)—half of it's on the roof in containers, half is in rack and roll on the ground floor—it ends up being about 28 kW a cabinet at the end. So it's funny how all these things started coming together with the amount of space we had to be able to do that density. And then when you look at the reality of what technology is doing, today the containers are landed on the roof, we found the sweet spot of about 450 kW because that is the maximum airflow that you can actually get across the equipment in that area of a contained box, to be able to continuously cool 28 kW. So we found the ceiling of air. Great.

On top of that we said we wanted free cooling year-round. So we went and took the hottest day of the year with a wet bulb and that was 85 degrees Fahrenheit (29.4 Celsius) and they designed a hot water cooling loop. And the hot water cooling loop is a supply of 87 degrees (30.6 Celsius) because that's eventually what it gets to at the server. But 87 degrees (30.6 Celsius) we're also looking at being able to plug in, not just today's air-cooled stuff but the future. I want to be able to have liquid cooled right to the chip. Because 87 degrees (30.6 Celsius) to the chip is cold.

So, you see all these pieces are starting to come together. We're building a very flexible Data Center that allows us to pick the tier level, pick the density as the business needs change. And they will change, and they did change literally overnight here. And as we see over the life of the Data Center we've given ourselves runway. Today's best air-cooled solutions I've got to the cap. I'm maximizing my floor space, I'm maximizing my supply chain, I'm maximizing my efficiency.

Because containers that we're putting in there, some are using 87 (30.6 Celsius) as the primary source, the other ones are using outside air and just regular swamp cooling and they're getting free cooling the majority of the year round. I've got PUEs of less than 1.1 at 28 kW density in cabinets. That's the kind of result we can get, that our overall cost per MW is going down because of all these variables that came together to build for what the business needs versus building what the Data Center needs and then just accommodating the equipment afterwards.

That's been the lesson really for us. We've created this multi-tier modular strategy that allows us to scale. By the way, the RFP process we did for the Data Center we followed with the actual compute equipment. So we put out that we're looking for 96 servers in the rack, 48 servers in a rack, for these two skus. We're looking for these CPU and memory configs and network configs, etc. So we gave them all the specs. Then we said you're going to be scored on your unit costs delivered, because they're going to package up and do everything else. You're also going to be scored on the wattage consumed with our average workload over its useful life. So we took the depreciation cost of the server plus the wattage cost—because I pay that bill—for that equipment over its 3 year life. And we made the decision on the IT equipment based on that. So, all-in TCO—a real TCO. We made a vendor decision, an IT decision. I was really pleased with that. And that yielded great results because the first round went to one vendor that was a surprise to everybody because they had the most efficient design. And then the other vendors saw that they'd lost and we told them why they lost and they tuned their equipment and a different vendor won the second round.

So I've got two vendors on the roof and two vendors on the ground floor, Day One, opening this Data Center in Phoenix. And they're both uber efficient. They're both highly cost effective. They're both dense. And they're both getting free cooling almost year-round.

Most people certainly wouldn't think of Phoenix as a likely candidate for employing outside air cooling. What prompted you to explore that?

My past, I came out of the IT side and what I saw was a lot of vendors coming up with really cool solutions on the IT equipment that never saw the light of day. Why? Because everyone had a phobia about water in the Data Center and about temperature and they assumed that air is the answer.

When I looked at the problem I'm like, there are two variables here: the surface temp of the chip and the outside air temp. Can we design to those two parameters to get free cooling? Yeah.

"I saw a lot of vendors coming up with really cool solutions on the IT equipment that never saw the light of day. Why? Because everyone had a phobia about water in the Data Center and about temperatures and they assumed that air is the answer."

Everybody buffers. You look at the chip manufacturers—Intel, AMD, etc.—they have to ship all over the world so they ensure that their operating temperatures of the chip are going to work everywhere. Which means there has got to be 20, 30, 40 percent overhead of temp, right? If you've got a really well tuned environment, you can raise those temperatures and stay within those boundaries.

Through the Chill Off 3 (a head to head comparison test of Data Center cooling products) we tested workload with both air and liquid. And we found out that there was no loss of performance at 87 degree (30.6 Celsius) inlet air. We found that there was a shadowing removal, meaning that the chip with memory in front of it and a CPU behind it the memory will heat up the chip further. That's from an air standpoint. But even with the shadowing it's a little less efficient but it still didn't have any errors and the boxes were running fine. And then when you put liquid to it—cold plate was one of our tests—the shadowing goes away so the efficiency gets even better. And then at that point you can now look at the chip and say 'Am I really optimizing that chip?' Because what I want is a gas pedal. I want to be able to raise the frequency of that chip or decrease the frequency of that chip just like I would have a Prius turns into a Ferrari, because when we need it we need it. I don't care if I'm paying more wattage for it, it just needs to stay within the thermal boundaries, which we can if we've got liquid to the chip. Boom—we can burst and use less machines to do the work and then back off in the times when it's not loaded. So, you take that parameter, too.

FIGURE 9-3 Illuminated panels at the end of each row reinforce the eBay Data Center's futuristic appearance.

Part of the RFP was we want direct access to the CPU to be able to adjust the voltage so that we can adjust the frequency of the chip as needed, so our engine can go back and adjust itself. So, we've got that hook in there. At the same time we now said build out the Data Center that I can roll in a cabinet that's going to use air, side cooling, or a passive door, or any other solution around it, or direct liquid to the chip, without having to redesign the Data Center. So we delivered two loops, the 55 degree (12.8 Celsius) loop and the 87 degree (30.6 Celsius) hot water cooling loop to every location in the Data Center. So the containers can use it, the racks can use it. I spent maybe an extra half a million dollars in capital to be able to do that Day One and that depreciated over 30 years is peanuts in what we're doing.

So here we've got the capability now to do from 5 kW to 40 in a footprint and an average scaling up to 28 kW a cabinet through every rack in the Data Center. So the useful life of a Data Center just extended. And the capabilities for us to go back and replace equipment that's air cooled today and roll in a liquid cooled one in the exact same footprint and get potentially two to three to four times the performance? Amazing. And I spent half the money that I did before.

What's the break point at which you want to change from air cooling to liquid cooling?

Anything over 20 to 25 kW. You're going to pay a little bit more for the liquid side. Again, there are products coming. We're pushing hard because they know what our workload is, they know what we're trying to accomplish, and if they can get that CPU variation it's a huge win on the TCO. It's not about power saving mode, where you turn on power throttling and those kind of things. That's in environments where it's just too hot. What if you have it optimized? Well you should now be able to go back and to tune it to what you need and when you need it. To me that is such a difference from what it was in the past.

If you start to get your arms around what compute workload is going to be on there and then you start to roll in say, if I use liquid cooling I can overclock these systems for three years because they're really optimized for that environment. So I can buy cheaper processors and use them like more expensive processors and still get the same performance. The unit cost may be about the same, but then at the times when I want to use it I'm turning it into a Ferrari. So I may use 120 percent of the wattage during that four hour period. But imagine at that point you back off. For the rest of the 20 hours I have less than that. And at other times I can either go idle with them or I can take them out of commission because I have less load than is needed.

So I've got a variable here, a gas pedal that I can go up and down. And instead of this constant in the Data Center from a load perspective it starts to vary. So the overall cost of running that equipment goes down substantially when you have control over the chip, when you're doing it with that temp. And everyone is going after this from an air perspective: we need to use outside air. Ok. But what I find is a lot of people are designing Data Centers with the equipment spread out. They're using the cheap processors and more of them. So they're using twice the amount of equipment to do the same workload in a cheaper building to get a PUE reduction of another .1 and they're missing the point. They're still using twice the amount of equipment. They're like 'Well, the wattage is two-thirds of what it was before.' But you're still using twice the amount of equipment. You're using more wattage than I would in a high density, high temp solution than what you've got in yours.

"A lot of people are designing Data Centers with the equipment spread out. They're using the cheap processors and more of them. So they're using twice the amount of equipment to do the same workload in a cheaper building to get a PUE reduction of another .1 and they're missing the point."

So it's a holistic view into the Data Center. When you really know the workload and the facilities infrastructure and you get those together and you start to tune it like a machine you get incredible efficiencies from that.

I understand eBay seeing significant variation in workload for its Data Center hardware. Do you think those trends are typical for other server environments? Is how you're designing your Data Centers—capable of alternating between Prius and Ferrari characteristics—a good solution just for you or is it applicable for most installations?

This comes back to being generic in the Data Center. So today you may have a business like a bank or just a traditional enterprise IT organization, right? And they don't change their equipment that much. It's fairly static at different times. But if you build up an infrastructure that's modular from Day One—a Data Center—and you have the ability to scale over time, it doesn't matter if you do it every 2 years or every 7 years. You still have the ability to add more capacity. Because the upfront cost to do larger pipe sizes, more outlet links and those things but not buy all the other support equipment is minimal. I have the ability to now take my 4 MW and go to 6 for almost half the price of what I did the first 4 MW for. And then from there I do it again. I do another upfront for the first 2 MW and the next 2 are almost half the price of that first 4. So I've given myself runway for that Data Center and I know that over time the densities are going to continue to increase.

It'll be different for everybody about how well they increase, but my point with this is the leading edge people, the ones that are pushing this—it's usually high performance computing—that is the leading indicator in the industry. What are they doing? If you look at the fastest computer in the world, it's liquid cooled. Why is it liquid cooled? Because they have the same chip problem that everybody does and so they've figured out how to optimize that environment. We've just taken it one step further and figured out how do I optimize for that chip and for

"When you really know the workload and the facilities infrastructure and you get those together and you start to tune it like a machine you get incredible efficiencies from that."

the outside air and build a Data Center that can manage both. And if you did that in all the regions? You know, the hardest one is going to be Singapore because of the humidity. But if you have liquid cooling direct to the chip in Singapore, you're going to get free cooling.

My point is: these practices about building a modular Data Center that is scalable over time, that does it up front—not everything but the ability to scale in chunks—applies to almost every Data Center out there. It's about how you're investing in your center. And if the centers are supposed to have a minimum life of 10 years then you should assume you're going to have a minimum of two to three tech refreshes. And others could have up to five. Like, we do tech refreshes every two years on a lot of our equipment because we're really pushing the boundaries here from a performance standpoint. But even if you did it every 5 years you have the ability now to double the capacity. If you could roll in a rack of the next stuff and not have to rebuild your Data Center and all the complexities around that that's a pretty big win for the company. And you're not spending 2x at the beginning, you're spending 15 to 20 percent more on piping and other infrastructure. It's just proper planning.

I was going to ask if eBay's rapid refresh cycle of its hardware—replacing about half of its computing equipment each year—influenced the design of the Data Center. It sounds like you consider the design applicable for any company that has a hardware refresh cycle, frequent or not.

The cycle's there, it's just how far in between is the cycle. Is it a long sine wave or a short sine wave?

I've been in the IT rooms. I've been in the labs, the server rooms, the Data Centers and all those pieces and they all have the same need. It's still compute equipment of some density somewhere that has to land in a place and you've got to power and cool it. Why wouldn't you build the most flexible infrastructure to be able to do that?

People that are building just for air today are going to be limited in the future. Will it work? Sure. Will they be able to take advantage of the technologies that come out? Not all of them. We're pushing the vendors to come back with these liquid cooling solutions because we know the answer already in our models, so I want to products that will fall in there. What I believe the industry is going to get from that is here is one of the leading indicators of what's coming. So if they're able to roll that into their Data Center and take advantage of it they're using half the equipment or less to do the same work. You talk to an IT person and say you can spend half the capital to grow in here if you use this solution, like liquid to the chip. But if they have a Data Center that can't take advantage of it, they're going to spend more in capital to enable it in the Data Center than it's worth.

I've said this for years: it's the organizational alignment. When you have these facilities teams and IT teams working together, and that's exactly I believe the secret sauce at eBay, We're all in it. We're in the same game, we have the same goals, we have the same budget. We all have to go lower the cost per megawatt to deliver capacity for the actual company. And that works out to be watts per transaction, or watts per user or watts per whatever variable. It's still watts. And the less watts I can use to do that and all the other knobs you turn for it—the efficiencies of the servers to the Data Center efficiencies to liquid cooling to air cooling, whatever—they all basically lower the amount of watts per whatever.

How are you delivering the infrastructure into the Data Center? Is it a raised floor environment?

Yeah. This is what's ironic. I didn't like raised floor before because it was kind of a waste. I don't need to have raised floor to deliver cooling, right? Modular cooling, I can put in sidecars or overhead, etc., is pretty easy. But what I found in this environment is it was worth it to put in a raised floor and we have an almost 6 ft. (1.8 m.) raised floor.

I know, it's ironic, I'm building one of the biggest raised floors out there and I don't like them. But the point is, there's no air underneath it. Everything under that is pipe work because we've got the two loops delivered to every one of the locations so that now I can snap in either a sidecar air conditioning unit or a passive rear door or I can plug directly into the rack as those liquid racks become available.

FIGURE 9-4 Liquid cooling piping is routed below a 6 ft. (1.8 m.) raised floor while power, cooling, and cabling are distributed overhead in eBay's Project Mercury Data Center.

In our next tech refresh I am pushing really, really hard that we are going to have liquid cooled equipment. And I think that's going to be here sooner than people think. When we roll it in and start seeing what we can get with that gas pedal, that's when I think the lights are going to turn on for people. Like, 'Wow, I today build infrastructure with DR that goes no more than 50 percent of my capacity. That's really wasteful. I'm only using half of what I can out of these servers yet I'm still paying the wattage penalty.' Imagine if you put in half the amount of equipment and you had the ability to overclock those to 130 percent when you need them. You've got the gas pedal when you need it, because it's really only four hours per day for us where it's the peak of the peak. The rest of it I'm going down to these low numbers.

What we're looking at is both horizontal and vertical scale. So, I've got 100 racks of equipment delivered for search. If I need all 100 racks for that peak of the peak and I overclock them to that point I can probably use 70 racks for it. The vertical scale: I can take my 70 racks and make them act like 100 racks by overclocking.

Then I go back and say 'Well, when I go down to here I can't go too slow because our search function requires a certain amount of latency to deliver a search result to a customer'. So there's the threshold at the bottom you say, 'Well I would never go below 2 GHz'. Ok. So downclock them all to 2 GHz. You're still delivering to the performance of the application. Then, if you only need 30 of the actual racks take the rest of them out of the pool and put them in hibernate. And as you see the triggers going up where it's starting to increase add another rack in. That's the horizontal scale.

But you see what I mean is we build the infrastructure to be able to have these cabinets scale up and down and horizontally as we need them, because we know what the IT workload is and we tie back in the infrastructure so that the engine runs efficiently. Think of a car. People are designing Data Centers without understanding how the engine inside operates and the people designing the engine are not expecting or worrying about anything in the cooling or what-not. So they drop an engine in and there's a disconnect. But when you have them designing the whole car, because the car itself is the Data Center, the engine is the IT and the control system is the gas pedal and everything else that takes advantage of it—you're tuning for all those aspects. That's what we're looking for. Ultimately it becomes one machine with all components working together and knobs that automatically turn themselves.

We're also looking to converge in the infrastructure and allowing the Data Center— because we've got I think over 240,000 points monitored in that Data Center in Salt Lake City and that we go into a PI System and that PI System is the stuff that runs nuclear power plants. It scales to millions and millions of points. We want to take that data and roll that back into our engine that is the application so they can start to understand, 'Oh, it's currently nighttime in Phoenix and I can overclock all my systems to here and ship the workload over there, because now it's even colder at night so I can get even more performance out of those chips because it's delivering 70 degrees (21.1 Celsius) instead of 87 degrees (30.6 Celsius) during the heat of the day. But the whole engine is tuned and the applications now can take advantage of that. The whole stack is connected. That's where our ultimate goal is, is to be able to have a finely tuned machine that only consumes the wattage it needs but can perform based on whatever business demand comes.

"Think of a car. People are designing Data Centers without understanding how the engine inside operates and the people designing the engine are not expecting or worrying about anything in the cooling or what-not. So they drop an engine in and there's a disconnect."

During most interviews for this book I ask about recommended Data Center design principles. I have taken away some from our conversation already: modularity, scalability, look at the Data Center from end-to-end, expect liquid cooling in the future. Is there any other advice that you would offer someone?

Multi-tier. If you build a modular infrastructure you should be able to deliver whatever tiers you're looking for. If you build out Tier IV, you're going to have Tier IV. If you build out a center that can scale to Tier IV or you build out a section that's Tier IV and the rest of them can scale between Tier I and III, you're going to give yourself a lot more flexibility. The majority of companies out there still have at least half or less of their equipment that really requires Tier IV.

Even the banking industry, certain transactional things and all of that it's the data where it's stored. It's the network that has to be in the Tier IV, but the compute engine that's doing that they've got to point it at multiple locations, the same thing as our search. You should be able to put that in multiple locations at a lower tier. So, right sizing your applications—there's another one.

I guess the other piece is still the same mantra: can the Facilities and IT teams work together? Are they approaching the design with a unified front? Are they looking at the problem together?

I participated in a Data Center project a few years ago in which building multi-tier areas was considered. The argument against doing it was the belief that once you paid for the foundational infrastructure to achieve Tier IV, you might as well build the entire Data Center that way because if you didn't you were overpaying for the sections with less redundancy throughout their design. How do you get around that? Or is that cost simply insignificant over the lifetime of a facility?

If you look at what we built in Salt Lake City: $287 million for a Tier IV center. Bulletproof. Big. Solid. It's just isn't going to go down and we need it. But I'm going to build right next to it almost four times the capacity at less than half the cost—almost a quarter of the cost—the capabilities of being able to do that. I would say over its lifetime I'm building half of that with almost four times the capacity.

I've got a certain amount of capacity inside of our Data Center in Salt Lake that because today I'm filling up the space, I would have consumed all my power already with compute equipment unless I now am building a center that I can pull out certain things that are lower tier. So, the capital investment of a Tier IV what you really probably need to do is how much would I actually build Tier IV, and I still would be really surprised if people would build more than 50 percent. If I am building 50 percent Tier IV and 50 percent Tier II I can build two to three times the amount of Tier II and give myself a lot more runway, up to four times the amount that I would within Tier IV. If I build that out modularly I should be able to now scale it up as I need. We're looking at 75 to 80 percent of our stuff is going to be removed out of our Tier IV. That's a big deal.

Talk about runway. I gave myself another 5, 10 years because I've just gotten rid of the majority of load in there. And I'm only putting the core network and the large storage devices and certain databases and other things that really can't go down, in there. And those scale a lot slower than everything else. But the ones that scale are the search nodes, are the front end nodes, the ones that we want to replace every two years because that's where all the workload is and they call the databases, they use the network. But all those computers are in the front, consuming a ton of power.

Again, it's the multi-tenant environment. If you have a generic footprint what we found is the smallest unit is going to be a rack. When we roll in a rack of whatever it's going to be allocated to, a business unit or a function. So if we've got generic cabling infrastructure, power infrastructure, etc., to be able to roll that in, then we don't really care. We want to have secure environments, we can still lock the cabinets, we can still put them in different sections but it's still anything can go anywhere at any density and attached to any project.

That requires the network team to figure out how they would isolate. That requires the IT teams to figure out how they would distribute for disaster recovery for failure domains inside of the equipment. They've got to think through it. But we've given them a flexible environment. Today in a lot of the centers I have to go figure out which blade slot in which chassis has enough power and enough connectivity to be able to add capacity. That's wrong. What I should be able to do is say, 'What capacity do you need in IT?' and I can accommodate it wherever I am. I can roll that into the Data Center and plug it in and go. That agility and that speed, that time to market, is what's really, really important to us.

That flexibility in a traditional enterprise IT organization makes it simple. You acquire companies, you downsize, you do a tech refresh—all those different activities you still have a flexible infrastructure that allows you to accommodate them. You may not have a high growth business such as an Internet based company as eBay or Amazon or Google and those things but you definitely have the same philosophy about modularity, enabling flexibility inside of a center to grow at your pace. And to do it very, very cost effectively both in capital investments as well as efficiency of operating them.

Were there any surprises throughout the project?

Oh, yeah. I'll tell you one that was very interesting to me. I was trying to get down to a single-corded device. If that device can go down then I'll design the infrastructure to be able to accommodate it. But I want a single cord that is concurrently maintainable. That's doesn't sound possible, right? A single power cord on a server that's still concurrently maintainable.

We said, alright, well, we've got a single cord. Then, upstream let's put in the ATSs (automatic transfer switches) and everything else so we can still do maintenance on the infrastructure but we can have all the single corded devices that don't go down. There's still more risk because when you're doing the maintenance and others it can go out, but the point is let's build it into the back end for flexibility. And what I found was all of this effort that we're putting in when you step back and look at it, I was saving a couple hundred thousand dollars in power supplies and PDUs and those things. Ok. But I was spending millions on the ATS infrastructure and massive power and everything else upstream to do that.

The lesson learned—and we literally changed it right in the middle and said, ok, the ATS is complex, we're not sure if it's going to work, it's at 4 MW. I mean it's big, big stuff that we have to flip so that we can do maintenance on infrastructure to allow these servers not to go down.

When we took it out of that and said 'Ok, we want two power cords from every one of them, on every server.' The power cords, though, one goes to a UPS supported gen-backed up feed the other one goes to street power that's conditioned. So I still have the ability to do maintenance on my A feed and I have the rollup capability to put a generator on my B feed if I really want to do it while I'm doing maintenance on the A. Ok. I get the exact same thing. I cut out $2.5 million or $3 million and netted a savings of $2.5 million because we had to still buy the power cords and the power supplies and busway stuff.

It was just one of those 'aha!' moments for us, that here we're trying to solve the problem by making it as flexible as we can up top but really we should be looking at what it is they need at the other end, simplify that. And so the two power cords

I'll do that on everything all the time. I won't get to the single power cord. You've got a lot of people out there that are going that way, too. Low wattage CPUs, low frequency, cheap commodity hardware with single power cords. They will go down. As long as you have everything that they can go down, ok. But if I don't have to go down why should I go down?

I am actually adding an extra power supply and those things in there, but I'm not adding all the UPS and gen and all the other stuff on the other side that cost a lot of money so I'm still getting all the major benefits out of it. The net-net is I have two power sources for every device in the Data Center and by the way we added additional UPS feeds for the things that really required more runtime like the network infrastructure that's inside of the building. It's Tier III because it still goes through the Tier IV backbone but I don't want those to go down. But that's like less than 3 percent of the load and the space in the Data Center. The rest of it, it's all two-cord, UPS gen on one, street power on the other. So that was a great learning for us.

Any other lessons learned?

It's great to put containers on the roof, but if you don't have to, don't do it. I would rather have a building that's twice as much area on the ground that has all container capabilities than putting them on the roof. We were bound by the footprint we had. We put in another 1 million lbs. (453.6 mt.) of steel in the building so we that could handle the weights, but the containers came in at almost twice what they were originally spec'd at. We got 98,000 lbs. (44.5 mt.) going up. We go 1,920 servers in there. It's big. We got a 100 ton (90.7 mt.) crane lifting it up on the roof.

They came in and it was as fast as 22 minutes to go from the truck to the roof and start plugging in power and data and cooling, but still it was a lot of work to make that happen. And then we found that the size of the containers—we wanted flexibility to orientation, size, dimensions, weight, whatever—so we had to build a secondary grid on the roof so that we could now orchestrate or land them however we wanted. Because we wanted the flexibility to say, well today it's going to be these two vendors but tomorrow somebody else may come out with a better container that we land up there. We wanted to be able to accommodate it.

A slab environment or an environment that allows containers to move around easily without it requiring a massive crane organization and structural steel to do it, you save a lot of money there too.

FIGURE 9-5   Half of the Data Center's capacity is provided by way of containers on the roof.

The other lesson learned in this is if you don't have to go that fast to build it, don't. If you can give yourself more time, do it. You do make compromises. This team has been really good, they haven't compromised on any of the major pieces we needed, but schedule did limit the amount of vendors who could participate. We couldn't use bundled or coupled gen-UPS units, because we couldn't get them in time or their size was a bit too big. So that limited some of the vendors from being able to be in it. Then we had to go back and now have decoupled gens and UPSs. It's working but I would much rather have those modular units because they work better when they're coupled together. The same manufacturer is responsible for that handoff between those units. It's just a finely tuned machine versus two independent vendors hoping that they're going to lock the bus and be able to switch.

Oh, and another lesson learned is leading power factor. Not a lot of companies are turning on a half a megawatt to a megawatt at a time of load. If you don't have an inline UPS that's adjusting the power factor so that the gens don't see any issue you have to figure out how to manage that. If the leading power factor is too high on the server equipment it will shut off your gens. The big players—you look at Microsoft, Google, us—when we're putting up these containers of 1,000 to 2,000 servers at a time you have to really consider that. So we had to put some stuff in the middle to correct that, to filter that to allow us to be within the tolerances of leading power factor. And that's primarily because of the way the design is, I don't have a double conversion UPS because that gets rid of the leading power factor.

Where did the name Project Mercury come from?

The closer you get to the sun the hotter it is, right? So, we're getting close to the heat. And then Project Quicksilver is, of course, liquid mercury that moves and changes very quickly. We want that capability in our Data Center. We should be able to adjust. And liquid mercury, liquid to the chip eventually. That's where the names came from.

You mentioned the Data Center's 14,000 sq. ft. (1,300.6 sq. m) hosting area. How much additional area is used for electrical and mechanical systems?

It's close to two times the floor space. Because we used larger units, we've got 3 MW gens so we're adding those chunks in three at a time and the UPSs are 2 MW. There was a kind of a mismatch in those sizes but we know that we'll be adding the next brick as we need it. Because we still have N+1 in the gens. So, 2x I think.

The way the design was put together is, we've got a 55 degree loop because we still have to have chilled water to some things. So, 55 (12.8 Celsius) and then the other one is the 87 degree (30.6 Celsius) loop, so it's a condenser loop. And both of them are directly accessible to the equipment itself. We can choose over time which one we're going to build out. So if we've got 12 MW of capacity that we need to deliver and then the N+1 in that I can now say 8 MW of that is going to be condenser so scale those up. Or if we realize that we're getting more efficiency of some of the chilled water you can scale that up too. Or we can scale the chilled water and then scale it back and scale it up with the condenser over time. Because not everything is going to fit on that 87 (30.6 Celsius) loop and we can't mandate that right now. We still need the flexibility.

If I look at the grand scheme of it, it's less than 5 percent (of our capital cost) that we put in there to be able to have that flexibility. Again, having it from the beginning, that the design is flexible and all of the design engineers are understanding the problem—because we spent a lot of time with them explaining the business challenge and then what the ultimate numbers are going to be. Finally we came down to a density per rack footprint that we needed to have based on the space and based on the available MEP yard space and that that we could say this is the sweet spot and then we'll scale it up over time.

The ground floor, we knew we would have stuff coming in at less than 10 kW in some areas. But other ones we're going to have rack and roll that's coming in at 25 or 28. Ok, well we can handle both and then we just scale them up over time by adding in modular units. As we get denser we add more modular units right on the floor. They take up space but as we replace those and potentially roll in the liquid solutions we gain all that space back again. So, the entire ground floor I can have 70 percent of it at 40 kW a cabinet and that'll work. That's a big deal, hundreds and hundreds of cabinets.

With all of the steel you had to put in place, what is the weight bearing capability of the Data Center building?

We can handle containers with all the supporting components at 125,000 to 140,000 lbs. (56.7 to 63.5 mt.). We can handle anywhere from 10 to 12 containers on the roof.

We have one vendor that's coming in at 98,000 (44.5 mt.), another one that came in at 112,000 (50.8 mt.). The next ones when they come in we don't know if they're going to be heavier or less if they're all liquid cooled because liquid would have more weight but we would have less infrastructure as well. We don't need all those air movers. We need liquid infrastructure to the chips and that's low flow liquid. So it's that same amount of liquid going to the container it's now just distributed directly to the devices instead of distributed to the air handlers. And then the other one that's using all outside air cooling, the swamp cooler stuff, that just is city water and not a lot of it.

I love this because the Data Center has 100 percent outside air cooled solution. Right next to it is a design that's using a heat exchanger with a primary source is the 87 degree (30.6 Celsius) loop and if we happen to go over 87 (30.6 Celsius) because of some fluke over time it exchanges with the 55 (12.8 Celsius) loop to cool down the 87 (30.6 Celsius) to 87 (30.6 Celsius). And everything's tuned.

It was a really cheap, innovative way for us to go back and get direct hot water cooling today to air based equipment in a container. I'm really proud of that. We pushed the vendors and they really thought about how to solve this problem. And we have two completely unique solutions that land in the same Data Center that are getting the same sub 1.1 PUE average over the year. Excellent.

Whoever comes up with the best mousetrap I want to land that mousetrap in our Data Center. And let the competition continue because the vendors love this. The HPs, Dells, Oracles, IBMs—you look at all of them, they're all competing for the business. But what they really want is the IT business. If we're tuning it to the infrastructure they understand that. They can win it because of their overall efficiency. It's really neat.

The other part is containers. We've gone through probably four generations or five generations of containers now. Everybody's trying to get in to the market but the reality is the IT equipment inside of this container has to be warranted by someone and the best to do that right now are the actual manufacturers. We've found that buying a full unit—it's like one big rack—a container with the power, cooling, and the connectivity infrastructure built into it that's warranted as one box and UL listed as one unit is the most effective way to deploy these things. It's also extremely cost effective. Somebody can build a cheaper container but if that container's not tuned to the equipment in it and you've got a failure and I've got $5 million or $10 million worth of equipment that's now damaged? Sorry, not going to happen.

I see that the container industry starts to shrink more. That's a prediction right now. Because the people that are building the equipment—this is just a big rack. They want to ship it. It's the packaging. I love it. We landed 1,920 servers in one day and then the next week we had another 1,500 servers come in and it landed in as fast as 22 minutes. And then we had another one come in the following week—bink—and we landed right next to it. So, I had almost 4,000 servers landed in less than 12 hours when you add it all up. That's insane.

We've never had that much equipment actually coming in to the Data Centers at eBay in the history of the company. But that's the whole point. We're doing it at half the opex, half the capex, and literally less than half the time, at four times the density. That's really cool. That's why I love my job, I get to do this stuff.

"Whoever comes up with the best mousetrap I want to land that mousetrap in our Data Center."

FIGURE 9-6   A computer circuit pattern adorns one of the Data Center entrances.

FIGURE 9-7   Additional accent lighting within eBay's Data Center.

FIGURE 9-8   Sliding doors at the end of rows 7 and 8 open (left) and closed (right).

FIGURE 9-9   Containers are pre-populated with more than 1,500 servers each and then placed on the roof by a crane.

FIGURE 9-10   Power strips glow in a darkened Data Center container.

FIGURE 10-1   Facebook's Data Center in Prineville, Oregon. Images by Alan Brandt.

CHAPTER 10
Facebook

ORGANIZATION: Facebook	
LOCATION: Prineville, Oregon	
ONLINE: May 2011	
NOTABLE FEATURES: 277 volt power distribution. Evaporative cooling system. Power over Ethernet (PoE) LED lighting. Custom servers. LEED-Gold certified.	
TIME TO DESIGN AND BUILD: 15 months for 147,000 sq ft. (13,656.7 sq. m) first phase	
SIZE: 307,000 sq. ft. (28,521.2 sq. m) total, with about 261,000 sq. ft. (24,247.7 sq. m) of hosting area and 46,000 sq. ft. (4,273.5 sq. m) of electrical room space. Mechanical systems are located in an enclosed area on roof and not included in size figures.	
POWER: 30 MW available for IT	
TIER: III	
CABINET LOCATIONS: Undisclosed	
INFRASTRUCTURE DELIVERY: Power, cabling, and cooling are all provided overhead	
STRUCTURAL LOADING: 250 lb. per sq. ft. (1,220.6 kg per sq. m)	
FIRE SUPPRESSION SYSTEM: Pre-action dry pipe system with VESDA monitoring	

Imagine having to create your company's first purpose built Data Center that is expected to not only support the online activities of millions of users at one of the most popular websites in existence but also be an example for other Data Center designers worldwide.

Such was the challenge facing the designers of Facebook's Data Center in Prineville, Oregon, during 2009. The social networking giant had previously leased space at various third-party sites in California and Virginia, leveraging wholesale Data Center properties as a way to quickly add capacity. This server environment would be different, though.

Facebook custom designed many elements of the facility, from an uncommon power delivery system—using 277 volt rather than traditional 208 volt configuration, thereby eliminating the step-down transformation—to building its own minimalist hardware. Facebook's server, slightly more than 1.5U (2.6 in. or 6.7 cm) in height, touts a vanity free design to reduce weight and materials. With no paint, logos, stickers, or front panel, the hardware use 22 percent fewer materials than typical 1U servers; the greater size was chosen to accommodate larger, more efficient fans and heat sinks.

Equally minimalist is the Data Center's mechanical design. There are no chillers or cooling towers. Outside air enters an enclosure above the Data Center, dubbed the penthouse, through adjustable louvers. The air flows through a mixing room where it is combined, as needed, with warm server exhaust and then passes through a bank of filters and into an evaporative cooling room where a misting system adds moisture. Fans then draw the air through a mist eliminator, capturing any water droplets not fully absorbed in the air, and push it down through openings above the Data Center's cold aisles.

Beyond the Data Center's infrastructure, Facebook has also taken a different approach in its lack of secrecy. Rather than treating the technical details of its Prineville Data Center as proprietary information, Facebook has publicized them, offering server, rack, electrical, and mechanical specifications by way of its Open Compute Project.

Jay Park, director of Data Center design, construction, and facility operations for Facebook, discusses how the facility was designed.

The Interview

Your company has rather famously gone public with information about its Data Center in Oregon, through the Open Compute Project. At what point in the project was it decided that you would be sharing your Data Center design information with the world?

We started this design back in early 2009 and developed it by end of 2009. It really came from our fearless leader, (Mark) Zuckerberg. He said, 'This is not our core business, Data Center design, and if we can share with the world and everybody can save energy...' He had this vision and he wanted to open it up.

The second thing is that as we developed this new power supply running at 277 volt and the localized DC UPS system. You know, if more people can buy this stuff quite honestly we can drop the price as well. The power supply is really the commodity, so the more people buy it the price will come down.

So those are really the two main drivers from the company perspective.

LEED Certification

Leadership in Energy and Environmental Design (LEED) is a rating system for the design, construction, and operation of green buildings. Facilities can achieve ratings of certified, silver, gold, or platinum based on criteria within six categories: sustainable sites, water efficiency, energy and atmosphere, materials and resources, indoor environmental quality, and innovation and design.

Did knowing that your Data Center information was going to be public influence the design? You were not only trying to design an effective Data Center for Facebook, you were trying to design something that was intended to be a model for others to emulate.

That is correct. If you look at the design, in all these years we knew that if we increased the input power voltage we will be able to gain some additional efficiency in these power supplies but industry in general they didn't want to develop a new power supply running at 277 volt that comes right off from the 480 volt system. They will continue to use this 208 volt system that requires additional transformation from 480 volt, perhaps to an inline UPS (uninterruptible power supply) system, things like that.

So, yeah, you're absolutely correct.

Let's talk about that power distribution system. If someone is looking to adopt the same approach that Facebook did, using 277 volts, they probably won't have the same customized servers. What do they need to do to be able to make use of that technology? Are there any hurdles to doing so?

That's a good question. As we open up this OCP (Open Compute Project) actually there are a lot of companies now developing power supplies running at 277 volts. Already HP and Dell are making that product available in the market. We are currently working with Samsung and other vendors—these are power supply manufacturers—and they are saying that this can be developed. They're really excited about this and they're developing this product. I think in general in the market you should be able to get this product fairly easy now.

They all knew that going with the 277 volts, getting rid of the additional transformation, you reduce the energy loss. I think everybody agrees with that concept.

FIGURE 10-2   Facebook's custom servers feature no paint, logos, stickers, or front panel, eliminating weight and materials.

Looking at your UPS configuration, you have dedicated battery cabinets to support your server cabinets. What prompted you to use that rather than traditional room-level UPS devices?

So, I wouldn't even call that as a UPS system. I called that a UPS system (in the Open Compute Project documents) because it's an uninterruptible power supply but if you think about it all it does is it provides 48 volt DC voltage. I see two advantages here. First of all, when you locate that UPS system closer to the power supply you increase the availability of the entire system. I actually ran some of the availability calculations. The truth of the matter is if you locate the power bridge system closer to the load you're kind of sort of eliminating the single point of failure. So you are increasing the availability.

The second thing is that the UPS system that we designed does not have all of the components like an inline system, like inline rectifier modules, you don't have an inverter, you don't have static bypass switches, you don't have maintenance bypass switches, and all that. The design is just the 48 volt DC battery banks in parallel, with the one common bus. That's basically what it is. I called it as a UPS system because it's an uninterruptible power supply but it does not have all of the components like an inline UPS system.

And, note that this is an offline system. It's not an inline system at all. During the normal operation the DC UPS system is basically all in standby mode.

How did the design for the enclosed mechanical area above the IT hosting space come about?

Originally we were going to install rooftop units, on top of our roof space, above the IT space. What happened was, when we started laying out all of the rooftop units, it was going to take a lot of roof space and we were running out of roof space. In addition, on cold days in the winter, maintaining this equipment up there it would be a very difficult thing to do.

So what we did is instead of buying packaged rooftop units we just built the penthouse wall around it and put all of the inside equipment in the penthouse. It's not a people space, you can call it a single giant rooftop unit if you want to.

What's the overall electrical capacity of the Data Center?

You've got 15 MW per each phase so it's a 30 MW site when it's fully built out and running at max capacity. With our PUE is running at about 1.077. Mechanical is very, very little.

If you look at it we don't have chillers, we don't have cooling towers. All we have is just a fan array and a misting system. The misting system is these Mickey Mouse high pressure pumps and that's it. It draws like 2.5 horsepower, something like that. It's ridiculously small. And so we don't have a huge mechanical system at all. It's very little. And fans, the bearings are all incredibly efficient. This doesn't consume a lot of power at all. So 1.077 is what we're seeing right now—this is accumulated PUE not a snapshot.

You mentioned the misting system. Can you walk me through how that's used and how the evaporative cooling system works?

Yeah. Let's start with the city water. We kill the bacteria, we eliminate all these substances. Then we pump that water up to what we call the pump skid. This pump will create the water pressure. The nozzle sprays in very, very fine water mist, which creates the misting system. Then basically the fan array will pull the air from outside. The system is horizontal, in parallel with the air stream, and it cools that air. Then it dumps it over into the Data Center.

The pump skid is right now configured as a 2N system. We got two pumps with manifolds and we come up with a common manifold and from that point on we have many misting zone lines. If you see the picture you will probably see it, the misting system you see a bunch of pipe lines, like a spiderweb. Each one or two lines are a zone. And then if you don't need to turn on all the misting system, like out of maybe one through seven zones, only zone one would be turned on and zones two to seven would be turned off, with everything in-between, because the skids are controlled on VFDs (variable frequency drives).

FIGURE 10-3
When needed, warm server exhaust is added to incoming air in a mixing room.

FIGURE 10-4
When the outside
air used to cool
the Data Center is
too dry, moisture
is added by way of
a misting system.
A mist eliminator
prevents water
that has not
been absorbed
by the air from
proceeding into
the Data Center.

You have the evaporative system in place and also an air economizer.
How many days per year do you anticipate being able to use outside
air for cooling?

Throughout the entire year we're going to be using outside air. This is it. The outside air and we just cool it with the misting system and dump into the Data Center. One hundred percent of the time.

During the wintertime, since bringing in 100 percent outside air would be too cold for the servers, we recirculate hot return air from servers to bring the temperature up to an acceptable range. So the outside air damper during the wintertime is only partially open and mixes the temperature up to a warmer setpoint.

What operational temperature are you using in the Data Center?

We're using the ASHRAE (American Society of Heating, Refrigerating, and Air Conditioning Engineers) TC9.9 standard 80.6 degrees Fahrenheit (27 Celsius) as the maximum inlet temperature and 65 percent RH (relative humidity) as the maximum RH.

I assume climate was one of the drivers for choosing where to locate the Data Center, enabling you to use certain energy-efficient technologies. What else lead Facebook to build in Prineville, Oregon?

The number one reason was that we could easily reduce the operating costs. And the utility rate was low because we were closer to the main transmission lines.

How long did it take to design and build the first phase of the Data Center?

The design and construction was one year. Well, a little bit more than one year because we kind of cheated—we actually started our design work a little bit ahead of time. We were doing a little R&D work here and there so we were able to use a lot of that design. I would say about 15 months from design to completion of this project.

Even at 15 months that still seems fast for a facility of this size that has a lot of innovative technologies and you're making your own custom server design as part of the project. As you said at the start of this interview Data Center isn't necessarily core to your business. For a company that doesn't have Data Centers at the core you seem to have done a pretty good job with it.

Well, let me back up. Our site acquisition stuff like that I did not count that time. I'm talking about the Data Center design and construction, probably about 15 months. Because we were doing this R&D site at the time we were doing a lot of engineering work up front. We were able to use a lot of that.

Let's say, if you have to build a Data Center and we're giving you all this Data Center information, you should be able to build a Data Center in 15 to 16 months.

Beyond the technical details that are included in the Open Compute Project documents, are there any particular Data Center design principles that you followed with the project?

When I joined two and a half years ago, there was no Data Center design team. I was it. I came from the Data Center design industry, construction industry, and then we started pulling a bunch of the experienced people on board. So, we knew exactly what we were doing. It's not like we were spinning the wheel or trying new things. That was not the case.

Certainly. Is there any general advice that you would suggest someone keep in mind as they embark on a Data Center project?

The only recommendation I would like to give industry is don't believe everything the server manufacturers say. Their nameplate data, obviously they are very conservative numbers. As a user I think they should really do a little more research on servers and understand the boundary of the server operating parameters. And then don't be afraid to push that boundary. I think that's the key to have a successful project.

"Don't believe everything the server manufacturers say. Do a little more research on servers and understand the boundary of the server operating parameters. And then don't be afraid to push that boundary."

During your project were there any surprises that came up along the way?

Yeah. Because when I came from another industry we built the Data Center but we never really built the servers. So when we started developing the servers and actually the servers they can take a much harder, harsh environment. You can push the humidity level up to 90 percent. It will work, no problem. Or the low side humidity condition. People talk about static discharge, it's going to damage the memory chip, CPU, blah, blah, blah. But the truth of the matter is that every rack has been grounded. With the proper procedure, when you touch the servers you can ground yourself. It's basic process and procedure to touch or remove servers.

You could do all that and you don't need to really worry about low-side humidity either. There are a lot of things you can do. Those are the kind of things I found out. I think the industry in general they're too conservative.

I was quite surprised actually how much we can push the boundary of server operating conditions. We didn't quite do that but next phase, next project we're actually pushing the boundary a little bit harder.

FIGURE 10-5   Power, structured cabling, and cooling are all provided overhead in Facebook's Data Center.

Your Data Center is obviously very new but if you go back and design it again what if anything would you do differently?

Maybe build it in phases and don't have to put all this capital cost from Day One. The entire building maybe you can build it in phases as business grows. We would have to think about that. You know, we are such a growing company and we need to meet the demand.

We are so there as far as the energy efficiency and the cost to build the Data Center. Yeah, if we squeeze it we should be able to get something out of it but right now our focus is meeting the demand.

I read about your Power over Ethernet (PoE) LED lighting system. What prompted you to use that particular solution?

First of all, as you know the LED light fixture lasts a really long time. Another reason we wanted to use that system is we have hot aisle containment doors, we have a ton of doors. Let's say somebody opens this door and doesn't shut it tight and leaves it open. All the hot air will be mixed with the cold air and we will not know about it. We could have put a door contact in and send it over to the Building Management System but even though we do that sometimes it's hard to spot these doors. So by using these LED fixtures you can actually integrate that with a door contact. If somebody leaves that door open the whole bay light we can make it flash.

So, there are a lot of controls. The functions are built into that system. And this is why we chose that system. And plus it's obviously energy savings and it's incredibly low power consumption. But quite honestly the ROI (return on investment) wasn't quite there. The truth of the matter is it's an expensive system and it wasn't there. We don't have to change the fixture every two or three years, it'll last almost 15 years.

If you leave the lights on all the time it might be a different story but we have what we call a lights out environment. If nobody's there we turn the lights off. When we ran that calculation under the lights out environment the ROI was not there. But the control system was very interesting and we were able to use that system to monitor the doors.

For your fire detection and suppression system you have VESDA monitoring and pre-action sprinklers. Is that a dry pipe system?

Yeah, it is a dry type system. As you know, if you leave that dry type system and you leave the pipe empty over a period of time you're going to see some condensation building inside of this pipe. If the pipe is perfectly sloped and if you have the drainage, that's not an issue. But I can guarantee you when these guys installed this piping it's never going to be perfectly sloped. So what happens is this condensation happens and you're starting to collect this water and it will collect in the low point. And then it will start corroding and you will have a little pinhole and then water will be starting to drip.

I experienced this problem with my previous employer and Data Center. Changing this piping in a live Data Center was a huge challenge. And so what we did here is that, not only is it dry type but we used nitrogen gas rather than compressed air. When you fill it with the nitrogen you don't have the oxygen so the corroding problem goes away. If you look at the National Fire Protection Association (NFPA) website they talk about this corrosion problem a lot and that's exactly what they recommend, too.

There are ongoing discussions in Data Center circles regarding whether or not to use a raised floor. Were there any reasons in particular that you didn't use one in your Data Center?

Yeah. To me it is a very expensive system compared to a slab. And also, when you do containment work you really don't need a raised floor because you're just containing the hot air and then you just throw it either outside or recirculate or whatever. And then cable management in the overhead in my opinion is much easier than under floor. Easy access and a faster installation. And floor loading, again, you don't need to worry about it. Especially when you're in a seismic zone area—we're not—the height of the raised floor has some limitation unless you do some serious bracing. So there are a lot of cons toward raised floors. I'm not a fan of raised floor design.

FIGURE 10-6 Outside air passes through multiple filters before entering Facebook's Data Center.

FIGURE 10-7 Mixing room fans.

FIGURE 10-8
Air passes through mist eliminators, at left, and propelled by variable speed fans, at right.

FIGURE 10-9   Cool air descends into the cold aisles of Facebook's Data Center.

FIGURE 11-1   Green House Data's facility in Cheyenne, Wyoming. Images provided courtesy of Green House Data.

CHAPTER 11

Green House Data

ESSENTIAL DETAILS

ORGANIZATION: Green House Data	
LOCATION: Cheyenne, Wyoming	
ONLINE: January 2008	
NOTABLE FEATURES: All power for Data Center comes from or is offset by locally generated wind. Virtualization, high-efficiency air conditioning, airside economizer, hot aisle enclosures.	
TIME TO DESIGN AND BUILD: 12 months	
SIZE: 9,500 sq. ft. (882.6 sq. m) total, with about 7,500 sq. ft. (696.8 sq. m) of hosting space	
POWER: 1 MW overall; IT usable capacity of 850 kW	
TIER: III	
CABINET LOCATIONS: 200	
POWER DENSITY: 4.25 kW average per cabinet, 12.5 kW maximum	
INFRASTRUCTURE DELIVERY: All infrastructure is delivered overhead	
STRUCTURAL LOADING: Undetermined	
FIRE SUPPRESSION SYSTEM: Novec 1230	

Wind isn't known for blowing in straight lines. It's appropriate, then, that Green House Data had to take an indirect path in its quest to run its 850 kW co-location facility on wind power.

The 7,500 sq. ft. (696.8 sq. m) Data Center is located in the capitol of Wyoming, a top wind site in the United States thanks to its high plains and powerful, long-lasting breezes. By late 2012, Wyoming had more than 1,400 MW of wind power installed and more than 5,700 MW of wind projects in queue, according to the American Wind Energy Association.

Despite those ideal conditions, Green House Data doesn't harvest wind on its own property or draw power directly from the wind farms in its vicinity. Its power instead comes by way of a 162 mi. (260.7 km) there-and-back detour into Colorado. Green House Data purchases renewable energy credits from a company in Boulder, Colorado, that in turn purchases energy from wind farms back in Cheyenne.

To keep power consumption low, the Data Center uses a variety of energy efficient elements including virtualization, high-efficiency air conditioning units, air economization, and enclosed hot aisles.

Shawn Mills, founder and president of Green House Data, explains the reason for its roundabout solution for securing renewable energy as well as what other strategies his company employs to make his server environment green.

The Interview

Let's start with some background about your facility. What prompted you to build your Data Center in Wyoming?

In 2007 a good friend of mine and I were sitting down over coffee in Jackson Hole, Wyoming, talking about how there were no Data Centers in Wyoming. We began researching and determined that Wyoming could definitely accommodate a high density, multi-tenant Data Center but it would need to be a nationally unique business model. This is where I had the idea of tapping into Wyoming's wind resources. This direction then lead me to research methods for Data Center efficiency for not only sustainability but also cost efficiency.

We ended up choosing Cheyenne as it was planned to be home to three or four relatively large wind farms. We also appreciated the proximity it has to the Denver, Colorado, area.

How long did it take to design and build the Data Center?

We built our facility in a highly modular fashion. With an unknown amount of demand and the desire to be an entrepreneur and build it and they will come, we went down the path of building it out in a modular fashion. We have a 9,500 sq. ft. building (882.6 sq. m) and we built out the first private suite of 1,000 sq. ft. (92.9 sq. m) to start and then have just grown modularly since then. Now we're launching another 3,000 sq. ft. (278.7 sq. m) of our facility as a suite.

Your facility doesn't have a raised floor. Did you forgo it for any particular reason?

We were retrofitting an existing building and the ceiling heights weren't high enough to allow us to use a raised floor. We were able to come up with a design in our building specifically that is relatively unique just because of our floor layout that allows us to use overhead supply and hot aisle overhead return as well.

Your company's reputation is built largely on its use of clean, renewable energy and you even have the word green in the name of your business. What's your definition of green, and in particular a green Data Center?

It's funny, because a lot of people ask 'How are you green?' From our perspective, at the end of the day we are a green Data Center because all of our energy comes either from locally generated wind or offset by locally generated wind. The unfortunate realities of renewable energy is that for the most part you can't be right next to the wind farm that produces at a price point that means something to somebody, a.k.a. has a payback. So we have had to leverage utility-scale wind farms in order to make sure that our pricing stays in line with the Data Center market. We couldn't afford to pay three times the cost of electricity for on-site generated wind.

So, we are committed to getting our wind energy a portion of it through the local power company and then offsetting it and covering it 100 percent through renewable, Green-e tags. That's one component of it from the green perspective.

Probably more important is—and what we tell our customers—the greenest electron is the one you didn't use. We operate at probably about 90 percent greater cooling efficiency than most Data Centers. And we're doing that by leveraging the outside ambient air in Wyoming to cool the facility almost 365 days a year.

You obviously wanted to be green with your facility. At what point in your design process did you decide that you wanted to be powered by wind energy? Was it because you were going to be located in Wyoming and therefore wind is an obvious choice?

We actually did a lot of research on solar, geothermal, and wind and at the end of the day cost per kilowatt hour is the least in wind energy production and so we went down that path.

We don't leverage any on-site generation. That said, why we chose what we chose is to maximize the cost savings we're able to pass along to our customers. The way our equation works is, we operate at about 40 percent less total energy consumption than an average Data Center but we have to pay approximately a 10 percent premium to be powered through wind energy. That net difference of 30 percent we share with our customers to ensure that they are 'green' as well as getting a good deal on Data Center services, because electricity consumption is one of the higher costs of operating a Data Center.

FIGURE 11-2   A row of hardware within Green House Data's server environment.

How can someone who wants to power their Data Center with renewable energy, but for whom on-site power generation is impractical, do so? What's the process for making that happen instead of just using the standard electrical supply from the local utility?

We talked to our local power company about how we can leverage their investment in wind energy. So it all starts with the local power company, working with them to figure out what type of accounting capabilities do they have to account for the wind energy production. Then what we've done to purchase our own renewable wind energy credits is gone through a company called Renewable Choice in Boulder (Colorado) that then actually purchases the wind back from other wind farms in Wyoming and specifically ones right near us that we're not able to tap into.

The main roadblock to you connecting to a wind farm right in your area is cost?

Yeah, absolutely. It's cost-related. Really, when you boil it all down, it's cost per kilowatt hour related. For me to produce it here on-site at my facility it's cost. For example, 40 cents per kilowatt hour, which is really expensive power. Where, literally across town, at utility scale they produce it at probably 4 cents per kilowatt hour.

Some people distinguish between purchasing renewable energy credits versus directly using renewable energy on-site. Do you think that the use of credits are somehow less green?

My opinion of it is that in an outsourced model nobody's willing to pay what it costs to provide an on-site generated electricity Data Center. Other than an enterprise that chooses to do that in their own Data Center for their own reasons. In the co-location market, the incremental cost of on-site—even with the energy efficiency that we have—still wouldn't justify itself and I don't think we could sell it in the marketplace.

Tell me about some of the energy-efficient features you have in the Data Center. I understand you have Coolerado air conditioners.

The Coolerados are a critical component to our energy efficiency. In the pod where the Coolerados are we operate about 200 kW of power IT load, and based on the manufacturer's specs the Coolerados operate on something like the 5 to 10 kW range, which is a shockingly low PUE.

Your website mentions 'aligning hot and cold aisles and redefining the cage space concept.' Can you elaborate on that?

In essence, there are zero cages in our Data Center facility and if we were to put a cage for security purposes it would still fit within our hot aisle, cold aisle containment scenario.

The problem with cage spaces is what we call the chaos factor. When you put a cage in there there's little to no control over hot spots and cold spots and containment of air to be as efficient as possible. What we've done is built it out into 20-cabinet pods where each pod is two cold aisles and a hot aisle and then it's all contained and exhausted out of the building.

FIGURE 11-3
Plastic enclosures above the cabinets isolate hot and cold airflow while door panels control physical access.

You're using a clear plastic enclosure at the top of your cabinets that acts as a chimney to exhaust the hot air, correct?

Exactly. That plastic keeps all of the hot air in the hot side of the cabinet and doesn't allow any mixing of the cold air with the hot air.

That hot air is ultimately vented outdoors?

Yeah. It's part of our 2N on the cooling system. We have 100 percent of IT load covered by our Coolerado system and then 100 percent on CRAC units. When we're running on our Coolerados the air is exhausted and if we had to for any reason switch to the CRAC units, all of the system shuts down and it becomes like a traditional computer room with CRAC units recirculating the air.

Were there any surprises during the design and construction of the facility?

Yeah. The biggest surprise—historically and not so much moving forward—was the lack of Data Center engineers' willingness to build a non-traditional Data Center. It was definitely us pushing them to think outside the box to build this the way we wanted to build.

Was there resistance to anything in particular that you wanted to implement?

Historical experience building Data Centers, really. Basically it came down to 'Data Centers are supposed to be this way' and their last experience with ASHRAE (American Society of Heating, Refrigerating and Air-Conditioning Engineers) standards. They've always built to the old ASHRAE standards and haven't kept up to the more progressive ASHRAE standards.

"The biggest surprise…was the lack of Data Center engineers' willingness to build a non-traditional Data Center. It was definitely us pushing them to think outside the box…"

With that in mind, what operational temperature do you try to maintain your Data Center at?

Our target is 50 to 77 Fahrenheit (10 to 25 Celsius) on temperature. The mean stays at 68 (20 Celsius). We're still able to stay in the general vicinity but it floats on a wider band on a temperature perspective and then with broader humidity. Depending on the suite you're talking about, from 30 to 80 percent humidity, or zero humidity control.

How did you overcome resistance to what you wanted to implement? Was it a case of 'I'm the client and we're going to do it this way' or did you have to demonstrate that what you wanted had some advantages?

It was a combination of both. There was a lot of hesitancy from the engineers, saying 'We've done it this way for the last 20 years. Why do you want to do it differently?'

I had to tell them that this is how we are going to do it. They needed to figure out how to make it work under the energy efficiency constraints. We are very pleased at how they were able to rise above their traditional Data Center experience to create what we have today.

We have touched on some of the energy-efficient elements in your Data Center. Anything else that you want to make folks aware of?

I think really the interesting thing is just virtualization and cloud computing. At the end of the day it's the single biggest impact on total energy consumption in the Data Center.

That's just for our managed cloud services. We're a cloud hosting and co-location facility. When a thousand servers doing a thousand different server tasks can operate on 100 servers using a tenth of the power that's a pretty amazing thing.

Do you think the various technologies in your Data Center are universal and can be implemented anywhere, or are some of them limited to what you wanted to accomplish at your facility?

Our cooling infrastructure can't be implemented anywhere, that's definitely a climate based thing. But just fundamental blocking and tackling things like hot-row containment, virtualization, even just hot-row/cold-row blanking panels, all those things absolutely can and they make a big difference.

The biggest challenge in corporate Data Centers is the need for speed and comfort. You don't understand how many times I was told by engineers 'We'll just do a CRAC unit, we can get it done faster.' There is a real impetus to not be energy efficient because of comfort level with doing it the way people have done it for an extended period of time.

So can it be done? Yes. Do you have to be diligent about it? Absolutely.

Your Data Center is not very old but if you could go back and start over again, what if anything would you do differently?

The interesting thing is we do get to start over, and we are starting over with this next 3,000 sq. ft. (278.7 sq. m) suite. What we are doing differently is that we won't have a full DX backup moving forward. We are comfortable with our ability to be cooled by 100 percent outside air and so are our customers. This is similar to Facebook's Open Compute Project, which is cooled by 100 percent outside air and yet still falls within the ASHRAE standard.

You're planning to open another Data Center, which will be online by the time this book is published. I assume you will make that facility green as well. What are your main site selection criteria for that?

It absolutely comes down to cooling capabilities and the ability to cool the facility in a similar fashion to what we currently use. It's not a small dollar value being able to cool using the outside ambient air. The savings are tremendous and it makes us more competitive when we're closing deals.

What type of fire suppression measures does your server environment have?

We have an early warning air sampling system as well as Novec 1230 gas. In our research it was the safest for humans, the safest for the ozone, and by far the greenest gas out there.

Any advice that you would give or design principles you would offer to someone preparing to start a Data Center project?

The biggest piece of advice that I would give is find engineers that agree with your principles, so that you don't have to battle the engineers to create the Data Center you're trying to create.

FIGURE 11-4
Power is distributed overhead to Green House Data's Data Center cabinet locations.

FIGURE 11-5   A closeup of the electrical bypass switch for Green House Data's server environment.

FIGURE 11-6   High-efficiency air conditioners cool Green House Data's Data Center.

FIGURE 12-1   The hosting area within IBM's Data Center in Research Triangle Park, North Carolina. Images provided courtesy of the IBM Corporation, all rights reserved.

CHAPTER 12
IBM

ORGANIZATION: IBM	
LOCATION: Research Triangle Park, North Carolina	
ONLINE: November 2009	
NOTABLE FEATURES: Modular design, extensive sensor network that monitors and manages electrical and mechanical system efficiency, use of both air- and liquid-based cooling. Rainwater harvesting. Ninety-five percent reuse of pre-existing building shell. LEED-Gold Certified.	
TIME TO DESIGN AND BUILD: 19 months	
SIZE: 160,000 sq. ft. (14,864.5 sq. m) total, with 100,000 sq. ft. (9,290.3 sq. m) of hosting space.	
POWER: Two 21 MW power feeds, 15 MW for IT	
TIER: Declined to estimate	
CABINET LOCATIONS: 960	
INFRASTRUCTURE DELIVERY: Electrical infrastructure, structured cabling, and cooling are delivered under a 36 in. (91.4 cm) raised floor	
STRUCTURAL LOADING: Undetermined	
FIRE SUPPRESSION SYSTEM: Wet pipe system, with VESDA detection	

When it comes to battles of man versus machine, it's clear which corner IBM is in. This is, after all, the company responsible for the supercomputers Deep Blue, which battled world chess champion Garry Kasparov in the 1990s, and Watson that topped uber Jeopardy! winners Ken Jennings and Brad Rutter in 2011.

"I for one welcome our new computer overlords," Jennings joked during his final answer on the televised quiz show.

IBM has a good idea of what it takes to make computer overlords happy, judging by the amenities of its Data Center in Research Triangle Park, North Carolina. At 100,000 sq. ft. (9,290.3 sq. m), it's the second largest of the technology and consulting company's more than 450 server environments worldwide and one awarded LEED-Gold certification for its energy efficient and environmentally sensitive design.

Tens of thousands of sensors within the Data Center monitor the operating conditions and energy efficiency of its mechanical and electrical systems. Still more allow IBM to continuously generate CFD (computational fluid dynamic) models of the Data Center to further optimize performance. Power can be provided in different quantities among the cabinet locations, with air- and liquid-cooling available as needed to keep computing hardware comfortable. The facility was constructed in modular segments, allowing for rapid expansion.

Chris Molloy, IBM distinguished engineer, discusses these and other design elements that are incorporated within the Data Center.

The Interview

What functions does this Data Center in RTP serve for IBM?

It serves two major functions. IBM provides a lot of outsourcing content for customers and it's an outsourcing source of our Data Centers. We have roughly 8 million sq. ft. (743,224.3 sq. m) of Data Center space in the outsourcing segment that we manage for our customers on their behalf. This is our second largest Data Center.

The second major purpose for this Data Center is our public cloud computing offerings, of which at the moment there are two offerings that are offered out of that Data Center.

What prompted you to renovate an existing building rather than build something new from the ground up?

There were basically three things that we were looking at, which were cost, schedule, and resources. In this particular case we were renovating old warehouse space and manufacturing space, which had the power characteristics already there at the site and also the hardened raised floor and a dual-story roof. That and the fact that we had been a part of the Research Triangle Park for quite some time.

As a result of those items a couple of things came into play. One, the schedule was shorter because we didn't have to go buy land or build a building. Two, the building was fully depreciated so the cost of the project was less. And three, the schedule in general came in because of the lack of needing to add things like power or hardened raised floor, that kind of stuff. Other characteristics of using an existing building made it very lucrative from the standpoint of schedule, cost, and labor.

You used 95 percent of the existing building shell and recycled 90 percent of the original building material. Presumably you made a conscious decision to incorporate those pre-existing elements into the Data Center's design.

Correct. Those were driven by the desire to have LEED certification. There are two pieces of that. One is submitting a proposal during the design phase, which will tell you how many points you're going to get and therefore what level of certification. And those items were a direct result of how many points we wanted to get for energy efficiency and the re-use of the building, the recycling of materials, the purchasing of materials from the local area to cut down on the carbon footprint of it, and then buying recycled materials as well.

LEED Certification

Leadership in Energy and Environmental Design (LEED) is a rating system for the design, construction, and operation of green buildings. Facilities can achieve ratings of certified, silver, gold, or platinum based on criteria within six categories: sustainable sites, water efficiency, energy and atmosphere, materials and resources, indoor environmental quality, and innovation and design.

All that work had to be done up front from the standpoint of determining how the project was going to be implemented in order to do those things during the project.

IBM uses a modular design approach to Data Centers to reduce build time and limit disruption to pre-existing server environments. Tell me about that approach.

The design itself is a 15 MW design. We also, in addition to using our Data Centers for outsourcing, we have a consulting group that builds Data Centers. They came out with a modular enterprise Data Center design which allows customers to build Data Centers in increments of space and power. This was a larger implementation of that reference material. It was eventually a 15 MW design, eventually 100,000 sq. ft. (9,290.3 sq. m) We started out at 6 MW and 60,000 sq. ft. (5,574.2 sq. m) and we could go from 6 to 9 to 12 to 15 MW and then we had another 40,000 sq. ft. (3,716.1 sq. m) that we could add to as well.

This ended up being better than what we thought because we don't build out until we need it. We thought we were going to add additional power as power density goes up on the equipment. So we thought we were going to add more power to the existing 60,000 sq. ft. (5,574.2 sq. m). It turns out our customers don't have that demand yet so we're going to actually build out more space than we are adding power to the existing space.

How does modularizing the Data Center's design help save time and scale capacity? I assume this is more than just building out a few rows at a time.

In this particular implementation we had 3 MW modules and we had room for five of them that we designed in, and the cooling that matches the power because the power turns to heat dissipation. So we created a 3 MW module that had the UPS (uninterruptible power supply), the generators, the chillers, and then we decided where those would go—either inside in an MEP (mechanical, electrical, and plumbing) room or outside as far as generators—and then we reserved the space for them but we did not install them. So right now today we have all the generators for the first 6 MW and we know in the existing 60,000 sq. ft. (5,574.2 sq. m) where the next set of generators are for the next 3 MW. We also had to pre-install some of the cable trays and make the water pipes big enough to be able to hold the eventual load, but the amount of additional cost to do that while you were doing the build was negligible compared to having to go back and add that after the fact.

The modular approach helps you bring in the 18- and 24-month projects down to under a year and it makes them smaller projects. Instead of building a 15 MW Data Center we're building five 3 MW Data Centers.

FIGURE 12-2
Thermal storage tanks for IBM's Research Triangle Park Data Center.

The Data Center had first 6 MW and later 15 MW of capacity for IT. What are the overall power feeds into the Data Center?

You figure it was designed with a designed criteria of a PUE of 1.4, so you can do the math on that.

The benefit there is we did some things that improve the reliability, decreased the risk, but decreased the cost. I'll give you an example of that in the cooling distribution system. Typically a cooling distribution system would have, even with a waterside or airside economizer, the chiller would be in line with the economizer which would be in line with the pumps which would be in line to the CRAC (computer room air conditioner) units out on the floor. So, there would be a kind of a one-to-one mapping of those.

What we did we criss-crossed the connectivity of those major components so that any chiller can supply any flat plate heat exchanger which can supply using any of the pumps to any of the CRAC units. And those were just water valves. That's not a very expensive thing to get that extra resiliency.

I can see how that would give you some additional redundancy within the system. Does that also increase the amount of power density or heat load that you can support at a given cabinet location?

No, that's predominantly just a resiliency statement.

One of the other things that we did was, traditionally you would size the chillers and put chillers on the UPS units so therefore increasing the amount of UPS that you needed in addition to the UPS that you needed for IT. What we ended up doing was running the numbers economically and deciding instead of putting the chillers on UPS we just put them on generators. And what we did was we built three 50,000 gallon (189,270.6 liter) chilled water tanks and we run the cooling distribution through the chilled water tanks similar to how we put UPS batteries in line, to use the cooling tanks to condition the water from a temperature standpoint. Those tanks have 30 minutes of ride-through time, which is more than sufficient to get the generators up and running and get the chillers running on the generators at a much lower cost point. That affected operational cost and capital cost but at the same time improving resiliency and reducing risk.

I understand the Data Center has different power densities from cabinet to cabinet.

Traditionally people have used the term watts per square foot. And watts per square foot is getting to be the worst metric of a Data Center because it implies that you've got uniform distribution of power and therefore cooling to a particular segment of the raised floor. And we have moved away from that. Instead of having, like, all 4 kW racks or 2 kW racks we wait until we actually need to run the power and we supply a certain amount of forced air cooling. But if we need to be able to cool past that we'll do something like add a rear door heat exchanger to have the supplemental cooling. So we've disconnected the amount of cooling you have to have for the amount of power. Also, we can run different capacity racks.

We did an analysis of how many of each type of rack in terms of power density our customers were currently using and then we extrapolated to say, 'Ok during this first revolution while they are filling up the Data Center how much power density will they have to have by rack?' So we support not only the low density racks but also support the 8, 16, and now 32 kW racks and we don't strand that power because we don't run it until the rack needs it.

Stranded capacity is a big challenge in legacy Data Centers. Not just low power density but whether or not you can deliver power where the demand is and not have any that's inaccessible. I imagine being able to distribute power flexibly really opens up the use of the server environment.

Yeah. The flexibility of how much power we can bring to a rack, like having a 4 kW rack next to a 32 kW rack, is one flexibility. The flexibility of decoupling the power from the cooling is another one.

I'll give you an example. In our Boulder Data Center we needed to install a high density rack. We had the power but we didn't have the cooling so we brought in a rear door heat exchanger to provide the supplemental cooling and we could continue to run that high density rack in a 40 watts per sq. ft. (430.6 watts per sq. m) rack space.

This Data Center was planned from the beginning to support cloud computing. How does that functionality manifest itself in the design?

A couple of things. When you look at the cloud computing model—and in this particular instance we're talking about IBM as a service provider of clouds—we are running our desktop cloud and now our smart cloud enterprise, which has production x86 based workload. Those are modular as well. So, we've got modularity in the power and cooling. We've got modularity in the space. Now we're starting to see modularity in the IT equipment that we're going to be able to put on the floor.

What we did when we designed the smart cloud enterprise was we built a modular footprint, which was a mixture of server, storage, and network, and we took that same footprint and mirrored it around to the different cloud sites around the world that we support. And we made that footprint small enough so it didn't require as significant an initial capital outlay and then now that we're coming back and reaching capacity limits at the different sites we're just adding another footprint. And we designed the footprint not to have to be contiguous to the existing footprint that was there, which is a big problem that other people have which is coming back later and either having to reserve contiguous space or not being able to put additional content there.

The implications of that is, knowing what the physical characteristics are of that footprint and knowing that our cloud equipment is higher density equipment and being able to support that. Also, from a network drop standpoint, as a service provider these are public clouds so our ratio of MPLS (Multiprotocol Label Switching) private network to public facing Internet network, the connectivity changed. So we had the discussion with our network service providers to make sure that they were bringing in more from a ratio standpoint Internet based connectivity versus MPLS private connectivity.

It seems that you have a lot of flexibility with the Data Center. In addition to the modular approach you can adjust how much infrastructure to provide at a given cabinet location based on what the demand is going to be.

Yeah. And the reason we have to do that is, and we've been extremely successful, we're an outsourcing group so we don't know which accounts are going to sign when and we don't know which accounts are going to have mergers or acquisitions and want to dynamically add content at will. So we don't want to make mistakes and we don't want to put ourselves at risk, so we do that by creating this module flexibility.

Tell me about your rear door heat exchangers and what functionality they provide.

Liquid cooling techniques are coming back to the Data Center. If you look at our Z10s, which are our mainframes, they've got built in coolers that you just don't see the external water connections. Old mainframes, circa 10, 20 years ago had water connections to them. So we're starting to see liquid cooling techniques come back into the Data Center and some people who have them are concerned about that risk. We're not because we've got a long history of using water in the Data Center not to mention the water that's in the sprinklers right above the equipment. But be that as it may we want to be efficient, we want to be cost effective. So if you look at the U.S. EPA (Environmental Protection Agency), which commissioned Lawrence Berkeley National Labs to go look at what the latest liquid cooling techniques are that come closer to the Data Center—obviously CRAC units are supplied by water but they're at the perimeter of the Data Center, I'm talking about within the rack—then you would look at the results they've had to what they call chill-offs.

The rear door heat exchanger is a device that fits on the back of the rack and has won the chill-off the last two years in a row, of all the liquid cooling techniques from the different vendors. Lawrence Berkeley National Labs did the independent analysis and it was the most cost effective technique for cooling per unit of cost. That device is a low pressure device and it actually contributes cooling to the room for every rack that it's on, because what happens is the fans from the servers or the IT equipment blow across a radiator. That radiator has cold water flowing through it. The net effect, if you put your hand on it, is that it ends up blowing cold air into the Data Center because it overcools the amount of cooling that's in that particular rack. The other thing is that is low pressure water and it's a closed loop sealed system, so should there be a leak it would not leak that much water and it would not leak it at high pressure. So, again, low risk for the additional resiliency.

The other thing is you don't need to put in on every single rack. You can just put it on the high density racks.

Some Data Center operators are hesitant to employ liquid cooling because of concerns about having a leak in the Data Center. It sounds like you definitely consider it a reliable solution and that, if a problem were to arise, it's anticipated to be minor because of the low pressure nature of the system.

Yeah. Liquid cooling is inevitable from the standpoint if you look at the major manufacturers and what they're designing equipment to these days and their future roadmaps, the density is going to get higher.

You look at the ASHRAE (American Society of Heating, Refrigerating and Air-Conditioning Engineers) charts which were recently updated, they continue to show that exponential trend in power density within a rack. At some point in time you won't be able to forced-air cool all the devices so you are going to have to do liquid cooling techniques. And that's why in the Raleigh Data Center in the 60,000 sq. ft. (5,574.2 sq. m) we only supplied cooling for 80 percent using CRAC units and forced air because the other 20 percent we were going to put liquid cooling techniques. As a result of that, every third CRAC unit we actually have taps off of the dual ring. We've dual rings of water that run in opposite directions around the Data Center so we can take out sections and turn them off to do CRAC maintenance. But we also have taps there to be able to have taps to bring cold water out to the floor for liquid cooling techniques like rear door heat exchangers.

"Liquid cooling is inevitable...look at the major manufacturers and what they're designing today and their future roadmaps."

Do you have a certain threshold—say 20 kW per cabinet—at which point you start using liquid cooling rather than forced air?

Economically it's much better than that. There's the physics involved and when do you have to. And that's a function of how you're spreading the forced air around and are you averaging it by putting a high density rack next to a low density rack. Even at the 6 MW over 60,000 sq. ft. (5,574.2 sq. m) with 32 kW racks, we could still air cool them from a physical standpoint. From an economic standpoint what we're finding is at less than probably 10 kW racks it may be more economically feasible to start using rear door heat exchangers. As that technology keeps improving it's going to go down to 6.5 kW.

Is there such thing as a common power density per cabinet now, or does that vary greatly based on individual need?

As you point out, it's more the latter than the former. It used to be we didn't care. The reason why we were able to do even level power distribution on a raised floor and measure average watts per square foot (meter) is because the servers, the network, and the storage gear were all the same power density so it didn't matter, you could mix and match and not worry about it.

If you look at the ASHRAE charts, the growth rate by family—whether it's servers, network gear, 1U or 2U standalone servers, tape equipment, network equipment—there's different exponential curves for each one and over time those exponential curves have more differentiation so the situation's going to get worse as far as uneven need of power as we build more equipment.

This Data Center has more than 30,000 utility and environmental sensors tied in with various software tools. What sort of data are the sensors collecting and how are you making use of the information?

To start with, you've got the up-down sensors and monitoring sensors for all the Facilities and the IT pieces of equipment. So, the CRAC units report information on up-down and how well they're doing. The generators, the pumps, pretty much any piece of electrical gear either on the Facilities side or on the IT side is reporting things. The generators report oil pressure or amount of gas left in the tank. So that's where theses tens of thousands of sensors are starting to report data and would create an information overload if all you did was look at the data. So from that you have to start having what's now called a class of Data Center information management or DCIM (Data Center Infrastructure Management) software that starts paring that down to taking the data and making it information and knowledge that you can use.

The other thing that's being reported from the IT equipment is temperature data and energy use data, how much energy a particular server is using, because the new Energy Star rating for servers requires that the energy fluctuate as the utilization fluctuates which means you'll have much more stranded power than you did before because usually when you turned a machine on it didn't vary much depending upon what utilization it was running.

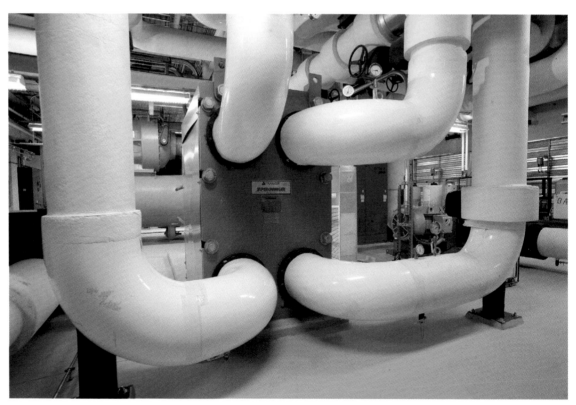

FIGURE 12-4   Use of waterside economization provides free cooling about 3,900 hours per year in IBM's Research Triangle Park Data Center.

IBM has airflow modeling technology associated with this Data Center as well. Is that accomplished through these sensors?

That's something that's a little bit different but integrated with our overall DCIM strategy.

IBM prides itself on having a very large investment in R&D, to the tune of $6 billion a year. A lot of that goes to our IBM Research organization and our IBM Research organization came out with this MMT (Measurement and Management Technology). Originally it was a mobile technology that had sensors at different heights and could build you a CFD model of the Data Center to identify hot spots. It's a temperature model and could model airflow as well. Well that was a snapshot and you would have to move the portable technology around each time you wanted a snapshot. What we've done now with the Raleigh Data Center is add permanently mounted sensors above and below the floor at different points in the rack and at different points in the rows and the aisles. And we can generate a continuous CFD model or snapshot dynamically.

Once you have that information you can tie that into hot spot analysis in real time or you can plug that into your decision making process on where you place the next piece of IT equipment in relation to the IT equipment you already have. So you in other words put it in the cold areas not the hot areas. And then you can also use that information for capacity planning for where do I need to put the next cooling technology or when we're doing analytics, what's the optimal cooling solution for the entire raised floor and should I eventually move workload around the Data Center to even out the cooling and mitigate hot spots?

When using that technology and examining what happens when hardware is deployed in different power densities per cabinet, does anything counter-intuitive or surprising emerge?

No. It's typically what you expect to see. We have hot spots around the high density equipment.

The other thing it points out to us is—and we've injected this MMT technology in some of our lower density Data Centers—as opposed to a CFD model where you put in your configuration MMT does real-time monitoring and can reconcile against what the model says and when there are differences you have loss. So that's where it helps us identify things like the fact that the blanking plates may not be there or the cable cutouts aren't filled with cushions or the perforated tiles are in the wrong place. It helps us do that type of analysis. Likewise it helps us to identify most older Data Centers, especially ones that had liquid cooled or a lot of hot equipment, there are way more CRAC units in a facility for redundancy than need be. It's actually also advised us on turning off some of the CRAC units and saving that energy and the life of that CRAC unit.

This Data Center has a raised floor. What infrastructure are you delivering overhead and what are you delivering by way of that raised floor?

Overhead we're running the water for the fire suppression system. Underneath we're doing the forced air. We're also doing the electrical and cabling underneath as well. We looked at overhead cabling. Our criteria for Data Centers has been better service at lower risk and lower cost. When all other things are being equal as far as same amount of risk, same amount of cost, we ask the hardware planners and the people who are working in that space what they prefer and if there wasn't a cost differential we went with what they preferred. They much rather prefer under the floor cabling because pulling cables under the floor is easier and quicker than moving a ladder around upstairs. And they were approximately the same cost.

The return air plenum is overhead. We have perforated tiles in the cold aisle on the floor and perforated ceiling tiles in the hot aisle, with a false ceiling therefore bringing the return air back to the CRAC units.

It's a 36-in. (91.4 cm) raised floor. We found raised floor being still the most economical way to cool the base set of equipment in the Data Center because the customers aren't investing yet in higher density equipment.

What sort of fire detection and suppression system does this facility have?

There's always been a raging debate about charged dry versus wet. IBM prefers wet. The insurance companies in the area don't care which one has a bias. We also use flexible piping where the head of the sprinkler is so that we can reposition it over the IT equipment. The other thing is the sprinklers themselves have individual trips so that if one trips it just trips over that equipment not over a section or an aisle of the rows of the raised floor. We've got VESDA early smoke detection systems as well installed there.

When you think about how this Data Center has been designed, is it a universal design that can be done by anyone for any facility or are certain technologies only appropriate based on the mission of this Data Center or where it's located?

There are a couple of things that are geographic specific, like the economic value that you get from a flat plate heat exchanger. In other words, we have a facility in Boulder that will use it more than the facility in RTP. The other thing we looked at was things like CHP or combined heat and power to have a gas turbine.

You've got to understand that some of those are economically driven not technology driven. If you've got a power source like a CHP system, natural gas, that is 8 cents a kilowatt hour that would be beneficial in the northeast where you're paying 13 cents per kilowatt hour but wouldn't be beneficial in Raleigh where we're paying 5 to 6 cents a kilowatt hour. The technologies have an economic component which cannot be ignored. So although some of the things are proven technology they're not economically feasible for that geography compared to other technologies.

So, yes you use a modular design. Yes it can go anywhere. The piece that some people can't do that we did, which we leveraged our Global Technology Services, Site and Facilities organization (the IBM group that provides Data Center consulting to external customers), was they did the analysis of what would a 3 MW module consist of from an electrical and a cooling standpoint. Not only the low initial cost of capital but the operating cost as well. They went through the major vendors' equipment and provided us that guidance on, this is what will match your electrical with your cooling and this is the model you need to invest in because of its operational characteristics, because of its variable speed drive, its variable speed fans. The variability that has the control content where we can control that variability so as utilization goes up and down on the floor and the heat goes up and down on the floor, the cooling can go up and down as well. A lot of people can duplicate that extensive analysis.

Any surprises that came up during the design and build of the Data Center?

Yeah. A recommendation that we make to everybody that's building a Data Center is that when you commission the Data Center that you actually put the type of load to test everything. So we actually did put a 6 MW heat load out on the raised floor in the different zones and tested it. What we found was our chilled water tanks lasted longer than we thought their design point would be, so we actually have more ride-through time than we thought that we would.

Is there any overall advice that you would offer to someone approaching a Data Center project? Any general design principles that are useful to follow?

Building Data Centers is significantly different than building a commercial building and certainly different than building a residential structure. It's in your best interest to get people involved in helping you build your Data Centers that have built Data Centers and have built Data Centers recently. If you look at the EPA report to Congress we're now building Data Centers more efficient than what EPA thought would be possible by this point in time. Some of the PUEs that are reporting now, the EPA said the improvements in technology wouldn't have even gotten there this far, but the things like any to any connectivity of the cooling distribution system, the modularity, the analysis—get somebody who's experienced in doing that. Obviously commissioning, the raised floor space, to make sure that it meets your design criteria. Look at not only the capital costs but the trade-off between capital and operating, because you can get some low non-variable facilities equipment, cooling and electrical, inexpensively but you'll pay for it in operating costs. So you have to do a total cost of ownership, not a 'I want to decrease my capital costs.'

FIGURE 12-5
An under-floor view of the piping for water cooling in IBM's Research Triangle Park Data Center.

FIGURE 12-6   Use of both air- and liquid-based cooling allows the Data Center to support different cabinet power densities.

FIGURE 12-7   Electrical switchgear for IBM's Research Triangle Park Data Center.

FIGURE 12-8   3 MW of wet cell battery capacity provide 15 minutes of ride-through power.

FIGURE 12-9   Six 2.5 MW generators provide standby power for IBM's Research Triangle Park
Data Center.

FIGURE 12-10   Cooling tower fans for IBM's Research Triangle Park Data Center.

FIGURE 13-1   Intel's pioneering use of enclosed cabinets in its Rio Rancho Data Center supports
36 kW per cabinet with air cooling. Images provided courtesy of Intel.

CHAPTER 13
Intel

ORGANIZATION: Intel	
LOCATION: Rio Rancho, New Mexico	
ONLINE: July 2006	
NOTABLE FEATURES: Converted wafer fabrication facility. First Data Center to employ cabinets with ducted exhaust to optimize cooling efficiency.	
TIME TO DESIGN AND BUILD: 20 months	
SIZE: 18,000 sq. ft. (1,672 sq. m) total, with 6,700 sq. ft. (623 sq. m) of hosting space.	
POWER: Redundant substation feeds; IT usable capacity of 8 MW	
TIER: II	
CABINET LOCATIONS: 268	
POWER DENSITY: 24 kW average per cabinet, 36 kW maximum	
INFRASTRUCTURE DELIVERY: All physical infrastructure delivered overhead; copper and fiber in separate cable trays and electrical wiring in dual redundant power busbars. No raised floor.	
COOLING SOLUTION: Air cooling, featuring enclosed cabinets with exhaust chimneys and air handlers located in a separate story above the hosting area.	
STRUCTURAL LOADING: 200 lb. per sq. ft. (976.5 kg per sq. m)	
FIRE SUPPRESSION SYSTEM: Wet pipe sprinkler system with VESDA detection system	

Intel Corporation has a reputation in the Data Center industry for innovation, often pushing boundaries to see what extra performance can be squeezed from the hardware and physical infrastructure within its server environments.

Company engineers have invented cabinet enclosures to improve cooling efficiency, constructed buildings that re-use server waste heat and even run hardware for months at a time in humid and dusty conditions to see how much energy could be saved—and how server reliability was affected—by operating without the extensive climate controls typically provided in Data Centers.

The result of the company's constant experimentation is a Data Center model that not only incorporates tremendous power density and optimized air-cooling but also coordinates networking, compute, storage, and facility elements.

Intel first employed its high performance/high density Data Center design in 2005, retrofitting a 25-year-old factory in Rio Rancho, New Mexico. Originally used for the production of silicon chips, the building now features a Tier II, 6,700 sq. ft. (623 sq. m.) Data Center capable of housing more than 22,000 servers in just 268 cabinet locations, thanks to 8 MW of electrical capacity and a power density of up to 36 kW per cabinet.

(Two other server environments are contained in the factory as well. A conventional 4,000 sq. ft. [372 sq. m.] raised floor space with hot- and cold-aisles and 7 to 10 kW of power per cabinet and a 60,000 sq. ft. [5,574 sq. m.] expansion space that is largely unoccupied save for the State of New Mexico's 28-cabinet, liquid-cooled Encanto supercomputer whose workload includes tasks such as projecting the movement of the Gulf Coast oil spill in 2010.)

Don Atwood, Global Data Center Architect for Intel, discusses how the old factory was converted into a high performance Data Center and why he envisions server environments with higher operational temperatures and greater power densities in the future.

The Interview

What drove the decision to convert a wafer fabrication facility to a Data Center?

The evolution of the technology within the semiconductor industry and the requirement to change footprints within the factories left us with available space. How we build chips, the different sizes of the chips and the different facility and physical requirements of the equipment to build the chips actually pushed us as a business into a substantially different factory footprint. Because of that we eventually end-of-lifed this facility and basically moved and it sat empty for many years.

Although the facility itself was used on and off for miscellaneous different internal purposes for many years, Intel was having substantial compute requirement growth needs globally. Our rate of growth in the Data Center from a space, power, and cooling perspective was very, very substantial. As we looked at our global footprint and where we needed to build based on where the right people were, what the bandwidth and latency needs are for the needs of our facilities, and what made sense financially—do we green-build do we retrofit?—we basically did a survey of our global landscape and said 'Hey, New Mexico is actually a good place for many reasons.' Geographically, from a power perspective, from a reliability and a cost perspective, it was one of our best locations globally. And here we had this fabulous, improved facility that was sitting empty that we could re-use as opposed to doing a green build at one of our other locations.

The lower cost and risk perspective was really great here, so we said 'Let's convert an old factory instead of building a new facility.' We have 150 sites globally and we had a lot of opportunities to go pretty much anywhere we wanted around the world but it made more sense financially to do a re-use of an old factory building and specifically do it here in Rio Rancho because of the low cost of energy and the high availability of power.

The fact that you were working with an existing facility, how did its pre-existing elements impact the design of the Data Center?

I think if we were to build a brand new Data Center and start fresh, there are certainly components that we would do differently. When you take a building that already exists and you retrofit it, you say 'Okay, these are the walls I have and these are the structures that we have and these are the investments we've made so how do we best make use of those?' So what we came out with is not necessarily how we would design a new one if we were building from scratch but what to do with infrastructure we already own.

The way that factories are traditionally designed, the top floor would be mechanical. Factories require a lot of constantly moving air to have cleanliness in the factory. The middle level is always the factory and the lower level is always the electrical delivery to the factory. Those are the three big pieces that Data Center's need—your Data Center space, your mechanical space, and your electrical space. So this facility was already fairly well established from a power distribution perspective. The water pipes were in the right areas and the electrical was in the right areas. We said 'This is what we have and it somewhat aligns to what we need from a design perspective for a Data Center.'

The only big gap that we had to look at was that we were building our first ultra-high performance Data Center. The design criterion was initially above 30 kW per cabinet—we ended up building 36 kW per cabinet. Our biggest concern was since we were going to have to put the compute on the second level, which is where the factory floor was, could the floor architecturally hold that much weight because we had pretty high density, high weight racks? Factories have very heavy equipment and it actually worked out very well. We did not need to make modifications to support the weight of our 2,500 lb. (1,134 kg) loaded racks. In many instances the building's weight-bearing capability was about double the capacity of what we needed, with even current-day technologies.

FIGURE 13-2   Air handlers on the third floor of Intel's Rio Rancho Data Center.

Thirty six kilowatts per cabinet is an impressive power density. What different cooling approaches did you consider along the way to accommodate that and what solution did you ultimately choose?

When we built this and designed it (in 2005), this was an interesting time in the lifecycle of Data Center design at Intel. We were moving from low/medium density Data Centers to extremely high density Data Centers, which at the time we were saying anything over 10 kW was very high. We were internally learning a lot about what high density meant and what the benefits of it were. We were kind of designing at the same time that we were testing the theory in other Data Center locations and also at this location.

We have multiple different types of compute within Intel. Some compute are not highly critical but other servers if they go down our stock will go down or our employees won't get paid; our finance and HR compute. High availability is different than a lot of our high density compute internally. The largest percentage of compute at Intel is high density that did not need that ultra-high reliability, just reliable services.

So, as we were going through the design to build our higher density, we kept asking ourselves what does that mean? Ultimately the cooling outlook was determined to be, if we ran our Data Centers and completely separated the hot air and the cold air and got away from hot spots or warm spots, we could gain about a 24 percent mechanical efficiency at the cooling coil. Meaning if I had 1,000 servers, for example, in a room that was 5,000 sq. ft. (465 sq. m.) or if I had 1,000 servers in a room that was 1,000 sq. ft. (93 sq. m.)—the same exact IT load—we could run about 24 percent more efficient with a high dense type of environment instead of spreading out the load. The tighter and the higher density we could go, the more efficient we were.

At that time there was not really a product on the market to cool 30-something kilowatts per rack without going to a liquid type of design, which was incredibly expensive. We actually designed the chimney cabinet that exists on the market today. Multiple vendors are selling it. We chose not to patent it so it would get out to the industry, but we actually designed that at this site for this need. We figured out that that was a great way to control the air completely and not let any of the hot air mix with the cold air. You can do it through hot aisle containment or chimney racks and there are multiple solutions today to accomplish this, but at the time we basically invented the Data Center chimney rack and we designed this room around it. When you walk in the Data Center today and you see many thousands of servers in a very small space what you find is that there are no warm or hot spots in the room because it's completely controlled.

The mechanical design was to totally control the air, have no leakage of hot or warm air into the room, and have the highest density to provide the hottest air to the coil. Instead of mixing hot air with cold air (pre-cooling), we want it as hot as it can get to the coil for the highest efficiency. There were some struggles. This was definitely the highest density we had ever done. In fact, outside of a few super-computers it's still our highest density design five years later. But it was extremely effective and worked very well for us.

FIGURE 13-4   Structured cabling and electrical infrastructure are routed overhead in Intel's
                     Data Center.

Why did you forgo a raised floor in your high-density Data Center design?

People do raised floors for a lot of reasons but the original intent of raised floor was to distribute the right air to the right parts of the room to manage the hot spots. We don't have hot spots because we 100 percent manage the air and we let no hot air into the room. If you control all the air in the room then you can dump the cold air anywhere you want and you can avoid the cost of building the raised floor. As long as you have enough cold volume in the room to meet the draw of the servers it doesn't matter where it gets in to the room. All network and power is done overhead for simplicity and agility.

What operational temperature do you try to maintain for the hardware in the Data Center?

At the time, which is different than what we do today and what we intend to do in the future, we were chasing the traditional thinking. I think our design set point was about 71 degrees (21.7 Celsius).

We now know, due to other tests we've done at this site with free cooling and a few other things we have done and published, that 71 (21.7 Celsius) is not necessary. The technology today is very tolerant to higher temperatures and we don't have hot spots to manage. Realistically, we want to get up to an average in a general Data Center in the mid- to higher 80s (27 to 31 degrees Celsius). We know we can go well in to the 90s or even into the high 90s (32 to 37 degrees Celsius) from a technology perspective today but there's a balance between risk and environmental controls and how many people are going to be working there. We know we're over-cooling the rooms even as we sit today but with some legacy hardware raising the room temperature is a net loss. Certainly at the time the Data Center was built lower temperatures were normal. We plan not to do that in the future and we plan to bring those temperatures up quite a bit.

I can go into that same room today and I can bring the temperature up to 93, 95 degrees (34, 35 degrees Celsius) and the servers would run fine. There'll be no problem at all, there's not going to be an increased failure rate. We're very confident in that and we'll save a ton of mechanical electricity by doing that. The problem is with the older technology, even generations just two years ago, if I raise the temperature the server fans will just spin faster and will actually draw more energy at the server than I'm saving at the facility level. So it's a balance. With the new technology the fans aren't going to spin as fast, they're not going to try and push as much air. To save a dollar, we don't want to spend $1.50 somewhere else. It's finding the right power consumption balance in the room based on the technology we're running.

FIGURE 13-4   Structured cabling flows through an overhead cable tray in Intel's Rio Rancho Data Center.

Assuming you don't encounter the problem that you mention, of server fans spinning faster, do you see 36 kW and high-90s operating temperatures as the maximum thresholds or do you see those numbers being driven up even higher in the future?

I definitely see it going up from where we are today. If we look at our (Data Center) strategy and where we believe we're going, and where we know we're going from a chip perspective, we definitely know that our footprint within Data Centers globally is shrinking substantially as our compute needs are rising. We have opposite vectors happening. A lot of growth needs are being driven through better utilizing general office and enterprise computers through virtualization and cloud technology. So instead of having 1,000 office servers that are 10 percent utilized, as an example, with virtualization we might have 100 servers or less that are highly utilized but our footprint and overall power consumption per CPU cycle used is substantially smaller overall. So we believe that certainly within the design side of our business, which represents about 70,000 servers, the higher density footprint with the latest technology is going to continue getting higher and higher in a smaller footprint and with lower overall power consumption.

Do you think the Data Center industry as a whole is going to be moving toward those super-high power densities?

When you look at the cost of building Data Centers per square foot, from a design perspective, it's going to be really hard for the industry to justify building mega Data Centers anymore. Unless you're one of the very few companies, the half a percent (of) companies that are building these monster Data Centers globally, which most companies aren't, I think your average company is not going to be building 20,000 sq. ft. (1,858 sq. m.) Data Centers much longer.

I consult with companies often, around the globe, who are looking at building 60,000 sq. ft. (5,574 sq. m.) Data Centers or 80,000 sq. ft. (7,432 sq. m.) Data Centers and after spending some time with them and showing them the model that we use, they often resize their design and build Data Centers at one-fourth of the size that are much more efficient operationally and reduce not only their capex upfront cost of building but their operational cost long-term. When it boils down to that there's a big savings both upfront and long-term, it's a hard sell to continue building these large footprints and low density Data Centers.

> "When you look at the cost of building Data Centers per square foot, from a design perspective, it's going to be really hard for the industry to justify building mega Data Centers anymore."

Coming with that higher density, is there a greater risk around thermal runaway? If something breaks, things are going to heat up that much faster. Or have we already crossed the point at which in most Data Centers things are going to heat up very quickly anyway?

That's a great question. That's something that we experienced early on with our really high densities. If you cool a Data Center in a very traditional manner thermal runaway is definitely an issue that people have to consider. But there's a multitude of ways of mitigating that risk.

I think what we're going to find and what you already see starting to happen, if you build high density Data Centers and you have alternative types of cooling like free air cooling all of a sudden that doesn't become such an issue because the normal mechanism of cooling your air is evolving. If you try to do high density with traditional cooling, it's a big gap to consider. I can tell you that as we went through this process globally we learned our mistakes the hard way a few times. When you have many thousands of servers in a very small square footage, you can have a runaway condition very quickly if you completely lose all of your cooling, for example.

You touched on liquid cooling and you're certainly at the power density levels at which people normally think about using it. It sounds like cost was a concern. Were there any other drivers that caused you to do this through air cooling rather than liquid cooling?

Initially, at the time, people thought anything over 10 kW you had to use liquid cooling solutions. But the cost was crazy high. We knew that we were saving a lot of money by going to high density but operationally we did not want to overspend money up front so we had to find the balance with a lower cost solution. Through the chimney design process that we went through we found out—and we're very confident with the chimney rack at least—that we can cool about 30 kW with completely passive cooling. No fans blowing the air. There are multiple solutions that have fans inside of chimney but we don't use any of these as they increase risk and consume more power. One hundred percent managed air via chimney cabinets or hot aisle containment solutions are all we need for less than 30 kW.

Beyond 30 kW chimney solutions, which I think the industry will see some day, controlled hot-aisle types of environment where you just dump all of the air into a room to cool or dump all of the air outside will allow us to go beyond 30 kW. Depending on what you're doing with the air when it comes out of the server, for example if you're just pushing it outside like some companies are doing in some instances, really sky's the limit. As long as it's not an environmental issue and you're not melting the cables behind the server, it's really not a gap.

How long did it take for the design and reconstruction of the building?

The design phase of the building was about seven months. A lot of that was going back and pulling up 20-year-old plans and validating a lot of the old systems that were in place and doing gap analysis of what we had versus what we needed to do this high density, high performance installation. The entire project from design to buildout was about 20 months from concept to funding to lights on.

FIGURE 13-5   Intel's Rio Rancho Data Center features 8 MW of electrical capacity.

Were there any surprises or challenges that arose along the way?

A whole bunch of them. Most of the gaps and surprises that we came up with I would call normal construction project issues. They were mostly around taking an old factory that was designed for extreme low density and converting that to a very high density power delivery and cooling design. Having the right chillers in the right places and the right air handling in the right places and how do we deliver enough power to every rack to support the high density? There were just some operational challenges. I wouldn't say anything major, but a lot of in-the-field decision making on how to get over obstacles using an old building that wasn't designed to do what we're doing with it.

If you could go back and design the Data Center again would you do anything differently?

It's all about the timing. So for example, from the power distribution perspective, at the time nobody was doing densities like this and you couldn't get enough power to the rack the way we wanted so we had to use vendors in some cases and suppliers in some cases that we just weren't completely happy with but (did) to get the densities that we wanted. This was kind of an untapped market to a certain degree so we worked with what we had or could get. So, I wouldn't necessarily say that we would do things differently, but the timing was such that we were leading the drive to go to high density and a lot of the products weren't in place.

The biggest challenge we had from a design perspective using this old facility is going back to the point that traditionally the factories we build are designed to have mechanical on top, factory in the middle, and electrical on the bottom. What that means is we had water on the top of the compute and electrical on the bottom. So making sure that we designed the pipes on the top to be contained and have the appropriate amounts of leak detection was a must. We had so many weld joints and so many solder points and so many pipe fittings, things were going to leak at some point with thousands of fittings so we needed to make sure leaks would not affect us.

With the super-high density and all of the technologies that come with that, do you feel that these are universal solutions that can be implemented everywhere or are some of these just corner cases that worked here but if someone else were designing a Data Center maybe it wouldn't be a good fit for them.

That's a good question. For us this was our big jump into extreme high density, we called it HPDC for high performance Data Centers. It has become our universal standard for designing Data Centers globally now and with virtualization, this will remain our standard for more traditional servers as well. I think that certainly there is evolution in technologies and vendors improve things and make them a little better so we see improvements year to year.

So this is certainly a repeatable model for you.

Extremely repeatable, yep.

If someone reading this book is looking to build a Data Center and they need 5 kW a cabinet or maybe 10 kW, do you think the chimney cabinet configuration and the other elements that you've employed are still an appropriate design for that or are we talking about different models based on different power density?

I've participated in many conversation with companies who are doing exactly what you ask, in general most companies when they have an opportunity to redesign or build a new facility from the ground up or a major investment upgrade, I'm seeing them go to much higher density designs using either chimney solutions or hot-aisle containment. I'm talking about the medium(-sized) companies, 500-servers to 5,000- or even 10,000-servers companies, most of them are converting to a much higher watts per square foot Data Center design similar to ours. Again it purely comes down to operational costs through efficiency and also a capex build savings.

The only exception I would say to that, and I would say this is an exception even within Intel, there is a small piece of our business that requires ultra-high availability solutions; reliability is critical and these systems cannot go down. In those scenarios we probably don't want to put all of our eggs in one basket, and there is a higher risk associated with putting all of our most critical apps and compute in extreme high density design. For that little sliver of our business, which represents today less than 5 percent of our total compute load, you'll find us in a more traditional medium density type of design, spread out a little more for risk avoidance.

So I think if you find companies like critical investment and banking companies, super critical businesses for which millions of dollars a second could be lost if they go down, I doubt that you'll see all of their servers in a small little closet just to save a couple bucks up front. They spread them out across multiple Data Centers and they have active-active clustering and synchronous replication for reliability. But for the vast majority of compute and traditional types of servers that aren't super critical to the business, I think what you're seeing is a high compression, decisions to move into much smaller spaces to maximize investment and experience high efficiency.

Any other lessons for people to consider from your high-density Data Center design?

Historically, we had traditionally built Data Centers without the larger IT needs clearly in mind. We have a team that builds facilities and they're focused on the physical stuff—the power, the cooling. The facilities have not always been built with a direct correlation of the complete use model and it wasn't always an optimal design.

What we've moved to and what you see in this design for the high performance Data Center, we built a room to function as a large compute solution. When we talk about Data Centers internally we don't talk about the 'facilities' anymore, we talk about the entire IT stack. We build our facilities in alignment with the compute and the storage and the network pieces needed to support the application layer. We are getting good about looking at the entire stack as a solution with less focus on the individual pieces, including the facility.

A fair amount of space in this building is unoccupied. Do you intend to eventually expand the Data Center?

Four years ago I would have told you 'Absolutely,' and I actually had plans to do that. But because of the high density and the reduced floor space requirements we're seeing globally, we will never use that space for Data Centers. Our footprint globally is being reduced dramatically at the same rate that our compute needs are ramping (up) substantially. Our biggest saving grace from a Data Center perspective and the game-changer for us internally in the way we build and run and plan for Data Centers, is (that) Intel's multi-core technology has changed what we do and what we need. We no longer build Data Centers for additional capacity. Our footprints are shrinking. We are focused on the larger stack perspective that I mentioned before. If I can spend $5 million on compute and avoid $30 million in facility, that's a good investment for our stockholders.

This was our turning point and we said, 'This is no longer about the facility specifically.' Data Centers for Intel mean the entire stack and how the stack works to deliver the right MIPS (millions of instructions per second) for the solution. There was a point that making investments in facilities made a lot of sense to us, but we passed that point about three years ago when our new technology came out and we were able to ramp up our compute by leaps forward and actually reduce our cost and footprint in the Data Centers by investing the right money in the right places. That's why we really don't focus so much on facilities anymore. Facilities are one component of the entire stack.

How does that manifest itself in your design? I think most companies design the physical layer of their Data Center to be very reliable but as essentially a self-contained set of infrastructure components. If you're considering the entire stack, how does that drive down and impact the physical design?

I think that's a really good question, and it took us a little bit to get good at that.

About 70 percent of our IT compute is designing next generation chips. Like airplane and car manufacturers will design concepts electronically and model them before they're physically built we design our chip and model it before we physically build it.

We basically take the business requirement/compute requirement and we associate that to our high-density knowledge. (We know) we can get X amount of cores out of a rack so we need so many racks to fulfill that design requirement. We build around the requirement. We don't build the facility and see what we're going to put in it 10 years down the road. We figure out what we need and we build the facility around it with the application layer clearly in mind. Three to five years out is the target. We're not building 20-year facilities; the technology is changing too quickly. So we try to be very adaptive. I think that goes back to the main point of, we build modular for cost and agility, because technology is changing too fast for us. We cannot build a Data Center today that is going to satisfy our need in 10 years so we would rather build small ones that meet the needs today and build another small one or medium one—whatever you call 8,000-ish sq. ft. (743 sq. m.)—five years from now when the technology has changed and we know what the 2015 chip and the 2020 chip is going to look like, for example. Our design target should be based on overall uptime of the stack; over-building costs too much money and under-building creates unwanted risk. When you consider the entire stack concept, reliability can be delivered in many different ways.

And then you refresh the Data Center modules as you need to?

Bingo. That's exactly right.

Any final lessons that you would like share about this Data Center project?

Internally, one of the 'Aha!' moments that we had through building this Tier II-ish facility is a strong design can deliver great reliability at a lower cost. We've had no downtime in almost 5 years—zero. I suspect at some point we'll have some downtime somewhere but what we are finding globally is you can build a Data Center without all the components you think you need and just do it differently with more intelligence and achieve the high availability numbers without spending the money.

We're building two Tier II-like Data Centers and getting Tier IV performances out of them. Really that's the sweet spot for us because we're not spending the money but yet we're getting the reliability consistently with the lower tier investment.

"What we are finding globally is you can build a Data Center without all the components you think you need and just do it differently with more intelligence and achieve the high availability numbers without spending the money."

FIGURE 13-6   One of the air handlers supporting the Rio Rancho Data Center.

FIGURE 13-7   Chilled water piping.

FIGURE 14-1   IO's co-location facility in Phoenix, Arizona employs time-shifted cooling to save millions of dollars per year in operating costs. Images provided courtesy of IO.

CHAPTER 14
IO

ORGANIZATION: IO	
LOCATION: Phoenix, Arizona	
ONLINE: Opened as a water bottling and distribution plant in 2006. Acquired by IO in December 2008 and brought online as a co-location facility in June 2009.	
NOTABLE FEATURES: Time-shifted cooling. Thermal storage featuring polyethylene balls of ice and a glycol-water solution. Patented cabinet enclosures. LED lighting. Ultrasonic humidification. Modular components.	
TIME TO DESIGN AND BUILD: 6 months for the first phase.	
SIZE: 538,000 sq. ft. (49,981.8 sq. m) of total space divided among two warehouses, including 360,000 sq. ft. (33,445.1 sq. m) of hosting space.	
POWER: 120 MW	
TIER: III	
CABINET LOCATIONS: About 3,000	
POWER DENSITY: Varies	
INFRASTRUCTURE DELIVERY: Cooling is delivered through a 36 in. (.9 m) raised floor. Power and structured cabling are provided overhead.	
STRUCTURAL LOADING: 700 lb. per sq. ft. (3,417 kg per sq. m)	
FIRE SUPPRESSION SYSTEM: High sensitivity smoke detection, pre-action dry pipe.	

Those who live in extreme environments must adapt to survive, developing new, useful abilities while discarding those that provide no advantage. That tenet of evolution has clearly been embraced by IO for its Data Center in Phoenix, Arizona.

When the co-location provider acquired the former water bottling plant in late 2008, it constructed a traditional Data Center in one of the site's two warehouse buildings. Leveraging Arizona's tiered power pricing, IO runs chillers at night when rates are lower, freezing water-filled plastic globes in a solution of glycol and water. During the day the softball-sized ice balls chill the glycol mix, which is pumped through a heat exchanger to chill water for the Data Center's cooling system.

The site's first adaptation occurred in 2009 when IO extended the Data Center's pressurized plenum into a patented server cabinet it developed, tripling the power density supportable at cabinet locations to 32 kW. Another came in 2011 when IO discarded traditional design for its second warehouse, improving operational efficiency by deploying Data Center modules. IO's business model evolved, too, becoming a modular component manufacturer as well as co-location provider.

Even highly successful species can have an evolutionary false start. IO in 2009 announced it would install a massive solar array capable of generating 4.5 MW for the facility. They later scrapped those plans.

George Slessman, chief executive officer of IO, discusses the evolution of its Phoenix facility, what caused the company to forgo solar, and why traditional Data Center designs are as outdated as a vestigial tail.

The Interview

IO began as a traditional co-location provider and has since expanded into manufacturing modular Data Center components as well. How does modularity fit into your Data Center strategy and what role do you see it playing in Data Centers going forward?

It comes from a place where we believe there are four things that are fundamentally wrong with Data Centers as they've been constructed for a long time. I come to this with a view that there has been what I would describe as incremental innovation in the Data Center over the last—let's call it 35 years or even longer—from the late '60s when the first data processing rooms were stood up for mainframes to today up until say a year and a half ago. They have essentially all been built the same way.

At the end of the day there are cooling elements. There are power distribution elements. It's a room. It's part of a facility in one way, shape, or form. Yes, the components have gotten more efficient individually. They've gotten bigger. They have more capacity than they've had before. There are more of them. There are more air handlers than less. There are bigger chillers than less. There are variable speed drives. But at the end of the day the overall architecture of the Data Center hasn't changed in any meaningful way in a very long time. If you look at the architecture of what we describe internally as Data Center 1.0, we believe there are four fundamental flaws of that architecture.

First, it's insecure, both physically and logically in most cases, meaning that the control software and the control tools that have been implemented typically in traditional Data Center builds have not been purpose built or designed for that outcome. As you well know, most of these came from being building automation systems or building management systems and not really from the industrial controls world, which have been mission critical to it. They have come out of the commercial building industry of managing HVA systems, managing office air conditioning.

Then the physical design of the Data Center itself, because of the complexity and the number of discreet components in itself makes it very difficult to secure. You have lots of doors. You have lots of openings. In every Data Center they're different. In some cases, Data Centers have been placed in to buildings with other uses, with people and other things. Holistically, we believe that the traditional Data Center environment is not well suited for managing security.

The second major flaw of the traditional Data Center is that it takes far too long to deliver. In the context of what they support, from an IT infrastructure both at the physical layer up through the application layer or the virtualization layer and then ultimately users, the speed at which IT moves is in months not years. So they take far too long for most enterprises in our experience.

"…we believe there are four things that are fundamentally wrong with Data Centers as they've been constructed for a long time."

In the government and even for service providers that tend to be a little more agile, from the day they first invent the idea of a new Data Center to the day that they rack IT, it's typically over two years to go through the whole procurement process, decision making, analysis, engineering, all the way through to commissioning and then finally a piece of IT being stacked. Because of that length of time to construct, it also then forces that asset to try to be more relevant for a longer period of time because you can't cycle it. It forces you to look at the Data Center in a 10 or 15 or even 20 year event horizon for utility. Again, in the context of the IT world every year you add you're adding an enormous amount of variability and complexity in calculating exactly what it's going to look like one year, two years, three years. Then imagine trying to look 10 or 15 years out. I always quip, 'What's a 10 year old cell phone look like?' It gives you a sense of the technology challenge there.

The third component that is broken in the existing model is that Data Centers cost too much. If you look at the total deployment from conception to acquisition of whatever the particular real property component is, the construction process all the way through to the non-IT fitup of the Data Center to then the point where you start to add IT is very expensive on a unit basis. Because it's based in the construction world—construction I believe is the only industry over the last 20 years that is less productive today than it was 20 years ago—you have productivity regression. In addition, construction in and of itself is subject to wage inflation and raw goods inflation and these sorts of attributes. You see that there's not a visibility in to that unit cost going anywhere but continuing to escalate over time.

Compare that to the IT world. Virtually every component of the IT stack is actually going down on a unit cost and there's visibility to continue unit cost reductions over time whether you're looking at storage devices or CPU cycles or network capacity. All three over time decrease in cost. In fact, the productivity of the IT department is the driving engine of productivity in the world today. IT department budgets, if you poll IDC or Gartner, have been essentially flat for 10 years and they're doing hundreds of times the amount of computational work they used to do. It doesn't match up very well.

FIGURE 14-2   Inside the first phase of IO's Phoenix Data Center.

The last component that we've attempted to solve with our technology platform and we believe is a flaw in the 1.0 model is the lack of scalability. The other ones are pretty easy to point at. Scalability is all of the things that we aspire to in the IT stack—modular design, modular components, in-place upgradable, just-in-time deployment. All of these attributes that we see in an EMC storage array or we see in a Cisco router platform or that we see in any of these other devices that make up the IT stack and the virtues of those devices that we as IT consumers have grown accustomed to having access to don't show up in the Data Center.

I boil it down to one basic concept from scalability. Everything in IT now is thinly provisioned. You have the ability to make very quick decisions and to provision an asset and then re-provision that asset, change its capacity rapidly and redeploy it to the same user, whereas the Data Center is a fixed provisioned asset, typically. You make a varied set of discreet engineering decisions up front. You apply discreet engineering principles to those and you deploy an asset that has—I'll boil it down to one metric that is the quintessential thick provisioned: this Data Center is 150 watts per square foot (1,614.6 watts per sq. m). You've now made a decision that impacts everything in the engineering.

This is the part that most people don't get and why I think there's been so many challenges in the Data Center—IT people don't think that way. IT people provision a router and then assume that if they need more capacity they can pull a blade out and put a new blade in that gives them more capacity. So when they buy a Data Center or use a Data Center that someone says, it's 100 watts per sq. ft. (1,076.4 watts per sq. m) the assumption is that 'Oh, two years later when I need 150 watts a foot (1,614.6 watts per sq. m) I should be able to just slide a blade out and put another blade in and have that capacity,' whereas we know in an engineered, construction-based Data Center you just can't do that. It's an integrated system. When you design x amount of power distribution that means x amount of cooling. When you say x amount of redundancy you get x amount of redundancy. It isn't that simple (to change). Hence why it takes so long.

The other component of scalability that I point to that we've attempted to solve is the ability to variably match the service level goals of the user—the applications inside the Data Center—with the resources being deployed. The other very challenging decision that's made in Data Centers today that affects scalability is you have to essentially decide what the resiliency tolerance you have for the entire Data Center. As we know, it's very difficult to have part of a Data Center in the Data Center 1.0 world to be N+1 and one part to be 2N and one part to be (something else). Or, more importantly, to have one part be five nines (of availability), one be four nines, one be three nines, and one be 'who-cares.'

So, if you take those four things, that's the state that we believe the current Data Centers are in. Having been in the Data Center world for a decade and having been in IT and technology for a decade and a half, we came to the conclusion about two years ago when we finished constructing the first phase of this Phoenix Data Center that this just wasn't going to be sustainable over the next 20 years. That continuing to build Data Centers, even though we build them much larger and we scaled them up and all these things. These four problems were going to adversely affect, if not become untenable, going forward for the IT consumer as we continue to see IT demand grow. The demand for IT cycles is exponentially increasing with no end in sight and in fact accelerating, I would say. Which means more and more and more Data Center, which if we keep building the way we've done we're going to paint ourselves in to the proverbial corner.

With that as a backdrop, that's the way we see the world. What we attempted to do then, and what we believe we've done in our modular product, is to solve those problems with two fundamental principles. Making the Data Center delivery component itself a manufactured and engineered component that is modular in aggregate—finitely modular and as a system modular. You can scale up vertically and horizontally. So you can go inside the module and you can upgrade components; you can in-place upgrade power delivery and cooling infrastructure inside the thermal dynamic module. You can also then add more modules when you need more capacity in that vector. And manufacture that so you get all of the benefits of having a supply chain, having innovation cycle over and over and over again rather than having all of the engineering skill that goes into a Data Center essentially go in to this Data Center and then moves on with the construction or engineering firm to the next one—and there's no incentive really to drive that innovation cycle over and over.

The real incentive for most engineering firms is to take the same plans they already spent the money on to build and just hand them to the next guy and charge him the same amount. Whereas in a manufacturing process we're incented and our customers are incenting us to manufacture better, faster, cheaper just like everything else. So cars today for essentially the same price as 15 or 20 years ago have 3x the functionality. From air bags to ABS, to all these things, are innovations that have shown up, and quality and cycles are better.

The second part we have attempted to solve in the approach to modularity in solving these four problems, is that now that you have a standardized delivery unit that's manufactured, on which to layer on top of that a software automation layer or control layer. In our case we call it a Data Center infrastructure operating system. That then gives you the ability to manage and actively and pro-actively control and then ultimately intelligently optimize that physical layer to match up with the IT stack.

So, taking those four problems into consideration we determined the way we were going to solve those problems was to manufacture the Data Center components and then software automate them. In getting there we now have a 300,000 sq. ft. (27,870.9 sq. m) factory that we operate where we produce these modules. Each module is roughly 200 kW of capacity. We have over a hundred frames in production. We've delivered over 70 modules to customers at our own locations in Phoenix and New Jersey where we host the modules for customers.

The punch line is, we've already recognized for customers anywhere from 50 to 60 percent reduction in initial capex in apples-apples environments. And we've also seen ongoing operating expense reductions in the order of 25 to 30 percent. In addition to that, we're able to deliver quickly. Just as one discreet example, Allianz, the German insurance company, we delivered a 3.6 MW Data Center system to them in 91 days from the day they signed the contract to the day they racked IT. So we symptomatically now are seeing the results of this platform solving those four problems.

Let's talk about the Phoenix site in particular. It seems this started as a conventional space and it has gone to using modularity throughout the facility. When did it first open?

We acquired the site in December of 2008. It's an interesting site in the sense that we repurposed it. It was previously a distribution and water bottling facility, owned by a company that had subsequently gone out of business. The structure and the site was developed and turnkey delivered to the water bottling company in 2006. We acquired the site in December 2008 and built out phase one, which is let's call it the first half of the site. It's a 538,000 sq. ft. (49,981.8 sq. m) facility and it's on about 40 acres (16.2 hectares) from a campus. It has a substation on site provided by the local utility.

We built out the first phase in what we call Data Center 1.5, which is a scaled deployment of capacity, bringing to bear all of the things that we thought was necessary to start to solve these four problems in a scaled way in a more traditional technology architecture. It's about a 250,000 sq. ft. (23,225.8 sq. m) raised floor space. It's all in one room, which is kind of unique, you don't see very often. Very high ceilings, 30+ ft. (9.1 m) ceiling heights in the space. We have 24.5 MW of UPS (uninterruptible power supply) online net of redundancy in that phase one space. We moved our first customer into the site in June of 2009.

We have 8,000 tons of chiller capacity, two 4,000 ton plants. This is phase one I'm speaking only to. We have two 16 MW Caterpillar generators through two sets of 20 MW paralleling equipment that power the phase one space exclusively. It's broken into four individual pods, but again all still in the same room. Each pod yields about 45,000 sq. ft.(4,180.6 sq. m) of usable raised floor. So out of that 250,000 sq. ft. (23,225.8 sq. m) in the phase one Data Center room there's 180,000 sq. ft. (16,722.5 sq. m) of net usable raised floor for IT.

We deployed a service gallery architecture so down the center of the room and to the north and the south sides of the room there are service galleys that have the power distribution power distribution units as well as the CRAH (computer room air handler) units located in those. It's a full chilled water system, bi-directional loops. We have a Tier III design certification for this site for phase one from Uptime Institute. One hundred percent concurrently maintainable across the entire system architecture, both power distribution as well as cooling infrastructure. We have a meet-me room on site, actually two that we operate. Today there are about 20 different telecommunications providers that are here on type 1 diverse fiber builds into the site. So it's a very large scale, kind of traditional-plus Data Center build that we completed.

FIGURE 14-3   Phase one of IO's Phoenix Data Center is a traditional build with power and cabling routed overhead and cooling delivered below a raised floor.

How long did it take to convert the building from its original use as a water bottling plant to a Data Center?

What was interesting was there wasn't a whole lot of conversion necessary to the space we use for Data Center. When we acquired the site they had cleaned everything out. It was really two 250,000 sq. ft. (23,225.8 sq. m) warehouses when we acquired it, with some office cap. We just went into that empty warehouse space and then built out the first phase Data Center. We completed the site, that phase one, in approximately six months from the day we took over to the day we moved the first Data Center customer in.

I confess I hoped that your Data Center retained some of the water bottling infrastructure, so anyone working in the room who wanted a drink could easily grab one off of a conveyer belt somewhere.

Everybody's like 'Water bottling in Arizona?' What's funny about it is, Arizona actually has really cheap water and has really cheap power. Because of that, the site was obviously also very well suited for a Data Center. We use a tremendous amount of evaporative cooling in our hydronic economization strategy so we consume a lot of water.

In addition to that, low cost power and high resiliency power is valuable as well. Arizona turns out to be a very, very good location for Data Centers.

I was going to ask what caused you to place your Data Center in Phoenix.

We have looked at obviously a lot of different places. We like Phoenix for its proximity to California from a commercial perspective, because there are lots of Data Center consumers and businesses in California. And Arizona, Phoenix specifically, is a short trip from Los Angeles.

In addition to that, from an environmental perspective or natural disaster all of the things that California is exposed to Arizona isn't. So earthquakes primarily, coastal risks, those sorts of things. It's a very, very stable environment in Arizona. It's also very dry most of the year, which makes the ability to use pre-cool and direct cooled hydronic economization very, very effective in this market.

The cost of power is very stable here as well. The power distribution in Arizona is still regulated by the state. Though it may not be as cheap as it would be in a competitive market, it's still very, very low cost because of the amount of hydro and nuclear power that feeds Arizona. In addition to that, because of regulation it provides great stability in pricing because the process to change rates requires government action. It yields pretty stable rates.

The only negative obviously people point to and ask us about, is, well, it's hot—very hot—during many parts of the year. But envelope load in a Data Center of this size, meaning the cooling load derived from the exterior heat, is not a 3 percent issue in a Data Center. And the bigger the Data Center the less of an issue it is. The dry environment more than compensates the additional cost that you would have to your cooling load during the summer months. And as we know, for a Data Center with 24 MW of IT load in it, it doesn't matter what the temperature is outside is it's going to overheat if the cooling turns off.

What operational temperature do you try to maintain your hardware at?

We've taken a very pro-active approach over the years, obviously working with our customers who have a significant voice in these decisions, but we believe that Data Centers for many years have been kept way too cold. That IT equipment does not need 60 degree (15.6 Celsius) supply air and in some places even lower. We target a supply temperature in the mid-70s (23 to 25 Celsius), with a plus or minus 5 degree range. We're more than happy to run a Data Center at 80 degrees (26.7 Celsius) on the supply side. I actually think you can go well beyond that. Data Centers should probably run in the 85 to 90 degree (29.4 to 32.2 Celsius) range on the supply side.

It's certainly the trend for Data Centers to operate at warmer temperatures now. The standards are catching up to what manufacturers have listed for a while as acceptable temperature ranges.

The manufacturers have been beating this drum for years and just haven't gotten ASHRAE (American Society of Heating, Refrigerating and Air-Conditioning Engineers) and some of the other organizations to pay attention. They have different mandates so it's a different outcome. Again, this I think is a little bit of the legacy-think. 'Oh, well the standard says this.' We've all see IT stuffed in a cabinet—not an IT cabinet but under a desk. It'll be running 120 degree (48.9 Celsius) air and it's perfectly happy.

With the amount of abuse that people subject laptops to, it does seem that Data Center hardware could withstand more severe conditions than they are typically subjected to.

Especially since it's the exact same gear for the most part. At least in your PC server environment, the Wintel boxes, there is not a significant amount of delta between commodity Wintel servers and what's in a desktop PC or a laptop. It's essentially the same, maybe a faster processor. Same manufacturer. Same architecture.

Where this comes from, though, is one of the things that we've attempted to address in our technology platform. There's no integration between the IT equipment and the Data Center in the legacy build. And I mean that from a programmatic or software management perspective. There are very few places where you can actually correlate the performance of the IT hardware with the performance of the Data Center. What's the temperature of the chip set? What's the temperature of the room?

What we've attempted to do and have done now in our IO. Anywhere product with our IO.OS on top of it is, you can go in and in one of our modules you can set an average planar temperature for IT to be the set point for the cooling. Rather than cooling the room you cool the chips, because the chips are what you're trying to maintain.

I read about plans for this Data Center to have a massive solar panel array—300,000 sq. ft. (27,870.9 sq. m) of panels. Has that been installed?

No, it wasn't, actually. None if it has been installed because the state of Arizona abandoned their incentive structure for solar and without the solar incentives it did not pencil.

Covering an 11 acre (4.5 hectares) roof with solar panels yielded less than 3 MW of peak power production during perfect operating conditions. This site pulls north of 15 MW of active demand, 24 hours a day, 7 days a week, 365 days a year. And from a kilowatt hour production perspective it was going to be less than an 8 percent contributor to our total power load here on site, if we kept all the power on site. When you look at the ROIC for the cost to deploy, if you try to do it without incentive programs it's a long ways from penciling. Especially in a state where I can purchase power for 5 cents a kilowatt hour from the utilities. It gets very, very, very challenging for solar to keep up with a scale, nuclear power and hydro.

On paper, this site seems to be a perfect test case for using solar in a big way. You have the option to employ it on a significant scale and you're in Phoenix where sun coverage is ideal. So if it's impractical for you, is solar just not a workable solution for powering Data Centers?

I think energy density is the primary problem. The amount of solar panels you would need to provide a significant enough load to actually create a valid alternative just isn't practical. And that's before you get to the cost analysis. If 11 acres (4.5 hectares) yields 3 MW, for what we would need here would be 5x. We would need almost 50 acres (20.2 hectares) of solar panels to match our peak demand. It doesn't really work physically from an energy density perspective.

The second thing is, when you get to the cost side of it, the cost per kilowatt hour fully amortizing the cost of the panels, the installation, the maintenance and everything else. And then appropriately assessing the panel risk, because if you go with the newer technology from a cell and panels it hasn't been in the field long enough to know what the degradation rates going to be over time on it. So your effective yield—today you may be yielding 100 GWh per year and if the degradation rate isn't 3 percent and it's 12 or 15 percent, 10 or 15 years from now that production has gone down 15 or 20 percent, which can massively impact the return on investment calculus. So with that you have two choices. You either abandon the newer cell technology, which is higher density and lower cost, and go with a more traditional cell technology, which has been proven and there are definitive, quantitative analysis and actuarial analysis around what the degradation is over time. In that case you're now paying too much and you're using older technology. The more we dug into it—and I spent a lot of time personally working on this—it's a very challenging analysis.

I think your assessment is dead on, that if it didn't work for us in this environment (it won't work for any site). And we're not shipping any of the power off-site. We were going to invert all of it and put it right here on site and use it all ourselves. Without a relatively massive tax subsidy it doesn't work.

I have seen some solar arrays deployed at Data Centers but they're just a fraction of the facility's overall power capacity.

Yeah. It's neat to point at, and it's a neat technology, and I guess it's one to at least start looking at—renewable on site and these things. But I think for industrial use, which is what Data Centers truly are is an industrial use of energy, it's going to be pretty challenging for it to meet the density needs. Those silicon chips use a lot of power per square millimeter and it doesn't make a lot of sense if you can match it up with things that produce a little bit of power across square meters of capacity.

I understand you're using thermal storage in a clever way to lower your energy costs.

What we did is, we have the capability to do almost 27,000 ton hours of thermal energy storage here on site. Because Arizona has variably priced power between day and night, and we were able to negotiate demand rates in the off-peak hours, and specifically during the hottest hours of the year, during the summer, we're able to make ice during the nights and then use that ice to either augment or completely carry the cooling load during the highest cost times of the day. It has provided a pretty significant impact for us to our aggregate energy costs and then also provides an additional layer of resiliency to our system from a continuous cooling perspective.

It's a solution everyone should consider. The problem is it requires scale. It's very hard to make it effective sub 10 MW just because 1) the physical space it takes up and then 2) the cost of deploying it. But once you've reached that 10 MW barrier it is a very, very good solution. Now, it only makes sense if you have variably priced power, or you're able to negotiate power purchasing rights, so you can time shift. The total amount of energy consumed is still exactly the same.

FIGURE 14-4   IO creates ice during the night, when energy rates are lower, and then uses that ice to cool the Data Center during the day. This use of thermal storage saves the company millions of dollars per year.

How much of a cents-per-kilowatt-hour cost delta in power prices do you need to make it worth doing?

You need to have at least a 15 percent delta between peak and valley. The bigger that delta the more pronounced obviously the savings are. And that's a fully loaded cost.

If you ever look at your utility bill, it's a relatively complex set of calculations the utility company does to get to the number. There are typically surcharges for peak demand versus off-peak demand, whatever your highest number is. So when you do all the calculus there, you have to have at least an aggregate delta split of 15 percent from your lowest cost power to your highest cost power.

Also what impacts that is what the length of those time periods are, because you obviously have to be able to recharge. The longer your off-peak is, the slower you can recharge your ice. This means the less demand you're putting on the meter in the off hours as well.

The other barrier to it is being willing to operationalize it and really put the time and resources into building the automation necessary to take full advantage of it—and then also having engineering and analytical skills inside your organization where you can keep on top of it. But it well in order pays for itself. We've saved millions of dollars over the last two years.

You previously mentioned the Data Center's raised floor. What infrastructure is delivered under floor versus overhead?

The architecture of the Data Center is it's a 36-in. (.9 m) raised floor. It's one common raised floor plenum among the entire 180,000 sq. ft. (16,722.5 sq. m) of raised floor, so you have an inordinate amount of shared plenum.

One hundred percent of the cabling is overhead from power distribution as well as networking cabling, fiber optic, everything. All of that's done in an overhead architecture.

The cold air distribution is a little bit different. We took the approach of doing static pressure, so we implemented variable speed plug fans across all of the air handling in the room. And we separated the air handling from the coil management in the air handlers. So we use 100 percent of our pumping energy before we deploy any fan energy. The coils we maintain almost at an 100 percent open state so that we can fully optimize the minimum pumping energy that we have to have on the chilled water loop. And then the fans actuate based on the static pressure delta between the IT space and the sub-floor plenum. The concept being, rather than blowing air like a desk fan does what we're doing is essentially making the sub-floor like a balloon which has a higher pressure than the room. If you stick a hole in a balloon, no matter where you put the hole you get airflow because it's flowing across a pressure differential rather than by using velocity. What it does is it gives you a much more even distribution of your airflow out of the floor.

It also enabled us to deploy a patented technology of ours which is called our ThermoCabinet, which is where we extend that pressurized plenum up into the cabinet itself so that the pressure differential then is across the server face rather than between the sub-floor and the room. We maintain a couple millibars of pressure differential and then the fans in all the air handlers just simply actuate against that pressure delta. We measure those deltas in a lattice across the entire room and then it actuates to the fans nearest the data point. The variability is really fluid across the entire room.

Some new Data Center designs aren't using raised floors. What prompted you to use a raised floor and this cooling distribution method, compared to other options?

We had a little bit different decision making criteria than others do. Because we don't know exactly what the customer fitup is going to look like because it's a co-location site. The raised floor provides a tremendous amount of flexibility. Anywhere you can take a tile out you can put one in to push airflow and so it gives you tremendous flexibility in where and how the individual cabinet rows and IT kit end up being laid out. I've built and operationalized Data Centers with no raised floor and it works fine. I don't believe there's any real operational benefit one way or the other, other than the flexibility you get in air movement. Where you have a room where you're blowing air essentially without raised floor and you're distributing it you have to lay out the IT kit ahead of time. Whereas in an environment where you have a raised floor plenum like you have here you can really make ad hoc decisions about where you're going to place IT kit.

There's a tremendous amount of value in having flexibility. Any time you can eliminate construction inside a Data Center you're eliminating an enormous amount of risk.

What sort of power density does the facility support?

When customers aren't utilizing our ThermoCabinet technology we draw the line at about 10 kW per rack. That's the natural threshold. In our ThermoCabinet product, because it's a completely sealed and heat and thermally isolated package, we're able to support way north of 24 kW per cabinet. When we have customers who need ultra high density, which we say anything north of 15 or 20 kW per cabinet, we provide them the ThermoCabinet architecture to deploy in.

We've talked a lot about the first phase of the facility. Let's discuss the design of the second phase and its use of modularity.

The second phase of the site is now essentially the second warehouse. The first 250,000 sq. ft. (23,225.8 sq. m) warehouse we turned into phase one. The second 250,000 sq. ft. (23,225.8 sq. m) warehouse is now a bidirectional chilled water spine that runs along the west wall of the warehouse. That spine then feeds modules that we set down. Also along that spine is a set of medium voltage unit substations that are tied to a 20 MW generator farm. The chiller capacity is tied to a 4,000 ton chiller plant in phase two that does both hydronic economization as well as traditional water evaporated, water cooled chiller. The power spine and the chilled water spine then connect to power modules or network or data modules. The power modules are 2 MW, integrated, manufactured, energy storage and distribution—so, UPS, battery and distribution panels that are in a module. You set down two of those modules which gives you the ability to up to 2N resilience for the customer. You set down a network module which is your meet-me room or carrier interconnection space for the system. Then we add data modules to the end of those three modules until we get to 20 and then we start the next row. It's a very, very different approach than you would see otherwise.

It's actually really cool here. What's great in our tour, when we take customers through, you can actually walk from what was legacy, traditional Data Center design and deployment and then somewhere in between that with the ThermoCabinet architecture and things like that, and then you can walk into what is DC6 and DC7 which is the modular. And it's a completely different experience.

The fire suppression in that room is just traditional wet pipe EFSR (Early Suppression, Fast Response fire sprinklers) because you don't need to put dry pipe in because the modules are each individually watertight as well as they're each individually fire suppressed. And it's a steel box. It's fire-rated as well. Each box has its own fire detection and suppression system which is gas based, inside each of the modules.

Each module has all the air-handling capacities, so one thing that's immediately obvious when you walk into the modular is that it's quiet because all the air-handling capacities are inside of each module. When you walk into the larger room it's dead silent. And then you walk into the module, and then the air handling capacity is modular, in and of itself and is inside of each module. The power distribution PDUs are inside of each module. And then you have up to 20 racks of IT equipment per module as well. And those modules run from 200 kW to north of 500 kW depending upon what the customer requirements. The minimum threshold is about 10 kW per rack and then can scale to well north of 25 and 30 kW a rack, depending what the customer's needs are.

FIGURE 14-5   IO's use of modular components reduced costs, quickened deployment times, and
improved scalability.

Were there any surprises along the way, during the deployment of either of the Data Center's different phases?

Unfortunately, one of the attributes of having done this for a long time is that the surprises are no longer surprises. They're expected. How they happen I think sometimes surprises you.

I've been surprised as we've deployed the modular—any time you deploy new technology and a new way of doing things, especially in as risk adverse of a marketplace as IT professionals tend to be, though they're tasked with technology which is always innovative and always new they tend to be very careful about it— how quickly customers as we show them the traditional way of doing it and the modular, how quickly they're willing to move to the new way.

I've also been surprised at the operational efficiencies that we've picked up that I didn't fully appreciate with the modular approach versus traditional. Most important in that is the standardization. All of the components are the same. They're in the same spot. They're manufactured the same way. That you can blindfold a technician and take him from one Data Center module to the next one and it's exactly the same. What has surprised me is not that it's standardized, because we knew that when we built them. What it has resulted in is the operational utility of a Data Center operations tech has been greatly, greatly increased.

I was also surprised at how quickly this very large Data Center was filled. I continue to every day be—not shocked because it's not surprising—impressed at how quickly we're building IT infrastructure. It used to be business drove these things and I think now what we're seeing is consumers are now taking over the driver's seat in technology. It's showing up in businesses but it is being driven by consumers. Technology like the iPad and the iPhone and the consumer user experience are driving business and commerce to keep up. And what it's resulting in is just an enormous amount of capacity being deployed and very, very rapidly. Phase one here, 180,000 sq. ft. (16,722.5 sq. m) of raised floor and 24 MW of UPS we essentially took to 100 percent utilization in 16 months. I think that probably during the whole '60s and '70s and '80s there wasn't much more than that deployed. It's an enormous amount of capacity. Then when you think about the computational capacity of 24 MW, it's pretty extraordinary. And this is one Data Center.

"Technology like the iPad and the iPhone and the consumer user experience are driving business and commerce to keep up. It's resulting in an enormous amount of (Data Center) capacity being deployed and very, very rapidly."

That's an interesting point. Many companies are using virtualization and other technologies to make their Data Centers more efficient but their demand for capacity continues to grow. I jokingly call it the diet soda syndrome: it's half the calories so people drink two. Data Center efficiencies free up capacity, but companies immediately consume the savings. They're doing hundreds or even thousands of times the computing than they did before but aren't reducing their consumption of capacity.

There's a famous maxim that came out of the Industrial Revolution in the late 1800s. It basically says that humans are pre-ordained to take productivity and turn it into more work. Efficiency never shows up in a reduction in use. It shows up in more use. To exactly your point.

I can never remember the gentleman's name. I think he was a professor. His whole assessment was, now we've mechanized everything and we just do it all faster. We just do more. No one used the telephone to reduce the amount of time that you talk to people. You talk to more people, right? I always point that out to people. It's the same in the Data Center.

Back in my early days when I was in IT at a very fundamental level, the old joke was 'the development server.' There is no such thing because the minute you plug it into the wall it's in production. The minute you give a developer access to a device that users can connect to it's going to be in production before you know it. I think similarly we've done the same thing in Data Centers.

The design elements of this Data Center have obviously evolved over time. If you could go back in time to when you started with the site is there anything you would do differently?

We no longer will even do traditional Data Center build anymore. It's all modular. And after seeing it and deploying it and operationalizing it and all these other things at this point in time and knowing the underlying economics of it and what's it's done for us from a commercial perspective, I would never go back to building a traditional Data Center again.

Is there any final advice that you would offer someone if they're setting out on a Data Center project?

Don't buy an eight-track tape, the iPod's out. There are companies that have modular technology, including ours. I'm now such a believer in the technology after it has been deployed and we have operationalized it that my advice would be think long and hard before you start down the path of a traditional construction-based Data Center. At this point in time you'd be better off to wait six or eight more months and see how this continues to play out than to start down the path that's going to cost an extraordinary amount of money and by the time it's done could be two generations or three generations old.

FIGURE 14-6   Overhead structured cabling bundles in IO's Phoenix Data Center.

FIGURE 14-7   Standby generators provide backup power for the Tier III Data Center.

FIGURE 14-8   Cooling infrastructure for a Data Center module.

FIGURE 14-9   Assembly of IO's Data Center modules.

FIGURE 14-10   Fire suppression controls and a badge reader adorn the side of a Data Center module.

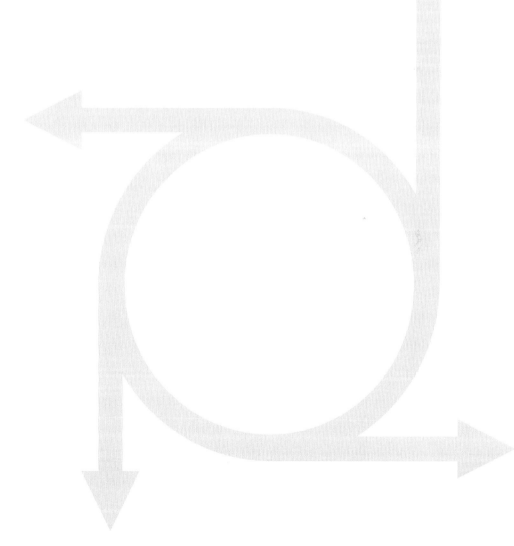

FIGURE 15-1   NetApp's Data Center in Research Triangle Park, North Carolina was the first to earn
the Energy Star for Data Centers rating from the U.S. Environmental Protection Agency.
Images provided courtesy of NetApp.

CHAPTER 15
NetApp

ORGANIZATION: NetApp	
LOCATION: Research Triangle Park, North Carolina	
ONLINE: March 2009	
NOTABLE FEATURES: Pressure control governance of airflow to cabinets, airside economizer, data hall cold rooms, 52U racks, rotary UPS system. Energy Star-rated Data Center.	
TIME TO DESIGN AND BUILD: 19 months	
SIZE: 125,000 sq. ft. (11,612.9 sq. m) total building space, with 33,000 sq. ft. (3,065.8 sq. m) of hosting space	
POWER: 25 MW	
TIER: III	
CABINET LOCATIONS: 2136	
POWER DENSITY: 12 kW average per cabinet, 42 kW maximum	
INFRASTRUCTURE DELIVERY: Power, cooling, and cabling infrastructure are delivered overhead	
STRUCTURAL LOADING: 185 lb. per sq. ft. (903.2 kg per sq. m)	
FIRE SUPPRESSION SYSTEM: Double-interlock dry-pipe	

Pressure, as the saying goes, makes diamonds. Air pressure apparently makes energy-efficient Data Centers.

Computer storage and data management company NetApp's innovative use of air pressure to regulate cooling helped its Data Center in North Carolina become the first ever to earn an Energy Star designation from the U.S. Environmental Protection Agency.

Although energy efficient the facility doesn't lack for power. The Data Center provides 25 MW for occupants—up to 42 kW in its 52U racks—and averages 770 watts per square foot (8,288.2 watts per square meter) of cooling.

Much of this is accomplished thanks to NetApp's use of an airside economizer as well as the vertical layout of the Data Center. NetApp placed the air handlers on the second level where they pump chilled air into designated cold rooms in the data halls below. Local weather conditions allow outside air to cool the Data Center about two-thirds of each year.

Mark Skiff, senior director of East Coast Tech Sites for NetApp, discusses the Data Center's unique air pressure control system and other features.

The U.S. Environmental Protection Agency established the Energy Star rating for Data Centers in 2010. Facilities are scored on a 100-point scale and earn the Energy Star designation if they are among the top 25 percent of their peers in energy efficiency.

The Energy Star Program, begun in 1992 to highlight energy efficient products, was initially applied to computers and monitors and later expanded—involving participation from the U.S. Department of Energy and applying to office equipment, major appliances, lighting, home electronics, new homes, commercial and industrial buildings, and more.

The Interview

What role does this Data Center serve for NetApp?

When we first set out to build this Data Center—it's a greenfield site on an existing parcel of land where we have some office buildings in RTP (Research Triangle Park)—the purpose was for it to support our internal research and development, so (it was to be) more of a lab environment. A lab environment is a little less rigorous in terms of infrastructure redundancy than a corporate Data Center.

But shortly before occupying the building, shortly before its completion, which was around January 2009, we were asked to retrofit a portion of it for corporate IT. So one of the things I think that is interesting or unique about the Data Center is that it's a multi-tenant Data Center. It has corporate IT, which is high availability with fully redundant on-site power systems with UPS (uninterruptible power supply), and that's physically about one-sixth of the Data Center. Comparatively speaking it's a relatively big Data Center. It's not the biggest in the world but it's about 33,000 sq. ft. (3,065.8 sq. m) of cabinet space and capacity of about 25 MW of equipment load. That's pretty good size and the corporate IT takes up one-sixth of that. So about 360 of the racks in the building—there are 2,200 racks, roughly, in total—are for corporate IT and the balance of the racks or about 1,800 are for product development R&D effort to support our product.

I assume those tenants have different operational models. What measures do you have in place that help them co-exist in your Data Center?

We have basically swimming pool rules, that there are certain things that you can do and can't do. For example, you wouldn't want to uncrate equipment up in the white space and create a lot of particulates.

Even though the space is all contiguous white space internally, we actually use a cold room versus a cold aisle (and in) our rooms for the corporate Data Center the front of the cabinets are card access controlled. So there's physical separation and security between the general white space and then the corporate IT white space. We installed doors on the hot aisles as well with card readers that, again, physically in a secure way isolate the space.

Like you say, the R&D environment is a little bit more dynamic than the corporate Data Center and the change control requirements are obviously a little tighter for the corporate Data Center but from a Facilities perspective we tend to do a lot of the same things. We're still concerned about let's say transformer load balancing loads compared to the rated ampacity of the breakers.

We don't treat them terribly different although our experience is that the Data Center people are more disciplined in terms of if you tell them how the infrastructure works they're going to adhere to it versus the R&D guys, for them to string cabling in a weird way or to connect things that are fed from different power services in a way that's not the greatest is more common just because there are a lot more people you're dealing with. That's how we deal with it. It hasn't been too much of an issue with having two users.

At what point in the design process was it decided to pursue the Energy Star certification?

We learned about the Energy Star portfolio manager initiative early on. I came here to NetApp in 2005. I was involved in a lot of the Energy Star work in D.C. with the EPA for commercial office buildings in my previous life so I was pretty well aware of the program. Through that we had certified our office buildings and we got to know about this benchmarking program and I think that was in the 2009 timeframe.

Ultimately the program rolled out in June or July of 2010 and we were part of the benchmarking program—I think there were around 100 Data Centers because they were trying to develop the parameters of what was large or small and was it important to take into account geography and climate or if you had UPS or not UPS, if you had economizers, et cetera. As they developed the program parameters and did their sensitivity analysis we were a part of that and as soon as we found out the program was alive we easily qualified. I think at the time we submitted our first year of data, where our IT loads weren't as quite as high as they are today, we were running an annualized PUE of 1.35. We recently surpassed 1.2 and now run a 1.17 PUE for the most recent 12 months of operating data.

FIGURE 15-2   Cold room enclosures isolate hot and cold airflow for greater efficiency in NetApp's Research Triangle Park Data Center.

Because you were able to easily qualify did the fact that you wanted it to be an Energy Star-rated site have a significant impact on the design?

No, because the design really pre-dated any information we had that they were going to roll out a program on the Data Center. Back in 2006 we actually developed a fairly high density Data Center in one of our existing office buildings. It was a 3 MW facility and the average watts per square foot was around 500 (5,382 watts per square meter), which was fairly high, 8 kW per rack. We were able to achieve that by enclosing the cold aisle and using at the time a fairly unique differential pressure control scheme for managing the air that was delivered to the cold room. This continues to be a pretty unique approach in the industry in terms of feeding only the quantity of air to the cabinets that the racked equipment is going to actually consume. That enables us, together with the direct outside air/free cooling, to keep our PUEs really at a minimum.

Back when we built a prototype lab we had proved the concept of metering exactly the amount of air to the cabinet as required based on differential static pressure and then when we built this new Data Center what we wanted to do is increase the density to 770 watts a foot (8,288.2 watts per square meter), which was 12 kW per cabinet. We actually can do up to 42 kW in a cabinet with the pressure control approach. The other thing we wanted to do was get the air handlers closer to the load, so rather than them sit at the ends of the hot aisles they were moved to directly on top of the cold aisles or cold room, with no duct work. Then we added the outside air/free cooling capability which enables us to cool the equipment about 70 percent of the year with no chiller.

Really, the desire was to make it more energy efficient and a higher density. The thing we found out by building a vertically-oriented building and compacting 25 MW in a 1 acre (.4 hectare) footprint our construction cost wound up being about a third what the Uptime Institute says it should cost for a Tier III Data Center. From a total cost of ownership this facility, both because it has a low PUE and because our construction cost was about $7,000 per kilowatt for Tier III, the cost as we measure it internally—we look at cost per kW per month delivered to our user—works out to about $60 per month for corporate IT here. That is about one-tenth the cost of what we pay at a co-lo and it's significantly less than what we pay internally in other sites where we have Data Centers that we have built and own within NetApp.

You bring up a feature of your facility that I definitely want to talk about, which is controlling air pressure to regulate air volume in the Data Center. I think there's the understanding in the Data Center industry that in many cases we're using a brute-force approach to cooling. We throw a tremendous amount of cold air at something and then hopefully evacuate hot air exhaust...

It doesn't work. You're only going to consume what the equipment is going to pass through it. And that was the 'aha' back in 2006 when I got here. I started looking at the cooling coil design parameters and then we did some measurements on the racked equipment. Our cooling coils were designed for 10 or 12 degrees and the equipment was seeing 20 to 25. What that says is you're delivering a lot more air and assuming that it's only going to go through a 10 degree rise on the coil. What happens is you oversupply, like you say, the equipment and you just get a lot of mixing and turbulence. We deliver everything from overhead. The more air you try to jam to the cabinet the more entrainment of hot air you get from the hot aisle when you don't have any physical separation between the cold and the hot as we've done with the cold rooms. What we basically do is put doors and a little bit of fascia above the cabinets and drop the ceiling down. The construction cost is miniscule compared to the mechanical and electrical.

That's how we got there. We said, 'This is ridiculous.' Even Liebert units and some other custom type air handlers, the coils are designed for 16 degrees or so and if the equipment's seeing 20 you're missing it by a pretty wide margin.

I think anyone designing Data Centers nowadays understands hot and cold airflow isolation techniques, but what's the best way for someone to determine if they're oversupplying air to their server environment or whether the air pressure is optimal?

When people are doing the containment, unless they exactly match the air they're going to have over-pressurization or they're going to starve the equipment. I haven't heard of really anybody doing it based upon differential static pressure. People are still trying to use temperature in the hot aisle or thermal information from the equipment maybe. For air conditioning, capacity is a function of temperature and flow. If the equipment only is going to take a certain amount of flow then that's really your only option then, to match the flow. And the temperature you select to provide, for us it's all based on our desire to economize our operation. We try to make it as hot as we can without cooking the people that are working in the hot aisle. Because the equipment can take much warmer air than the people can stand.

"We try to make it as hot as we can without cooking the people that are working in the hot aisle. Because the equipment can take much warmer air than the people can stand."

I'm not out there every day looking at Data Centers that have containment but everything I read online tells me that they probably do have an issue with pressure and flow. If they're doing it with an air curtain, let's say, probably their curtains are flapping open or whatnot.

So, to answer your question, I hear a lot as people come through the facility and we have hundreds that come through here in a year's time, organizations that are customers or partners or prospects. They talk a lot about temperature control and they look at what we've done and it's an 'aha' to them that this is the way it should be done or one way that is an effective way to do it.

FIGURE 15-3
Pressure differential transmitter used in NetApp's RTP Data Center for cold room pressurization (right) and mezzanine pressure controlled relief air (left).

What made you decide to operate your Data Center at 74 degrees Fahrenheit (23.3 Celsius)? I know of many companies running their server environments warmer than that and of many companies running them cooler.

There are several drivers for that. Of course the warmer we can make the cold room the more we can use outside ambience, because if it's 75 (23.9 Celsius) outside and we're using 74 or 75 (23.3 or 23.9 Celsius) degrees supply as long as the outside air is cooler than the return air we're going to use the outside air. And with a 20 degree rise—let's say it's 85 (29.4 Celsius) outside—it still makes sense to take 85 degree (29.4 Celsius) air and cool it to 75 (23.9 Celsius) because the air coming back is 95 (35 Celsius), right? Obviously we want to make it as warm as we can but the limiting factor, like I said earlier, becomes how warm can you make it in the hot aisle before people get too hot?

We found that 95 degrees (35 Celsius) is about the limit, and particularly when you're bringing in outside air in the summertime that has a fair amount of humidity in it. It tends to get pretty warm. In fact, even though it's cooler in the winter and we could make a 60 degree (15.6 Celsius) cold room if we wanted, our folks working in there would get used to that 80 degree (26.7 Celsius) air in the hot aisle and then they would really complain a lot. And 95 (35 Celsius) in the summertime is certainly not an OSHA issue and if you dress appropriately it's not a hazardous condition. It's more a personal preference. We try not to float things too far down in the winter—we might go down to 70 (21.1 Celsius) because it's still free and then we'll float up to 75 (23.9 Celsius) in the summer.

The other thing that we're doing is by having higher temperatures we never really try to get to the dew point where we're taking moisture out of the air, which from a Data Center perspective the equipment doesn't really understand latent cooling and humidity as long as you don't have it too high or have a condensing environment. Our objective is not to do any condensing at the cooling coil and waste more energy.

Again, if you look at the typical Data Center that's running a 55 degree Fahrenheit (12.8 Celsius) supply, about a third of the work being done could be latent cooling, or at least the rated capacity of that cooling coil is based on about a third of the work being latent cooling. That's probably not the case because most Data Centers are built pretty tight and there's not a lot of moisture infiltration but there's going to be some because you're introducing outside air for ventilation and whatnot. Those are really the drivers for why we picked 75 (23.9 Celsius).

The other thing is, if you get up to 80 (26.7 Celsius) what you see is a lot of the equipment the way it's built will actually internally speed up the fans and the fans can be a fairly high proportion of the energy used by the racked equipment. We haven't had a chance to study it to a high degree but we know that the incremental energy used, once we get to 80 (26.7 Celsius) and we start triggering these fan speeds up, offsets the gain we get on not running the chiller.

Is the design of this Data Center a standard for NetApp going forward? Are the technologies that are being used repeatable at other locations or are they specific to this particular site and its climate and other conditions?

That's a really good question. In 2006 we built this prototype room with the differential pressure control and high density and then shortly after that we built a lab in Sunnyvale, California, based on that concept and added a free cooling capability to it. It was sort of the next generation to what we did here in '06. They have some issues there with trying to get the exhaust air out of the building because it was built within an existing office building and they had to create a chase—as you bring in outside air you got to get rid of air you're not using anymore from the hot aisle.

There are a few hiccups but this building, because it was a green field, we didn't have that issue. The whole second story of the building is the air handling that is able to get the air out of the sides of the buildings as we bring raw air in from the roof.

So, to address your question, would we do (this design) in any location we choose to build another Data Center? It depends, because some locations—it gets back to the issue of using ambient air for free cooling—if you have salts, if you have corrosives, if you have high particulates, maybe not such a great idea. This is a great location for doing free cooling in that we're in a suburban business park with pretty good air quality. The only issue we run into about a week a year is pollen. Not that pollen is difficult to filter, but pollen is just pervasive and we found that it gets around some of the filter rack. One thing we did here is we used a commercial type air handler and saved a lot of money by using it and it does by and large a pretty good job but the filter rack that the filters sit in have a lot of bypass so we've had some issues with the filtration of the pollen. That being said, it's probably cheaper to run the chillers one week a year than it is to change 3,500 filters.

If you could go back and design the Data Center all over again what, if anything, would you do differently?

Functionally, the only thing we would do differently is to add a pre-filter to the filter rack to address the pollen issue.

There's probably a half a dozen things we could do to make the building work a little bit better. They're so minor in some respects that I don't think it would be meaningful to really go through them.

On the other side of it there's a few things we could do cost-wise to even reduce the cost beyond where we have it today and still have the functionality. But the building, when we built it, the total cost was around $66 million and we had less than 1 percent change orders. So, it was a pretty interesting process and I would say by and large we haven't really done anything in two years to address any issues. We're wrestling with this filter-rack thing now and it's probably a couple-hundred thousand dollar type of fix but when we started the whole process actually back in March of 2007 (when) I was told to build this building I interviewed some name-brand Data Center consultants and each of them that came here wanted to build a single-story building about 15 acres (6.1 hectares) in size to handle 25 MW.

At the end of the day we built this 1 acre (.4 hectare), three-level building and we did it with a local architect and a design firm that does a lot of biotech, because to me it was more of a high-volumes-of-air, big-chilled-water-plant design issue for mechanical/electrical plumbing than it was a Data Center. We actually used a general contractor that had never built a Data Center, somebody that we had worked with on some office fit-ups. The message there is we didn't buy into any pre-conceived notions. NetApp was very involved as the project manager of the building and every decision that was made.

We didn't even know for sure what it was going to cost us. We're not in this business, right? We just used the prototype building costs and sort of said 'This is going to be four times bigger and we're going to need a shell and we think it's going to cost x.' Prior to the modification for the corporate Data Center we had a $45 million budget not including the racks and PDUs and we brought it in at $44 million. It was just an interesting project, but not knowing what it would cost every step of the way we looked for opportunities to save in the construction. At the end of the day, functionally it has worked (with) very high availability and low cost of ownership.

What helped you get from those original estimates of a 15-acre (6.1 hectares) Data Center down to just 1 acre (.4 hectare)?

Well, most Data Centers are 150 or 200 watts a foot (1,614.6 or 2,152.8 watts per square meter), so you're talking about 4 kW a rack. Maybe a more modern

Data Center might be trying to get to 7 or 8. We were doing 12. By using the pressure control we were able to get the higher density, the 770 watts a foot (8,288.2 watts per square meter). Being able to get two or three times the kw per rack that most Data Centers can get shrank the footprint and then by going with a three-level building where the air handlers sit right on top of the load and the utilities are all in the basement, you divide that by two-thirds. Those two things really enabled us to get from 15, 17 acres (6.1, 6.9 hectares) down to one (.4 hectare).

FIGURE 15-4
NetApp installed commercial grade air handlers rather than customer Data Center models, saving about $10 million in capital costs.

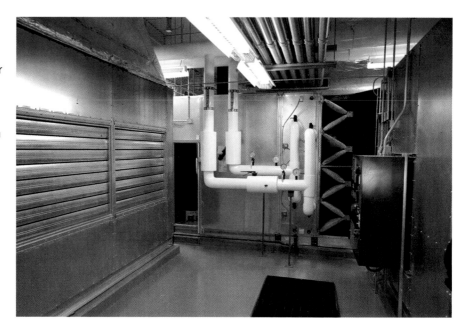

I saw that you scored 99 out of a possible 100 points on the Energy Star scoring. First, let me say congratulations. Second, though, I have to ask: what was the one point that you missed?

It's not a point based system, it's a performa that they create. We've gone back in and put in our numbers today and we're at 100 based on our PUE being lower.

I'm not a proponent of someone chasing a higher score on a Data Center metric—PUE, LEED, et cetera—by doing things that don't truly make their Data Center more efficient, but was there any point in your project where you had to make a decision whether to incorporate certain design elements to achieve a higher score versus its cost or merits?

That's a good question. Really the thing that drives the cost effectiveness of the Data Center is the airside economizer. It's going to give you a lot more free cooling hours than a waterside economizer. There are pluses and minuses to each. If your ambient air is not good quality or you could use one in combination with the other, but we know at 25 MW even in a moderately priced utility state like North Carolina the free cooling, the PUE difference between let's say a 1.8 and a 1.2 is $6 million a year and that's going to buy a lot of features. Frankly, putting an economizer on an air handler is almost no cost. It involves a connection between the air handler and outside air and a mixing chamber. You're talking something that's clearly less than $1 million to do that.

Another things we've done is the containment. The cost to do that is 1 or 2 percent of the project cost so, again, it's a no-brainer to use the pressure control, limit your fan horsepower, et cetera. It wasn't anything where we modeled a lot. We looked some different things up front but we were also trying to build a building pretty quick. We interviewed architects and engineers in April of 2007 and delivered a building in December of 2008 so we didn't have a lot of time to say 'We're going to explore or model A, B, and C.' At the same time, we had the prototype and we had a clear vision of what we were going to do.

Is there any advice that you would offer someone as to how to approach a Data Center project?

The whole project teaming is the most critical element of doing this. NetApp, being a relatively young company without a lot of baggage and pre-conceived notions and being rewarded because your boss did it a certain way, we had an advantage, I think. The culture of the company is innovation. Probably the fact that it started off as a lab versus a Data Center, it was a lot easier to convince the R&D guys who were my customers than it may have been corporate IT which tends to be more conservative. I think just generally based on what I've seen talking to people, the more mature cultures look at this and say 'I get it, but I would never be able to make this happen' versus younger West Coast-type companies where the early adopters they tend to be doing these sorts of things.

All of the Data Center's physical infrastructure overhead—there's no raised floor—and you're using very tall cabinets, at 52U. Did you encounter any challenges in routing and terminating it all?

No. Most of the cabling is all fiber and we're heavily into the Cisco Nexus switches so if you look at the cable plant it's actually pretty minimal. There is a cable tray system that connects everything, but like I say it's fiber. You wonder why we have all these big heavy cable trays for a little bit of fiber.

If you look in to the cold room through the door what you're going to see is 30 cabinets on the right and 30 cabinets on the left separated by a 46-in. (116.8-cm.) aisle. Up above that, down the center in about 6 in. (15.2 cm.) in a drop ceiling is your lighting and fire suppression. And then on either side of that is basically an architectural grid that simply is there for aesthetics and the air handlers sit above that on variable speed drives and they pump the required amount of air based on the static pressure.

That's all that's going on in the cold room, it's pretty clean. It's about an 8 ft. 9 in. (2.7 m.) ceiling. When you get into the hot aisle, now you have a 16 ft. (4.9 m.) clear height where you have above the cabinets the busways and the cable plant and then some lighting. It's very clean.

The one by-product of having the containment is it's very quiet versus most high-density Data Centers are very noisy—you can't talk. Here because you have doors on the cold room it's really an effective acoustic treatment.

If someone wanted to fully load one of your 52U cabinets, what's the greatest power density you can support at a given individual cabinet location?

Here's what I always tell people. You look in the cold room, through the door, there's 720 kW of power. You can use it however you want in that room of up to 60 cabinets, you just can't have more than 42 kW in a particular cabinet.

The reason we can do that is, if you take a bathtub and you stick your arm into it you're not going to change the water level in that bathtub as much as you try. You might make some waves. If you put a cabinet in there with 42 kW of power and it's able to move the air through that cabinet the pressure in that room immediately backfills. You can't change the pressure in the room, it's physically impossible to do it.

Our only limitation with this pressure control idea is based on power distribution. The reason we get the 42 kW is every cabinet in this Data Center has two 21 kW power strips in it.

Your cooling system includes the capability to use wastewater from a nearby municipal treatment plant to serve as makeup water. Were there any challenges with incorporating wastewater?

To be quite honest with you, we're still waiting for them to turn the system on. So, we'll see. The issue you might have is the availability or are the contaminants higher than they're telling you? Are the contaminants variable?

With water treatment you sort of assume you got the same stuff you're having to treat. With wastewater, who knows if that will be the case. The reason we're using it is we don't want to be relying upon city water and we would like to have two sources.

Having this wastewater system—it's the town of Cary, Wake County and Durham County are developing for the RTP (Research Triangle Park) Business Park. It was a no-brainer for us to ask to be connected to it and use it as a primary source.

Any final advice?

Work closely with your internal customers and pick the right partners. In our case I think having partners that were doing the design for us be local was really important, versus somebody that had to fly in and it would have been a hardship to get together. Particularly in the beginning you're doing a lot of brainstorming in the design concept phase. Picking the right team and having a good partnership internally with the user is really critical.

FIGURE 15-5
A walkway between two server rows in NetApp's Research Triangle Park Data Center.

FIGURE 16-1   Syracuse University's Data Center is both a production server environment and a research facility. Images provided courtesy of Syracuse University.

CHAPTER 16

Syracuse University

ESSENTIAL DETAILS

ORGANIZATION: Syracuse University	
LOCATION: Syracuse, New York	
ONLINE: December 2009	
NOTABLE FEATURES: Microturbines powered by natural gas. A trigeneration system that produces cooling, heating, and power for the Data Center and nearby building. Use of direct current and alternating current power. Closed-loop water cooling system using rear-door heat exchangers and sidecar heat exchangers. LEED-Silver certified.	
TIME TO DESIGN AND BUILD: 14 months	
SIZE: 12,000 sq. ft. (1,114.8 sq. m) total, with 6,000 sq. ft. (557.4 sq. m) of hosting space.	
POWER: Two redundant 750 kW feeds; IT usable capacity of 600 kW	
TIER: II	
CABINET LOCATIONS: 70	
POWER DENSITY: 8 kW average per cabinet, 35 kW maximum	
INFRASTRUCTURE DELIVERY: Structured cabling above cabinets. Electrical conduits, piping for liquid cooling system, and air cooling delivered under a 36-in. (91.4 cm.) deep raised floor.	
STRUCTURAL LOADING: 450 lb. per sq. ft. (2197 kg per sq. m)	
FIRE SUPPRESSION SYSTEM: Novec 1230	

Most modern server environments feature their share of redundant systems but few can match the belt and suspenders deployment of physical infrastructure solutions at Syracuse University's primary Data Center.

Built in 2009 to host IT academic and administrative systems for SU's 1,500 full- and part-time faculty members and nearly 20,000 students, the facility features both alternating and direct current power topologies, both liquid- and air-cooled cooling systems as well as both on-site power generation and utility power feeds. Such technologies are typically either-or choices for Data Centers, but here they're all used simultaneously.

That's because the 12,000 square foot (1,114.8 square meter) production facility also functions as a sophisticated test bed for University researchers to analyze Data Center electrical and mechanical systems at work. Researchers are using the collected data to develop models and simulation tools to monitor, manage, and even predict Data Center energy usage.

Not surprisingly, the Data Center has been designed to be extremely energy efficient. It employs twelve 65 kW natural-gas powered microturbines for primary power, two 150-ton absorption chillers, and two heat exchangers that together form a trigeneration system that not only provides chilled water for the Data Center but also warms the 92,000 square foot (8547.1 square meter) building next door. (In all, the system generates 4.1 million BTUs of byproduct heat.)

Chris Sedore, Vice President for Information Technology and Chief Information Officer for Syracuse University, discusses the challenges and lessons learned from designing and building the dual-purpose Data Center.

The Interview

I understand that in addition to this Data Center being a production facility, you use it to measure the efficiency of Data Center systems. It's almost a test bed for what other Data Centers can do.

It absolutely is. I'm not aware of another facility that's been built like this, with that intent. I've seen ones that are pure research-oriented, in which you build it and you put test loads in and experiment. And there are obviously lots of production Data Centers. But this merger I think is fairly unique.

It really drives a lot of the analysis and design choices we made here, to say 'Where do we need to instrument and how do we need to instrument to make sure we can measure this?' A lot of the benchmarks that are out there now, they're good but they're maybe not as scientific as our researchers would like them to be.

Can you give me an example of some of the things that are being measured with this Data Center?

I say tongue-in-cheek that we measure everything. That's a little bit of an overstatement, but we have a lot of instrumentation. If you look on the power distribution side, all the way from the grid connection or the turbines down through that power distribution chain to the outlets in the racks, we can measure power consumption. For the servers that we're installing, the majority of them, you can also ask the server 'How much power do you consume?' So, you can look all along that chain at what the performance of the system is. Similarly, in the cooling space it's heavily instrumented to let us know how the cooling system is performing. It's really this notion of collecting large quantities of data about performance of different portions of the system. The piece we're working on now is basically how do we take all this data, crunch it, and use it for both operational purposes and also for research ones.

LEED Certification

Leadership in Energy and Environmental Design (LEED) is a rating system for the design, construction, and operation of green buildings. Facilities can achieve ratings of certified, silver, gold, or platinum based on criteria within six categories: sustainable sites, water efficiency, energy and atmosphere, materials and resources, indoor environmental quality, and innovation and design.

For that research portion, once you have that data and you've been able to do with it what you want, what's the intent? Is this something that is to be shared with people who you might host in the facility? Is it to be shared with the public so that the Data Center industry as a whole can learn from it?

Certainly that's our hope, that we will share what we learn in various ways. One of our traditional outlets, of course, is academic publishing. So we hope to produce articles from our researchers and graduate students talking about various ways to be efficient in the Data Center. One of the drives there is to understand—and this is an issue with construction of Data Centers as well as buildings in general—(why) designs don't often perform exactly the way that they say they will. We really want to be in position to help refine those models so that they're more sophisticated in terms of what outcomes you get based on particular design inputs.

What is Syracuse University's overall Data Center strategy? Is this facility going to meet your needs for the foreseeable future or do you have plans for building out additional server environments?

From a prime computing perspective, what I said (when planning the Data Center) was 'I expect that this will comfortably meet our needs for 5 years, from a power and cooling perspective. And I believe that it will meet our space needs for 10 years.' The power and cooling is a lot harder to predict than the physical space is. I didn't have to sign in blood on those things, but the projections led us to that place.

So, I don't see us constructing additional Data Centers as prime capacity items. However, we are likely to build a secondary Data Center that is smaller that houses core network equipment for our North Campus and also serves as a backup Data Center for key systems.

FIGURE 16-2
The data hall
within Syracuse
University's Data
Center.

Your facility doesn't neatly fit into the traditional tier classification system for Data Centers. What drove your decisions regarding which physical infrastructure components to have redundant?

That's a great question. One of the things we did in constructing this Data Center was to not necessarily be driven by rules of thumb or best practice. And I don't mean to say that those things are necessarily bad. But we were really looking to try to optimize everything that we could in the design of this facility. When we looked at where to build in redundancy it was a risk-based approach. What components do we think are likely to fail? We looked at service history for microturbines, for example.

"One of the things we did in constructing this Data Center was to not necessarily be driven by rules of thumb or best practice...we were really looking to try to optimize everything that we could in the design of this facility."

One of my big pieces in Data Center design is, I need it to be flexible. So, if we need to make a change to the power system, I want it to be a pluggable infrastructure. It's the same design principles we use for IT, but at least in some places—and fortunately that's not true here—facilities (components) don't necessarily get designed with the same notion. You pour the concrete and that's what you deal with rather than saying 'Well, if we design this a little differently we would have a lot more flexibility.'

Back to your question, from a redundancy perspective we tried to look at the known performance characteristics, known risk characteristics for all the elements of the system, and then base our redundancy decisions on those characteristics.

You mention microturbines. Tell me about those. That's one of the features of this facility that I think is interesting and an element that you don't see in a lot of Data Centers.

Microturbines, they're really fascinating pieces of technology. They're essentially small jet engines. People run them on different things: natural gas, diesel fuel, landfill gas, and lots of other input fuels. In our case, we have 12 of these units. They're nominally 65 kW per unit and they produce electricity and they produce hot exhaust.

Ours are a little unique because the way that ours are assembled they also serve as the UPS (uninterruptible power supply) for the facility. Because of the nature of how the inverters in them are constructed, we can plug a battery array in the center of the flow of the turbine and let them draw from batteries to also produce the power needs of the Data Center.

FIGURE 16-3
Primary power
for Syracuse
University's Data
Center comes
from twelve 65
kW hybrid UPS
microturbines.

What prompted you to use microturbines as a primary power source rather than going with the conventional setup of commercial power feeding your Data Center and a generator behind it?

When you look at on-site electrical generation, if you look at it straight from a 'I need electricity and how can I best get it?' perspective, it's hard to beat the grid in most places. But you have to look at the full picture of where the electricity is generated to the point of use in your Data Center facility, to look at the losses all the way along that chain. This is a concern for us as an institution because we're a Presidents' Climate Commitment signatory. We're really trying to look at our environmental footprint.

The American College and University Presidents' Climate Commitment is an initiative to make higher education campuses sustainable and reduce their greenhouse gas emissions. Syracuse University was one of 152 charter signatories of the ACUPCC in 2007. As part of the initiative, the University in 2009 issued a Climate Action Plan that includes the goal of becoming carbon neutral by 2040.

NOTE

If you're running a coal-fired electrical plant, you're sending a lot of heat out the stack as waste, essentially, where in our case we're actually able to use that byproduct of the generation process either to provide cooling for the Data Center or to provide heat for the adjacent facility. So we actually get a better full utilization of the energy than we would otherwise and it makes that cost picture look different.

Please explain your trigeneration system, which encompasses cooling, heat, and power for the Data Center.

If you look at a flow picture, you have the natural gas flowing into the microturbines, electricity coming out to feed the Data Center floor, and then the heat byproduct goes to one of two places. One is just a heat exchanger that turns that hot exhaust into hot water that we can use for heating next door. The other is to this really neat device that's called an absorption chiller that takes that hot exhaust and turns it into chilled water. It's like a propane refrigerator, if you've ever heard of such a thing. It's really a heat-driven engine that produces chilled water. Our chilled water capacity is about 300 tons, so it's a lot of cooling in that space. Probably not enough for every possible scenario in terms of the adjacent building, but it's enough the majority of the time to cool the Data Center at full load as well as the adjacent building.

FIGURE 16-4   Electrical switchgear for Syracuse University's Data Center routes power from turbines to hardware, from turbines to backup batteries to keep them fully charged, and from batteries to turbines to restart any that are idle.

If someone was building a Data Center facility and they were looking to use this sort of system, but they didn't have a building nearby to be able to use the excess capacity—say they have a standalone Data Center—does that reduce the benefits of this solution so that it's not advantageous to use?

It's a great question. It depends. There are really a couple of dimensions that you look at there. One is the cost of electricity where you're constructing. We call this spark spread, which is the difference in cost between buying it and generating it. If you happen to be in an area where you can buy natural gas very inexpensively and electricity tends to be quite expensive—and there are places like this—then the system can make sense just based on the power needs for the Data Center as well as the byproduct cooling. So, you're not getting full advantage but you get the cooling out of it.

There's a climate aspect to it. If you're in Arizona where you really need cooling all the time, then it works well. On the other hand, if you were in northern Canada then all you're really getting is electricity because you can use outside air for cooling a good portion of the time so maybe it doesn't work so well. So, you have to factor those things in.

The other thing that matters for some Data Center owners is that their utilities can't give them any more power. For whatever reason, their location in a metro area, et cetera, they may not be able to get enough power into their facility. So if you have a Data Center in let's say Manhattan, and you've got 30,000 sq. ft. (2,787 sq. m) that you can't put equipment on because you don't have electricity, it may be worth doing this even if you're throwing away some of those byproducts because otherwise the real estate utilization is such a problem. You really have to understand the investment in many dimensions in order to know whether it's the right choice.

Another thing that you can do with this (trigeneration) is, rather than use it totally as prime or only as backup is you use it as a base load piece. So let's say I had a 1 MW Data Center facility, I might put in half a megawatt worth of generation capacity, use all of the cooling—because then I can use 100 percent because essentially every bit of power used in IT equipment turns into heat. So, I'm not going to generate 100 percent of my electrical need but I'll generate 50 percent that the byproduct gives me 100 percent of my cooling. That's a very common way to use cogeneration or trigeneration systems because they do a nice job of providing that mix.

When outside temperatures are low enough, you can leverage outside cooling for your needs. How many days per year do you anticipate being able to use it?

We anticipate 120 days per year of cooling will be possible from using heat exchangers with outside air.

What operational temperature, at the server inlet, are you aiming for in this Data Center?

It's interesting that you ask that. One of the analysis tasks for us is to look at what is the optimal inlet temperature. There are these interesting issues that happen. There has been a lot of work to say we should be raising Data Center floor temperatures. The consensus is that that's a good thing and I don't intend necessarily to argue with that consensus. But, with the way that we're doing cooling it isn't necessarily clear what the optimal point will be on the curve. You start to look at what the efficiency profile of your air conditioning units is. In a traditional Data Center you have to look at your air handlers, whether they're CRACs (computer room air conditioners) or CRAHs (computer room air handlers), and the energy you're spending blowing air around. That optimization can look a little different when you're using rear door or sidecar heat exchangers because it might make sense to maybe run it a little higher, it might make sense to run it a little lower. You really have to analyze this to know the answer to that question.

I can't quote any of these for a variety of reasons right now, but I know that when we've done some of the modeling work some of the results have been counterintuitive. So we want to make sure that before we set that design point that we're getting the optimal efficiency from it.

You have hinted at the liquid cooling solution that you're using in the Data Center. My understanding is that this was customized for this site. How was that developed?

The partnership behind this was really Syracuse University and IBM. The rear door and sidecar exchangers are an IBM creation, at least the ones that we're running.

We partnered with IBM to look at how to put this cooling system together. IBM has been doing liquid cooling since the '70s. It's kind of fun to work with them because they pull out documents that are literally 30 to 40 years old that talk about issues and concerns and design parameters for these. But we also did some things that are new and unique that were brought both by our own experience with building facilities as well as IBM's in terms of variable speed drives for our pumps and newer ways of doing instrumentation. I would say it was a partnership between Syracuse, IBM, and the two engineering firms on the project.

FIGURE 16-5   Hardware within Syracuse University's Data Center. Shown are an IBM storage array, a mainframe that uses direct current power and a supercomputer with liquid cooling to the chip. The liquid cooling is integrated with the building's chilled water system. The three full-height rack doors on the left are rear-door heat exchangers.

In the Data Center industry the general take on liquid cooling is that it's more efficient than an air system but that it has a higher capital cost. There's also a lingering concern about water in the Data Center. Many folks have worked hard to keep liquid off of their floor and are hesitant to bring it back to the cabinet. Did you have any concerns along those lines?

Well, I'd be lying if I said I didn't have some concerns at least when we were starting down this road. But when you actually look at the systems that we're putting in place here, the truth is that there really is not a significant increase in the risks in operating a Data Center. If you look at our rear door exchangers, for example, we're doing the chilled water distribution under floor and the connections for the rear door and the sidecar exchangers are both down at the bottom. So, if you look at where we were likely to have a leak, it's all down below the place where we have equipment.

You go back and actually—again, IBM is a great resource in this—we did this for a long time and the record of these liquid cooling systems is actually pretty good. Were there zero incidents of problem? No. But frankly we have water issues in a number of places. One of the things that was interesting to me as we were beginning this design process was the number of Data Centers I visited that have sprinkler systems in them. The basic thing is, look, we're very unlikely to have a fire here and they have dry pipe systems, but when we looked at the cost of other fire suppression, we decided this is the better risk/reward ratio.

So, is it a concern? Yes. But I can tell you that if it's up to me I won't build another raised floor Data Center. I will do distribution overhead just to avoid the capital cost and other issues associated with a raised floor. And that includes putting chilled water overhead. If it's done right I don't think it's any significant risk profile we can't deal with.

You're using a direct current power topology in your Data Center. I have heard a lot of people talk about employing DC power because you can avoid the losses from converting from DC to AC and back to DC power again, but this is the first production Data Center I'm aware of to actually implement it. What prompted you to use it and what sort of savings are you seeing?

What prompted us to use it is really when you look at the chain of what happens to power in Data Centers. It is the conversions you speak of that are of concern here. Even down to the power supply of a machine where the first thing that happens when you enter a typical switching power supply is you take 120 volt or 240 volt AC and turn it in to nominally 385 or 400 volt DC so that you can step it through to produce what the machine needs. This is another place where the partnership with IBM mattered in the sense that we're working with them to look at next generations of this technology. We decided that we think there is a future for DC.

Certainly there are concerns about what equipment is available to run on DC. There are some folks who have vested interest in AC power saying the savings are really smaller. It's a case of, we think this is a direction that makes sense to go in the longer run. It's going to take some changes in the market space.

The other thing that's relevant here goes back to our conversation about on-site power generation. We did turbines because turbines are proven, their performance profile is well known and well understood, but also on the horizon is fuel cells. One of the things that's interesting about fuel cells is that they produce DC natively. So when we look at this developing in the next 10, 15 years we think that there's going to be an even bigger play for DC because you have the potential to go straight from the generation to the machine without any intervening steps. Fuel cells have a particularly great story in this regard. They work essentially like batteries, they're lots of small cells. If you want 400 volts you just assemble the right collection of them and you can have 400 volts output. The other thing about fuel cells that's really attractive from a Data Center perspective is that they are very, very reliable. So as that technology evolves and develops, as I think most of us expect that it will, there's going to be an even stronger play for DC power in the Data Center than there is now.

I should also say that the turbines can also natively generate DC, and this is something we're going to be playing with in the Data Center as well.

Do you have the option to provide AC power for the Data Center as well?

Oh, yeah. The distribution is that we have 500 kW of AC power and about 100 kW of DC power available to the floor. We can't get everything that we want to run in our Data Center DC power-equipped. So, the majority of the equipment in there we anticipate being AC-powered for at least the next few years.

Were there any special steps that you needed to take because you have both types of power going in to the facility?

A little bit. You want to make sure it's clear to your electrician what's what. In a typical Data Center you can look at a cable and know what it is. But in ours, given that we have both AC and DC power distribution, those folks have to be oriented. The distribution systems are a little different and there are some things that you have to know, but I was actually pleasantly surprised both in terms of the folks that worked with us on the construction but also our own (Syracuse University) electricians that this is not as big a deal in terms of a transition.

As a side note, that is also true because in the larger mechanical systems for buildings they're sort of blurring these lines anyway in terms of the large blowers and pumps and things you use as part of normal infrastructure. So, these electricians have to be pretty sophisticated folks generally. This is not as much of a curveball as you might think.

What lessons did you learn during the design and construction of the facility?

One of the things that I learned is, boy do you have to have the right team to do this kind of project. There are lots of architectural and engineering firms, Data Center design firms. You can hire them and get a great conventional Data Center, and even a reasonably efficient conventional Data Center, but if you want to color outside the lines, you really have to have a team that's comfortable with coloring outside the lines. That includes the CIO who has to be willing look at things and say 'Well, I know no one else has done this, but I'm looking at the way that this is arranged and the nature of the components and the track record and what's proven, et cetera. And I am willing to certify, yes I will run my production systems on that.'

Another piece I often mention, and this is particularly true for larger companies or institutions, is that you really have to have a great working relationship between your IT and your Facilities folks. I've had exposure to other institutions or organizations where that relationship is not so great. There's a clear black line between those two organizations—'I'm the provider and you're the consumer and what I do you don't need to worry about what I do.' Well, if you want to optimize Data Centers those things are intertwined in fairly sophisticated ways and that relationship needs to reflect that sophistication in terms of if you want to optimize you have to link those things at a pretty sophisticated level.

Were there any challenges or surprises that came up that you didn't expect when you started?

I was actually surprised at essentially how straightforward it was to get all of these folks working together on something that was so out of the box. The people were great, but also it was really a willingness to look at all of the different components. Most of what we have in this Data Center is stuff that's off the shelf from somewhere. There are a few things in there that we've done that are unique and you really can't find anywhere else in the world. The particular microturbines that we have out there now I believe they were first of a kind and so far are only of a kind, but they're going to be an off-the-shelf item now from Capstone (Turbine Corp.). Outside of those things, this was 'Let's look out there, find all these things and let's put them together in a way no one else has.' And that was maybe easier than I thought it would be at the outset.

This is a relatively young facility, but if you could go back and start the design all over again what, if anything, would you do differently?

Let me answer that question two different ways. If I look at doing it with the same mission—in other words I want it to be a research facility as well as a production Data Center—probably not very much. We really need all of the different aspects of what we have there to satisfy both of those missions.

If you said 'Hey, Chris, I want you to start again. I want you to build something that's equivalently efficient but it's really going to be a production Data Center' I would look seriously at dropping the raised floor. There probably are some other minor things we would look at. One of the things that we did do relatively quickly after we constructed it was we built some caged space inside the Data Center to accommodate researchers and others. We basically had to double the amount of caged space we had on the floor pretty quickly after we opened because demand for that kind of Data Center space was stronger than we had anticipated.

The other thing is that, this whole densification/virtualization has been playing out as we have been working through this process as well as the cloud side. My own analysis of buying cycles out of the cloud: if your utilization is above 60 percent, it's a pretty clear case you can do it cheaper on premise if we're just talking cycles. But I certainly would want to look at all of the options for providing the services that we have to provide if I was going to start again and do this today. We did look at leasing space, we looked at lots of other different options for doing this rather than construction. Even excluding the research part of what we wanted to do, it was really difficult to meet the needs that we had with what was available when we started this process a couple years ago.

This world is evolving pretty rapidly. For institutions Syracuse's size and maybe a little bigger and maybe a bit smaller, the ongoing Data Center strategy is going to be an interesting space to try to choose the right investment.

FIGURE 16-6   Two 150-ton absorption chillers help cool Syracuse University's Data Center.

I know you mentioned that the technologies in your Data Center, if they're not out-of-the-box now they soon will be. But you do have a lot of elements that I think set this Data Center apart from a traditional server environment. The microturbines, the trigeneration system, liquid cooling, the DC power—which of these do you see as being universal solutions that are appropriate for anyone to put in to their Data Center going forward and which do you think someone would need to pick and choose depending upon specific circumstances?

It really depends on some of the dimensions we talked about earlier. What does your electrical supply look like? Where are you located in terms of climate? I did a presentation for a tech conference for New York State folks and I said 'Look, if you're in New York State and you don't have an economizer, either an air economizer or a water economizer using outdoor cooling, you're really kind of crazy because you should always have this.'

My view is if you're building a Data Center of any size, I think you're going to have to do liquid cooling. It's not even really a matter of is it cost effective. The reality is when you get up to a range where your racks are, say, 30 kW it's very, very difficult to do that with raised floor airflow. You get to a point where the temperatures and the rate of flow, how much energy you're running with blowers, it just can't make sense any more. There are some who are looking forward further in to the future arguing we're going to have to go inside the boxes with the liquid once again. We have an IBM P575 where we've got liquid to the chip because that was the way that they needed to do it to make this work. I think on the liquid cooling side, that's another one from my perspective that you're going to have to do it because physics is going to demand it, but I also think from an energy perspective it works pretty much everywhere. Unfortunately for a lot of the vendors who send me offers to do CFD (computational fluid dynamic) models of my Data Center, all of those issues worrying about hot spots and the rest of that stuff, they just go away. So, operationally, in terms of risks and other sorts of concerns that you have those become non-issues.

I think that if you look across the spectrum at the generation side, that is less universally applicable. It's really a local optimization that you have to look in to and understand.

To DC power, I think this is a market evolution question. I had a conversation with one server manufacturer that I won't name and they said, basically, 'Look, if I can't sell a million units I can't make a business case for this.' There's going to need to be some instigation in the market that really drives an efficiency gain here and that may take 5 or 10 years. When people ask 'Should I put DC in?' I say generally if you have equipment that you know you can run on DC and it's sufficient to pay for itself at this point yes I would put in DC. If you don't have those characteristics in what you're doing, I would make provisions so that if you're planning on having a facility life that extends beyond 10 years that you're able to install it and operate it in that facility but it isn't something that I say generically everyone should be putting in now.

You have the goal that at some point this Data Center will be able to flexibly provision both its application workload and its cooling. Move the IT load, move the facility resource to be able to support it. How do you envision being able to accomplish this?

That's a great question. There really are two dimensions to that. One is the IT dimension. How do you distribute workload across the compute resources and storage resources and network resources that you have in your Data Center. For us, the big play here is in the virtualization space. We're doing experiments with VMware's vSphere product. They can automatically load balance, they can consolidate, they can actually turn physical servers on and off to add capacity or subtract capacity based on load. So, on the IT side it's really leveraging the tools that we have there to provide the right mix of redundancy and performance and energy efficiency.

On the Facilities side the challenge and the opportunity is to, number one, factor in the Facilities parameters in to those choices so that you can say 'Well, it would be best from a Facilities systems perspective if we could consolidate load geographically within the Data Center as well as just picking 10 different servers that are in 10 different racks as the destinations for it.' The other thing is, it's nice to be able to tell the Facilities systems what you're doing from a consumption perspective so that they can produce that optimally. And I'm not claiming that we have this now, but it's this kind of optimization that we're working to be able to perform. Some of it is here. VMware can do it, and we have a pilot environment where we're doing this auto-scaling experimentation.

If you're looking at larger enterprises, we already do this follow-the-sun approach with tech support. You could do maybe the reverse of that with your Data Center load and say 'When is electricity most available?' Well, typically it's most available at night in a particular region or continent, where people are asleep so energy usage goes way down. Why not just move your workload to where energy is the cheapest or the most available or maybe the greenest? That's the bigger scale version of this. Yeah, we can say that we can do it within Data Centers and optimize, but I think those same models and algorithms should be able to drive that on a global scale as well as within the Data Center scale.

Do you have any final thoughts that you would like to share regarding this facility or Data Center design practices in general?

Probably the parting thought that I would share is a challenge to CIOs, to be willing to try new things and, with appropriate due diligence, take some risks to build facilities that are new and innovative rather than sticking to what's known to be safe.

"Be willing to try new things and, with appropriate due diligence, take some risks to build facilities that are new and innovative rather than sticking to what's known to be safe."

FIGURE 16-7   A closeup of the Syracuse University Data Center building's outer wall.

FIGURE 16-8   Hot exhaust (585 degrees Fahrenheit/307 degrees Celsius) from microturbines flow through heat exchangers, shown here, producing hot water that is then piped to an adjacent building to heat it.

FIGURE 16-9   Air- and liquid-based cooling are delivered in Syracuse Unversity's Data Center below the 36-inch (91.4 centimeter) raised floor.

FIGURE 16-10   An IBM Rear Door Heat eXchanger "cooling door" removes heat from the hardware within a cabinet inside Syracuse University's Data Center.

FIGURE 17-1   Rooftop satellite dishes provide backup connectivity for Terremark's NAP (Network Access Point) of the Americas building. Images provided courtesy of Terremark.

CHAPTER 17
Terremark

ORGANIZATION: Terremark	
LOCATION: Miami, Florida	
ONLINE: June 2001	
NOTABLE FEATURES: One of the largest single-building Data Centers on the planet. Capable of withstanding Category 5 hurricane winds. Lightning prevention system that defends against strikes by discharging static electricity flares.	
TIME TO DESIGN AND BUILD: Ongoing	
SIZE: 750,000 sq. ft. (66,677.3 sq. m) total, with 600,000 sq. ft. (55,741.8 sq. m) of hosting space anticipated upon buildout.	
POWER: Designed for 70MW upon buildout	
TIER: III	
CABINET LOCATIONS: Varies by customer configuration	
POWER DENSITY: Varies by customer configuration	
INFRASTRUCTURE DELIVERY: Power and cooling are delivered under a raised floor, structured cabling is provided overhead.	
STRUCTURAL LOADING: 180 to 280 lb. per sq. ft. (878.8 to 1,367.1 kg per sq. m)	
FIRE SUPPRESSION SYSTEM: Pre-action dry pipe	

Terremark's flagship Data Center is a testimony to thinking big.

When the massive co-location facility known as the NAP (Network Access Point) of the Americas was proposed for construction in 2000, Terremark was a real estate development company with no Data Center design or operations experience. The dot-com bubble burst early that year, making the outlook for Internet-related companies—and co-location centers that rely upon them as customers—grim.

Despite that, Terremark moved in to the business in a big way, constructing one of the largest Data Centers on the planet. (The company now has about 50 facilities.) At 750,000 sq. ft. (66,677.3 sq. m) and with an anticipated 70 MW of electrical capacity upon buildout, the six-story building's capacity dwarfs what some high tech companies have for their entire global Data Center portfolio.

The immense structure features Tier III standby infrastructure, server cabinets up to 10 ft. (3 m) tall, and almost unlimited power density—as of this writing, two U.S. government agencies are in discussions with Terremark to host a hardware deployment requiring 1,000 watts per sq. ft. (10,763.9 watts per sq. m) of power and cooling.

Although the scale of the Data Center seems daunting, the abundance of its physical infrastructure elements—space, power, and cooling—are actually its greatest strength, providing design and operational flexibility not usually available in smaller installations.

Ben Stewart, senior vice president of Facilities Engineering for Terremark, discusses why bigger has proven to be better for the NAP of the Americas.

The Interview

What drove the decision to locate this facility in Miami?

If you look on the Eastern seaboard of the U.S. all the transoceanic cables come in to New York or Florida. Most of the Florida cable systems service Central and South America, though we do have Columbus 3 which comes over from the Mediterranean into the South Florida coast.

All those cable heads come into south Florida and they had to find a place where they could peer their traffic. They were buying tail circuits up to Ashburn,

Chicago, and other major peering centers to conduct that. So, a consortium pooled their money to build a facility in Miami where all these cable heads turn up in to and actually staged their traffic right here in Miami. Terremark, a real estate development company at the time, won the contract to build this facility and then somewhere through that process decided that it was going to shift its business model and become a designer, operator, and owner of these kind of facilities around the world.

So that's really the genesis of the facility. It was the cable heads coming in to South Florida and needing a place to terminate in to and exchange their traffic with all of the terrestrial carriers as well. We now have 172 carriers inside this building who are exchanging traffic with each other.

So it was as part of this Data Center project that Terremark decided it wanted to get into the co-location business?

Yeah. Manuel D. Medina was our CEO at the time. That was right at the time when Internet was really getting hot and heavy and also when it busted, in the 2000/2001 time frame. Nonetheless he saw that as the absolute future for telcos and everybody and that's when he shifted gears. He had the vision and he wanted to dive into it and certainly must have had hundreds of doubts.

I didn't join the company until 2003 but during 2000/2001 right during the dot bomb when you build a facility of this size—750,000 sq. ft. (66,677.3 sq. m)—and all those cable heads coming up and carriers coming in and to have the Internet bubble burst on you just as you open your doors had to be a very trying time but of course over the years has proven to be the secret sauce. It was just a brilliant move.

As a huge co-location facility you obviously support a variety of customers with different physical infrastructure needs. What's the upper limit to the power density that you can support for a given customer space?

Most of our co-location floors are in the 40,000 to 50,000 sq. ft. (3,716.1 to 4,645.2 sq. m) range and with that kind of floor space we can accommodate almost anything.

We don't meter our power, we charge by the whip. And the more power you buy the more cooling you're obviously paying for with that. So it's really up to us to figure out how we're going to deliver that cooling.

Obviously each floor is designed and built to some power density. For instance our second floor, which is the first floor we built more than 10 years ago, it was designed and built to 80 watts per sq. ft. (861.1 watts per sq. m). But that's over roughly 80,000/90,000 sq. ft. (7,432.2/8,361.2 sq. m) of white space so we can move that cooling around very easily. And in the early days we had a lot of carriers coming in at about 30 to 35 watts per sq. ft. (322.9 to 376.7 watts per sq. m).

On the other side of our floor we've got a customer pulling down about 300 to 400 watts per sq. ft. (3,229.2 to 4,305.6 watts per sq. m). And we have no problem delivering that because that's just static pressure under the floor. You throw more tiles down and you get the air in there that they need to cool those servers.

With such large floors we don't dictate that to our customers. We're in the business of making this space work for any customer that could ever possibly want to come in here and we've built and designed that sort of flexibility into our floors.

What's the most extreme request that you have had to accommodate?

A customer came in with some mainframe type of equipment, some real high power type stuff and they're running probably in the 300 to 400 watts per sq. ft. (3,229.2 to 4,305.6 watts per sq. m) range in a very small area. That's probably our heaviest one in this facility.

How does it influence your Data Center design, knowing that you're going to have to accommodate a range of client needs? How do you ensure that you have flexibility within your infrastructure?

On the cooling side, which is usually the more difficult side because you can distribute power from other floors and things, it's really the raised floor. The raised floor and the ability to move our cooling around by moving perforated tiles.

I read a lot about people talking especially on the enterprise side going away from raised floors and building directly on the slab and ducting the cold air and ducting the hot air out. That's a great idea, energy efficiency-wise that's probably one of the better ways to go. But when you do a build-it-and-they-will-come model where you've really got to have the flexibility and you don't know who is coming or how much they're going to need and you're designing their layouts on the fly, that raised floor just provides an enormous amount of flexibility.

FIGURE 17-2   An unoccupied hosting area within Terremark's NAP of the Americas facility.

How long did it take to design and build the NAP of the Americas facility?

We're really designing it on an ongoing basis.

When the site was originally built we only built out the second floor, so the design basis and the build was only to power and cool the second floor. As we go from floor to floor we continue to modify that design basis as we learn things and try new things on an energy efficiency basis. Each floor is just a little bit different as we go.

The time period to design this, they started construction in August of 2000 and opened the doors operationally in June of 2001 so it was less than a year to put this entire structure up. It was built on a parking lot so it is a purpose-built building. But the design was only about 6 months and design was ongoing as they constructed the facility, to include adding floors.

You mention changing your design and build approach based on what you have learned. What are some of the things in recent buildouts that you didn't do originally?

The second most recent one is that we put in a drop ceiling so we have a hot air plenum as well. Now not only do we move our cold aisles by moving our perforated tiles we move our hot aisles by moving egg crate that's hanging in the drop ceiling above. So even on a better basis we're separating our hot air from our cold air and then taking the CRACs (computer room air conditioners) and putting them straight up into the hot air plenum. We're sucking the hot air out of the hot aisle instead of letting it just naturally convect up in the overhead and pull off to the perimeter coolers.

I say two times ago because we improved on that a little bit more. That proved to be very difficult for our cable management systems because, again, we build it out in advance. Having that drop ceiling in there and trying to put Allthread up into the overhead to drop trapezes and ladder rack and stuff down to run cable management to where our customers want to be proved to be pretty challenging. We modified that a little bit by using something called Unistrut. We put in a big green grid overhead of all of our floors where we hang our lighting and our cable management and everything. When we did the drop ceiling that conflicted with that so we got the Armstrong drop ceiling folks together with our Unistrut folks and now we actually build the drop ceiling into that Unistrut so it doesn't conflict with our cable management in any way, shape, or form. So we can still have the benefit of the hot air plenum without the operational complexity of trying to calculate your cable management in advance so it doesn't conflict with the drop ceiling—it's all one now.

When I interview most Data Center designers I typically ask what they would do differently if they had an opportunity to go back and design their facility again. That doesn't seem applicable here because you're getting to design sections of the facility on an ongoing basis.

Excellent point. That's exactly right, because as we do each floor we learn a little bit more.

We have a facility up in Culpepper, Virginia, where we're building individual 50,000 sq. ft. (4,645.2 sq. m) pods on 30 acres (12.1 hectares)—in fact, we just bought another 30 acres (12.1 hectares) so it's going to be a 60 acre (24.3 hectares) piece of property. The original design on the original 30 was to build five 50s. So A was our first one, we built B and C, we're in the process of D. I tell people that by the time we build E we're going to want to burn A down.

FIGURE 17-3   Clients use cabinets up to 10 feet (3 meters) tall in Terremark's Data Center.

Are there any early installations where you can't wait for them to become vacant so that you can go back and re-design them because you know much more now?

On our second floor, back when we were first just trying to stay alive and put customers on the floor, we kind of allowed customers to go on the floor wherever they wanted, however they wanted, oriented any way they wanted. So our cold aisle/hot aisle orientation is not optimal in the way that we actually had some customers come in and orient their servers. They're sucking air in from the hot aisle and blowing hot air out into the cold aisle. We've had to come in and take them down and turn them around because we just couldn't tolerate that.

I would love to distribute the carriers around a little more. When we built out the second floor we built from the west to the east so on one side of the building we've got a whole bunch of 35 watts per sq. ft. (376.7 watts per sq. m) customers and on the other side of the floor we've got a whole bunch of 400 watts per sq. ft. (4,305.6 watts per sq. m) customers. Kind of would liked to have mixed that up a little better, but when you're in a constrained revenue environment there are certain things you have to do to just stay alive.

That makes sense. Even for companies with in-house Data Centers if they undergo huge growth surges it requires discipline and foresight to closely manage installations and not allow the drive to bring hardware online rapidly to take precedence over everything else.

You're absolutely right. Engineering and Operations, one group wants to stick to the rules and the other ones say they can't stick to the rules. It's a constant battle. It's a yin and yang sort of thing, but the business model will vet out what the right answer is.

Although you're building this facility incrementally its capacities are much larger overall than most other Data Centers. Did any challenges come with designing and building a server environment on such an immense scale?

To be honest with you I would say the opposite—it made it a bit easier. Because we have so much power and so much cooling that we can spread around to so many different places, that kind of flexibility has made it easy for us to bring customers in and when they wanted something very unique show them the unique things we could do for them. A lot of the other places they have been to take a look (they are told), 'Here are your three choices, which one works for you?'

We've got all this white space and all this pressure under the floor and all this power distribution capability that we haven't distributed yet. You tell me what you want and we can work with you. Having so much capacity in terms of space, power, and cooling to move around—the built-in flexibility to do that—it's proven to be pretty powerful. If we just had a bunch of 2,000 sq. ft. (185.8 sq. m) rooms that would be a lot more difficult to do.

Your standby infrastructure includes to rotary UPS (uninterruptible power supply) systems rather than conventional battery UPS systems. While those are becoming more common for new Data Centers today, they weren't the default choice when your facility came online in 2001. What prompted Terremark to use them?

I can go on for hours about that. Quite honestly, in your book *Grow a Greener Data Center* you address that pretty well: the smaller footprint, no need to environmentally control at 77 degrees (25 Celsius) the large battery strings and to replace the battery strings every 3 to 5 years to the tune of $100,000 per battery system, et cetera, et cetera. All those things apply here.

When we talk to people who say 'I've got to have my 10, 12, 15, 20 minutes of UPS' I always ask why. Because nobody's mechanical systems are on UPS. And with the power density you've got in Data Centers nowadays—our floors start heating up very, very quickly if we have a bump in our cooling. I don't think we can go a minute before we're going to have servers start shutting themselves down or overheat. So if you have anything more than a minute of UPS it's wasted money, wasted capital, wasted maintenance because the floor will not tolerate anything more than a minute.

We say we've got 15, 20 seconds worth of flywheel backup at full load, which we're not at so we in fact have something larger than that. The generators here start in 1.2 seconds. Generators at some of our other sites that are on a little different topology start in 10 seconds. NEC (National Electric Code) requires a generator to start in 10 seconds. Give yourself 50 percent margin, call it 15 seconds. Who needs more than that?

And if you've got proper redundancy built in to your systems, as all quality Tier III/Tier IV sites have, you don't need anything more than that. You can even tolerate failures and still keep the load up.

Your facility has satellite dishes on the roof that provide backup connectivity in the event a problem occurs with your fiber cabling. What can you tell me about them?

The dishes on the roof, there are two 16.4 m. (53.8 ft.) C-band dishes and then the smaller one that looks more like a geodesic dome that's an 11 m. (36.1 ft.) Ku-band dish. Those are all pointed to commercial satellites and on the other side wherever the customer is—I really can't talk too much about who's actually using those services—they just put a small VSAT (very small aperature terminal satellite communication system) up on the side of their building and if for any reason they were to lose their terrestrial connectivity—a fiber system went down, a central office caught fire, or something—we can just switch over to the satellite modems. It's obviously not at the same bandwidth but at a lower bandwidth reestablish that connection to the VSAT terminal sitting on the side of their building going across that commercial satellite.

That's not a technology commonly used at a co-location facility, is it?

No, none of our other centers have done this. This one customer that I'm speaking of is unique and very risk averse. Even with our large customer base—we have thousands of customers deployed at this facility here in Miami—there are only two or three using this service and they're all kind of linked. It's not common at all.

Was this something you had in mind during the initial construction of the facility?

No. Absolutely not. We've learned so much from this facility. For instance, when it was first built we never envisioned in a million years that the U.S. government would want to be inside here, however in retrospect the Southern Command is here (so) it makes perfectly good sense for them to be here.

The Southern Command's area of operations is Central and South America and all those cable systems come into this building. So when they're running it off down there sometimes they need to hook up some terrestrial circuits in a real hurry. If you want to hook up to something in a real hurry—what they call zero mile connectivity—all the carriers are right here in the building. We put in a cross-connect and you're up as long as the tail circuit is on the other end, you're up and running right away. We're turning up circuits for the Southern Command in hours that used to take them 6 to 9 months.

We never envisioned that before. Satellite dishes on the roof? Absolutely not. In fact we had mapped out the entire roof because we don't have a lot of equipment yard here. Everything has got to go on the roof. We had mapped out the entire roof for 7,000 tons of chiller up there, how we would lay it out and how we would grow into it.

When the need for the satellite dishes came around we had to consume an awful lot of that real estate on the roof for the dishes. That was not planned. However, all the dunnage was built onto the roof of the chillers and as luck would have it we were able to saddle off the weight to the columns straight down to the bedrock. We were able to pull it off. Again, that flexibility for these customers that wanted it here. And now we've gone to a more vertical style chiller to account for the lost square footage on the roof.

FIGURE 17-4   Four inch (10.2 centimeter) conduits turn up into Terremark's building from an outside underground vault. In the conduits are innerduct with fiber optic cable and pull strings protruding from the innerduct.

A lot of what's built at your facility is driven by the needs of specific customers, but do you feel that the design elements overall are universal and can be installed in any Data Center or are they point solutions that are only appropriate in certain circumstances?

There are point solutions, but these are things anybody can use anywhere and they are being used anywhere and if they had floors this size they would be doing it this way. Like I say, it gives you that kind of flexibility.

When I refer to point solutions, we do have some customers that are in 2,000 sq. ft. (185.8 sq. m) suites. We do have some of those here, which incidentally were originally designed to be the battery rooms and instead we went with rotary UPS and we opened them up to be sold as private suites.

Sometimes it gets so hot in those rooms that if you put downflow coolers in there you wouldn't be able to put any cabinets in because they were going to consume so much power. So we went to cold aisle containment and in-row cooler technology inside those rooms. That would be a point solution example of how we accommodated high power density in a very small room, where we just couldn't get enough air handlers in there to handle it directly.

With all of the retrofits and expansions that you have done along the way, even though you're only working with one facility it seems like you have actually built multiple Data Centers.

You're absolutely right.

Do you have a Data Center design philosophy or general advice to offer someone as they approach a Data Center project?

Yes and no.

We build co-location centers, which are a little different animal. So there are things that I would say are true for co-location centers which would probably be absolutely not true for an enterprise builder. For instance, I get all the Data Center (industry) newsletters and when I read about the Facebook project in Prineville, I drool at that. They own all those servers—they're building their own servers with big heat syncs on them, really cool stuff. With a co-location center, what are we going to tell our customers, 'We love to have you come here, we'll sell you some square footage but you've got to build your own servers.' We've got to meet everybody's needs.

If we had a customer come to us and say 'I need about 30,000 sq. ft. (2,787.1 sq. m). I need you to fence that off for me, and I need you to help me come up with a really, really energy efficient solution just for my 30,000 sq. ft. (2,787.1 sq. m),' what a ball that would be, because now all that flexibility isn't required anymore. We can do anything we want inside that space because we know the hardware that's going in there, all of the variables that we have to consider on the outside somehow suddenly become fixed constants and we can design to that.

I love it when people say 'I've seen Data Centers, they're all the same.' I disagree. Data Centers are like fingerprints, they're all so very different. You can class them and categorize them but even within their categories they change they're so very different. In a co-location environment it's very simple, we're in the business of selling space. We want to consume as little of it as possible yet keep it as flexible as possible—(those are) almost diametrically opposed, but nonetheless that is our goal when we go out and look at white space to develop and grow. Use as little of it as you have to for your own stuff but keep it as flexible as you possibly can. And that doesn't work for an enterprise. That would be ridiculous.

"Data Centers are like fingerprints, they're all so very different. You can class them and categorize them but even within their categories they change they're so very different."

That's interesting to hear. Data Center capacity was primarily defined by physical space for decades, until the 2000s when high-density hardware made capacity about power and cooling for most companies. But you're saying that for your business Data Center capacity still comes down to physical space.

Correct. Well, we'll usually run out of power and cooling before we'll run out of space but we are very, very careful about how we carve up our space for our customers.

I'm sure you've read about our cloud environment. We're very virtualized and virtualizing increases your power density. You're putting the same amount of compute into a smaller area. It doesn't really save you a lot in the way of energy, although some people are quoting about 15 percent of power savings by piling it all over into one corner. But by piling it over in one corner just complicates your cooling solution. Yet that's a good thing to do because it frees up more white space that you can build more power and cooling and customers in to. It's a dynamic.

When most people think of virtualization I don't know if they necessarily think it being offered by a co-location facility. How does virtualization play into your facility?

Well, virtualization on our side is on our own IT equipment. You've got these huge facilities full of IT equipment and people always ask us 'How many servers are you supporting?' I don't know. They don't belong to us. And when we calculate our PUE and our efficiency people ask 'what are you doing on the IT side of the equation?' Nothing, because it doesn't belong to us. It belongs to our customers.

It would behoove our customers to put in more efficient power supplies in their servers so they had to buy less power from us. It would lower their opex and all that does is really give us back power we can sell to somebody else. But we do have our own IT infrastructure and that's the cloud, managed services as well as our cloud computing.

What we found is the cloud computing environment, which is a very small part of our floor because it's virtualized, it actually gives us an opportunity to do that enterprise thing. Now we can take that IT equipment that belongs to us—all our customers care about is they can get into it and turn up compute, down compute, storage up and down, network up and down. As long as they can get into it and do what they need to do and it is up 100 percent of the time, they don't care what we're running our cold aisle at. They don't care how we're managing that room in there. So suddenly we now have the freedom to go in there and do some of the things like they're doing up in Prineville. In fact, if we wanted to build our own servers to support that cloud environment we could do that, too. In this huge floor we've got this little area over on the side which is our cloud footprint that allows us to do some of that enterprise stuff. It's actually kind of exciting for us, but we have very little of it on a percentage-of-floor basis.

You are, by necessity and design, getting to use a lot of different Data Center technologies in your facility.

This is a playground.

FIGURE 17-5   An enclosed hosting area within Terremark's NAP of the Americas facility.

Anything out there that you haven't had a chance to employ that you're hoping to?

I keep reading about more and more of these places like the Yahoo! Data Center in Lockport or Facebook's Data Center in Prineville using this evaporative cooling where they're actually building a center with no chillers. They aren't installing any chillers at all. We aren't building up in those latitudes that allow us to do that, but we do use waterside free cooling, airside free cooling. Obviously no free cooling here in Miami but some of our other sites where free cooling makes some sense we're able to do that.

But we really haven't been able to get into the evaporative cooling part of the world yet. It's something we're always looking at because it's obviously going to save us a great deal of money in terms of utility, a lot of opex savings. The other side of it too, though, we don't evaporate any water at all. All of our chillers, everything is air cooled. We see that as a risk. Right now all of the focus is on Data Centers and the amount of energy they consume. You're already starting to read some things about how much water they're consuming and where their water sources are and where their backup water sources are. It's kind of nice when we have a customer come to us and grill us about those sorts of things and we get to the water piece and they ask 'What's your backup water supply?' We don't need any water. We don't use water. We don't evaporate water. We have no evaporative cooling.

So, right now we don't have that anywhere. Yet I keep reading about the benefits of it and places with no chillers. How exciting is that? Would love to explore that a little bit further, but currently we're just not in any area dry enough to allow us to do that.

Any final thoughts that you would offer someone approaching a Data Center project? Any lessons learned as you have solved issues for various customers needing Data Center capabilities?

When we solve them for our customers usually they're coming to us because they're tired of trying to do it for themselves. But I do talk to and deal with other companies and people in professional associations, people who are trying to still roll their own, trying to do it for themselves.

My only advice to them is, Data Centers have a lot of moving parts. People think they're very simple, they're very straightforward and there really isn't that much to it. Even if you just break it down electrically and mechanically, there are a lot of moving parts, a lot of options. There's no one model that's perfect for anybody. There are tradeoffs, there are pros and cons. They really need to partner with somebody else who has got that kind of experience or take the time to develop that experience on their own through their own study to really make those kinds of decisions for themselves. I have seen so many Data Centers designed for an enterprise that did not take into account anything to do with their business model or what it is they were trying to do. And they were just miserably disappointed with the product that they got because it doesn't support their business because nobody took that into account.

Even some of your large companies out there will just go to a major A&E firm and say 'I need a 100,000 sq. ft. (9,290.3 sq. m) Data Center.' The firm says 'Ok, well what for?' 'I don't know, I just need it.' And they get a Data Center and it's built to Tier III or something to that effect and they get in there and say, 'This isn't working for us at all. It's not shaped right, it's not powered right, it doesn't have the flexibility.' Yet all those things seem to come out afterwards, and that's because the people doing the buying and the people doing the building didn't shake hands very well.

There are just a lot of moving parts, a lot of things to consider. I love it when someone comes to me and says 'Ah, a Data Center is a Data Center. Yeah, there are some differences but in the end they're all the same.' I just smile and say 'My God I hope you never build one.'

FIGURE 17-6   Distributing cooling beneath a raised floor and strategically placing perforated floor tiles gives Terremark maximum flexibility to support customer deployments.

FIGURE 18-1   The Yahoo! Computing Coop in Lockport, New York employs no chillers or mechanical refrigeration. Images provided courtesy of Yahoo!

CHAPTER 18
Yahoo!

ORGANIZATION: Yahoo!	
LOCATION: Lockport, New York	
ONLINE: September 2010	
NOTABLE FEATURES: No chillers or mechanical refrigeration. Airside economization and evaporative cooling system. Hot aisle containment. Rotary UPS. Shared space for electrical and IT infrastructure.	
TIME TO DESIGN AND BUILD: 9 months from ground-breaking to commissioning	
SIZE: 190,000 sq. ft. (17,651.6 sq. m) total	
POWER: 20 MW	
TIER: Varies	
CABINET LOCATIONS: 2,800	
POWER DENSITY: Undisclosed	
INFRASTRUCTURE DELIVERY: Power, cabling, and cooling infrastructure are delivered overhead	
STRUCTURAL LOADING: Undisclosed	
FIRE SUPPRESSION SYSTEM: Dual interlock, pre-action dry pipe	

Twenty miles east of Niagara Falls sits a cluster of pre-fabricated metal structures. With louvers on two sides, angled roofs and a cupola rising above their centerline, they are oriented to maximize space on the property and take advantage of prevailing winds.

The buildings were designed with a nod to chicken coops and their natural ventilation, but shelter powerful computing equipment rather than poultry. Welcome to the Yahoo! Computing Coop.

Thanks in part to western New York's cool weather and Yahoo!'s willingness to exceed ASHRAE (American Society of Heating, Refrigerating and Air-Conditioning Engineers) temperature and humidity guidelines, the facility operates without chillers or refrigeration. An evaporative cooling system is in place but typically used less than 3 percent of the year.

The online search giant created the coop design after testing hardware in extreme environmental conditions and challenging a fundamental design issue: could they build an effective Data Center without mechanical refrigeration? Doing so has resulted not only in reduced capital and operational costs, but also improved availability by not relying on a complex mechanical system.

Yahoo! has subsequently deployed the design, which earned a $9.9 million sustainability grant from the U.S. Department of Energy, at Data Centers in the state of Washington and Switzerland.

Yahoo!'s Christina Page, Global Director, Energy and Sustainability Strategy; Nick Holt, Director Global Data Center Facilities Operations; Paul Bonaro, Data Center Facilities Manager in Lockport, New York, and Bob Lytle, Data Center Development Project Manager, discuss the design and operation of the Yahoo! Computing Coop.

The Interview

What factors prompted you to locate the Data Center in western New York?

Paul: One of the criteria the site selection committee looked at was the weather. To implement this design requires a certain weather profile. That was the number one driver in being able to deploy this technology. The other was proximity to renewable energy and hydro power. That was a major factor. And a location where all the other criteria that would go into a Data Center site could be met.

Chris: Access to power that was both green and affordable was a key component. Some other factors were network connectivity from multiple providers and reasonably priced land. Tax benefits and the first-rate workforce present in the state of New York also played an important role.

That's interesting. You didn't choose the site and then come up with the design. You planned to use this design and went looking for a place where you could leverage the climate to accomplish it.

Chris: Correct.

This Data Center is best known for how it's cooled. Can you walk me through how that's done?

Paul: Essentially there's an air handling system for the computer room segments that takes in outside air, filters the air, and then there are fans that move it into the room. That air handler makes use of return air from the IT equipment to mix with outside air to achieve the set point. That's all done through building controls and automation with outside air and return air damper systems.

The only means of cooling that we use is the evaporative cooling system, which we deploy when we exceed our desired set point. The evaporative cooling system is a passive cooling system that uses tap water—no artificial means of pressurization or anything like that—and evaporative media to cool the air that's coming in through that air handler.

That creates the cold aisle temperature or inlet temperature to the racks that we desire, and then we use hot aisle containment. Hot aisle containment captures the heat off of the back of the cabinets and discharges it through the top of what you may have seen as the chicken coop in pictures of the site. That air is not recycled unless we want to use it to warm the air in the cooler months to reach our set point.

I understand you were very precise with the cooling design, down to the point of how the buildings are oriented so as to take advantage of how the wind blows across the property.

Nick: The reasoning for the buildings being tilted like they are was actually two-fold. One was position on the land that made the most effective use of the land itself. Additionally, you didn't want a building that dumped hot air onto itself. Positioning the building in a certain way would allow the prevailing winds to push the exhaust heat away from the building. When you placed the building you wanted to make sure you didn't locate it where the prevailing winds would push the hot exhaust into the intake. So the alignment of the building was based off prevailing winds but it wasn't a major design factor, but rather a positioning factor.

FIGURE 18-2
Yahoo! positioned its Data Center buildings to maximize space on the property and to ensure exhaust heat was blown away from the structures.

I've seen both hot and cold aisle containment used in Data Centers. What caused you to favor hot aisle containment?

Nick: As you go through the history of the change of the Data Center model from more of an open floor plan to more of the hot and cold aisle configurations, initially cold aisle configurations were set up because the distribution of the cold air was via raised floor, under that floor to the front of the aisles. As soon as raised floors went away, and we moved away from distribution of air under the floor tiles to air from in front of the servers, it became possible to do hot aisle containment.

So, a big change that came from cold aisle containment to hot aisle containment was because we were no longer distributing with a raised floor. That allowed you to open the front of the servers up and not have to wonder where the air was coming from specifically but wonder where it's coming from fundamentally, because as you open the room up the whole room became the cold aisle versus just right in front of the cabinet. So, that was the reasoning behind transitioning from cold aisle containment to hot aisle containment.

Was the decision to forgo a raised floor tied to the use of the cooling design?

Nick: The reasoning for removal of the raised floor was that it was not needed. Designs that do not have under floor distribution of air can still use raised floor—we do that in some locations, for cabling and for infrastructure under the floor. But you can do cabling above the cabinets, so in most cases raised floors aren't needed.

Paul: It's a huge savings on construction, too. Massive.

Nick: And structurally as well. You had to make all these cabinet positions be structurally sound on a raised floor and it's a lot easier to do it on slab.

Bob: And when you're building from a green field you actually have the option of running it all in conduits under the slab, which you wouldn't be able to do in, say, an existing building which might make it tougher to go with a non-raised floor. You would be running so much overhead.

Do you consider the design elements of this facility to be universal? Could anyone implement this in a Data Center, or is the design meant to serve a particular function in a particular location?

Nick: Here's my input regarding the design and implementation. It has to be done in climates that accept outside air economization. Period. That's the bottom line. It has to meet the fundamentals, to utilize the air outside.

Let me discuss co-location. You as a co-location provider can provide a YCC (Yahoo Computing Coop) pod to somebody. You could sell pods versus rows and racks.

The YCC building design is universal. It's not just enterprise companies, it's not Fortune 500. It can be your mom and pop co-los that can use the same technology. It's really just about understanding the fundamentals of air distribution and also the dynamics of thermodynamics.

Paul: And it can work on any scale. You can go down as small as you want. The building is essentially a modular design just repeated over and over again. It doesn't have to be a multi-megawatt facility to utilize the techniques.

Is there a maximum power density that this design can accommodate, leveraging outside air, either per cabinet or on a watts per square foot basis?

Nick: I'd say no at this point. Because you're controlling the cold aisles, but the (ultimate) control point is the hot aisle. So as long as your hot aisle doesn't overheat then, yeah, you can deploy anything you want in there.

What was the inspiration for the Data Center's cooling design? I love the thought of someone at Yahoo! sitting at their desk, looking out the window and suddenly thinking of a chicken coop, but was it that easy?

Nick: I'll take you on a short journey of how we got there. We start with YTC (Yahoo Thermal Cooling), which is our design regarding cold aisle encapsulation with cooling coils. Basically, take the cooling coil out of a CRAC (computer room air conditioner) unit, place it between the two rows of servers, and let the servers move the air. That design was based off of getting rid of CRAC units because CRAC units of course draw a lot of energy. They take up a lot of space and they're maintenance intensive.

That was to resolve an issue regarding CRAC units. When we went into the YCC design the basis was basically like a circus tent. Why do we need all these components that we have inside the Data Center? Why can't we just use the fresh air that's outside? Utilizing different tests that we did by placing cabinets outside and all these other tests that we completed prior to the mockup of the actual design, we decided we didn't need all those components that currently were inside a legacy Data Center. It was really trying to think outside the box and decide can we do this? Well, we determined that we could.

We also determined that we didn't need all the control points, the stringent humidity requirements, the stringent temperature requirements. They were no longer needed and were a legacy from punch card days when keeping humidity between 45 and 55 percent was required to keep punch cards from sticking. That wasn't required anymore. As long as we keep a consistent temperature and a tempered humidity we were going to be fine. And that's what drove us to this design.

FIGURE 18-3   Power, cooling, and cabling infrastructure are delivered overhead to cabinet locations in Yahoo's Lockport Data Center.

Was it a case of realizing that hardware is robust enough that you don't need to follow strict operational guidelines?

Nick: See, we still stay within the guidelines. The manufacturer's specs are the manufacturer's specs. It's just that we realized that those specs are pretty wide open. When you tell me you can run a server at very high temperatures, then I'm going to run it that high.

That's additionally the internal distribution of the electrical system. If the manufacturer tells operators that a PDU (power distribution unit) can operate at high temperatures, then we push the equipment temperatures to the higher temperatures.

That drove the industry to a) recognize some great opportunities that were available and then b) it was an opportunity for the server manufacturers to understand that 72 degrees (22.2 Celsius) isn't always the best and required. Now, granted, at 72 degrees (22.2 Celsius) the servers do run at a lower temperature, which makes them run at a lower load, but it's not required for operation 24 hours a day, seven days a week.

Paul: There was the wide discrepancy between the server manufacturer operating ranges and the ASHRAE guidelines. You see ASHRAE consistently expanding their guidelines to accommodate designs like this and I think this just took that a few steps further.

Having looked to the manufacturer's specifications during design, now that the Data Center is operational have you had any hardware that hasn't performed under those conditions?

Nick: We've found no gear—we're talking strictly servers, we're not talking tape libraries, media, stuff like that, that's a different story—we've found no server that's not able to withstand the temperatures and humidity ranges that we're operating in, no.

How long did it take to design and build the first phase of the site?

Nick: We went from YTC design straight in to YCC. So, for the design length of time is kind of a fluid number, because of the different types of testings that we did complete. To go from a fundamental theory to an actual design was probably six months and then you've got to work yourself in to engineering and all that stuff to get an actual design.

What did some of that testing entail?

Nick: The local testing, what we did basically is a mockup. We mocked this entire building up and basically had inlet restrictions. We created restrictions with filters and stuff like that and laid the configuration of the racks a certain way that we wanted the air to flow past them. And we tried the atomization of air with water, which didn't work. Basically it got the servers all wet like a rainforest.

We then went to a media which is like a swamp cooler media, versus the atomized air concept that saturated everything, and found that when we tested the swamp cooler approach everything worked great. During that day we did two tests. One was heat the building up really, really high, to about 104 degrees (40 Celsius), and then allowed the moisture to cool the air. We additionally added humidity to the air to see the fundamentals of what happened at the server level with elevated humidity as well as elevated temperatures. We were able to get a full swing of data from from one extreme to the next extreme.

Additionally, we tested the low temperature side, using recirculation. When you put in cold air to a Data Center that's actually worse than putting in hot air, because if you have a Data Center sitting in high temperatures and you blast it with low temperature air you're going to break some stuff. So, the solder joints will be sitting at high temperature and you'll hit it with extremely cold air, the solder joints will retract and the servers will break themselves.

So testing the high temperature as well as the low temperature as well as the air distribution flow, in a controlled environment with data collection, were all important.

Did you find a sweet spot? Conditions that were ideal to operate within that you then wanted to try and find in nature?

Nick: It's not so much a temperature you create; it's the consistency you create. You can run a server at 90 degrees (32.2 Celsius) inlet if you'd like, but you need to do that continuously and consistently. Don't go up and down, up and down, up and down. You can run a server at 50 degrees (10 Celsius) but don't do that inconsistently. It's all about consistent temperatures is what really is the saver.

Paul: Like Nick was saying, controlling the rate of change is obviously a big concern when you're talking about outside air. I described that recirculation feature before where we can hold a set point. That rate of change is very easy for us to control during most conditions throughout the year. And then when we are subject to the rate of change that the outside air throws at us, it's really not an issue at that point, which would be more toward your summer months.

We also find that in western New York, for most of the year you can run at however low a temperature you want in the computer rooms without having to increase mechanical loads, which is kind of a unique feature of a building of this design. Whereas a server might consume less power at lower inlet temperatures, if the server fans are driving off of server inlet temperature, most Data Centers would have to increase their mechanical horsepower to drop that inlet temperature. Here in Lockport, we can mix the temperature to wherever we want without increasing any mechanical loads. The dampers just adjust to a different open or closed position. It's kind of a unique feature we're taking advantage of here, to find like you said that sweet spot for a computer room and for the servers within it to operate.

And this still is well within what would be considered a traditional kind of environment for them temperature-wise. In the summer we don't get extreme dry bulb temperatures too often. But what we do look at that affects a lot of our systems here would be the outside air dew point. Because we lack humidity control, we're subject to whatever the outside air dew point is, so monitoring that and understanding how that will affect our building systems is more important in a facility like this than it would be in a traditional Data Center.

FIGURE 18-4
A worker stands inside the cupola atop one of the Yahoo! Computing coops. Hardware exhaust is discharged out of the building from here.

You obviously wanted this Data Center to be energy efficient. What other design principles did Yahoo! follow when designing the facility?

Nick: We wanted to operate it with the least amount of mechanical load possible. We wanted to basically eliminate cooling. That's the bottom line. It sounds simplistic but that was really the design principle, just completely eliminate cooling.

Paul: Along with that, the elimination of complex mechanical systems. Once you identify all of the failure modes of the new design, your availability is increased because you're not dependent on complex mechanicals. I've been in Data Centers where it's winter outside but they've overheated because a chilled water pump failed. You can't just open a window in those kinds of Data Centers. But that is what we do here—we can open those windows.

If you're asking about availability perspective, that's one of those things that I don't think you had to have this design criteria per se because it was inherent within the reduction of that complexity.

Chris: Frequently reducing your complexity increases reliability; it also reduces cost. That was one of the things here. Cost effectiveness and reliability were priority one. I think people have this mental model that when you're talking about energy efficiency or green, it's going to be more expensive up front and you really have to sweat the payback period. In some cases, especially with the simplicity of design, it can be cheaper and faster to build.

You're supporting this Data Center with a rotary UPS (uninterruptible power supply). What prompted you to implement that rather than a conventional battery UPS?

Nick: If you look at a typical battery system, you've probably got three fundamentals that are consistent. One is the size of the installation. We've addressed that with reducing from 10 minute batteries to 5 minute batteries, which was just a fundamental reduction in battery capacity, the amount of batteries you have deployed. When we went over to a rotary system—it's called a Hitec, which is basically an induction coupling—you retract the kinetic energy out of the flywheel.

We were familiar with rotary power systems and had used them before. We liked the efficiencies with them and we looked at a couple different manufacturers and determined that Active Power is what we wanted to deploy. Our first Data Center we deployed it at was one of the largest deployments of that product in one single configuration in the world at the time. Then when we went to Lockport, we went toward a more distributed system.

Paul: The flywheels are associated with smaller loads than you typically see. Typically, in the past when they've been deployed, you see megawatt or greater chunks of flywheels grouped together and feeding out to large sections of computer room. The units here are distributed more in like what would be traditionally seen as a PDU-sized segment of power. This for us reduces some of the risk associated with operating those systems by virtue of affecting a smaller chunk of power with each transfer or whatever we're doing with the system, such as maintenance. It also fits into the modular philosophy of the building very well.

You've got a group of equipment associated with one system, associated with a segment of the cooling system. It makes it very repeatable here. It allows you to scale in a more controlled fashion, versus building out a massive segment of power and then filling it up we can reduce the time needed to deploy a segment of this thing.

Were there any surprises that came up during design or construction?

Nick: Yeah, it actually worked. Some of the testing we did I looked at and I thought to myself, 'Wow, there's no way.' Then you would look at it and think 'Hey, that's pretty cool.' There were a lot of people in a big room looking at each other, thinking 'Wow. This actually works.' It was enlightening.

Paul: Last summer would have been our first summer really operating with a significant load in the building. If you look at the weather history for western New York last year it was a very, very hot summer. It was like the third hottest July on record. So right away we got to validate the design in what you would call extreme or design conditions.

I think that was fortunate, that we weren't living with something for three or four or five years and then got hit with something extreme and maybe at that point had to question how we do things. It was still relatively new. The team, we're constantly learning about the building, obviously, but at that point we knew we were going to have some challenges in the summer just trying to figure out how best to tune equipment and to optimize equipment. We were already in that mode. We had a lot of the resources available at our headquarters with Nick and the team there, as well as members of the design team that were still engaged. It was nice to have a challenge like that come along right away.

Nick: That was one of the blessings that we got. We got that early enough in the design that we were able to play with it before we were playing with it with a full deck.

Chris: Paul has a really nice slide summarizing some of the extreme events of July 2011. I'm looking at it right now. It mentions things like it was the third warmest July in 141 years of data, warmest single month in 56 years, 30 of 31 days over 80 degrees Fahrenheit (26.7 Celsius) high temperature.

It was like Mother Nature gave us a little test run. That was pretty extreme, and the Data Center functioned really well.

FIGURE 18-5   A view from inside one of the Yahoo! Computing Coop's contained hot aisles.

This is a still a relatively young facility, but if you had to go back and do the project again is there anything you would do differently?

Paul: We live with it every day and, there are small things always, but I wouldn't say anything with any of the components that were selected or the sequence of operations and things like that. We're constantly changing, but there is nothing that we would change fundamentally or that is a major hindrance for us operating the facility.

Once you kind of reset your mindset—you've been working in a traditional building for that long, you can step away from that and look at it with a fresh perspective—I wouldn't say that there's anything that we would really change too much.

Nick: This design and this build were done by operating engineers. Not by design engineers. Not by construction managers. This was done by people that actually operate Data Centers. And so with that in mind we were able to identify the stuff that we already know about. We didn't walk out and say 'Could somebody design us a Data Center?' We were actually the operators that designed the Data Center.

As an operator we know the fundamentals that we're challenged against and we were able to incorporate those in the design. Additionally, we brought Paul Bonaro's team on board so early in the process that they were able to incorporate the operational side of the Data Center immediately. Not 'We built a Data Center' and then 'Here, go run it.' Paul and his team were incorporated Day One. As soon as we identified Paul as the guy for the Data Center he was put right into the process with full authority to make decisions. I think that was one of the fundamental things that made it this way; it was built by operators.

What steps were taken in this project to coordinate IT and Facilities goals? If you're trying to design a Data Center without a conventional cooling system, that presumably requires buy-in from both IT that owns the hardware and Facilities that maintains the physical infrastructure.

Nick: Since 2005, we as an organization have run IT and Facilities under the same VP. There's no win-loss. A lot of our designs, going back to YTC designs and also the cold and hot aisle configurations, come from a true partnership between Facilities and IT. A facilities manager does the infrastructure and Site Operations does the servers and those two sit in the same office of that building.

There's no 'Oh, it's your fault,' 'Oh, I need this,' 'Oh I can't get that because Facilities…' It's one voice, one answer. And we involve IT in the design. Hell, the servers move the air. Part of our design incorporates the IT side because that's how we move the air. The fans are only to get it past the filters if we need it. And during recirculation that's not even needed. So, this was a true partnership between IT and Facilities from conception to commissioning.

Paul: I would say the same thing on the project side. I've been involved in construction projects before—not in the capacity I was here, but—a lot of times your decisions are made by a design engineer who is not an operator, who hasn't been an operator. Not that they're wrong, but without an operator's input to challenge some of the assumptions if you're not involved in the process at that point you may get handed a facility where there's a disconnect between the operating principles and the design principles.

Bob, being the project manager, was really able to facilitate a lot of that. The decisions that were made during the construction phase and getting the input from the operations teams so that the decisions made were what the operations team wanted to operate. Not what the mechanical design engineer or electrical design engineer wanted to implement because that was their principles. More so than any other project that I've worked on it really integrated into the design phase and so you knew what you were getting at the end, which is almost a luxury.

Nick: Here's an example. People stand around a table and say 'Let's go build a Data Center' and then they hire someone to do it. And what happens is, that person that actually designs your Data Center is a guy that sits in a room whacking on a keyboard on a BMS (building management system) that decides how you're going to operate your building. That's reality. Reality is that somebody who has a history of building legacy systems—if he even built a Data Center before—is the one coding your BMS or coding your controls.

We took that away. We said 'You know what? We want control of that, and we want to be able to say how it's going to work.' That was a fundamental design change for us. We took total control. And we didn't allow somebody else to come in and decide what they felt we needed to do. We just did it.

It was a change in the industry. It was very complicated at first. This guy was saying 'What about my years of experience?' Well I don't care. Because I don't need to know how a fundamental Data Center works, I need to understand how my Data Center works. And so that's how that kind of change came about.

Chris: I think an ongoing theme is the idea that the status quo isn't necessarily going to work for the Data Center of the future. And yet another good quality of the modular design is being able to continue to push the status quo. But, the status quo is tied to a lot of operations systems and BMS to a lot of things. And so challenging in design in some ways is just the first step.

Any final advice that you would offer someone who is taking on a major Data Center project?

Nick: Yeah. Get the operators involved. That's my best advice. What happens is the design engineers design things the way they have done for years. So get the operations team involved early.

"The status quo isn't necessarily going to work for the Data Center of the future."

FIGURE 18-6
The U.S. Department of Energy awarded Yahoo! a $9.9 million sustainability grant for its computing coop design.

FIGURE 18-7
Outside air is drawn in, filtered, and then moved into the Data Center with fans.

FIGURE 18-8
There are no raised floors in the data halls, saving material and construction costs.

FIGURE 18-9
Yahoo! made sure to involve its Data Center operators when developing its computing coop.

Appendix

Although this book is aimed at a general audience, a handful of Data Center industry terms crept into the conversations. Here is a brief overview of them, and why they're significant.

Availability—A Data Center's availability is the time the facility is operational and capable of providing services.

Delta T—Difference in temperature. For Data Center infrastructure, the term is typically used in reference to the difference in the inlet and outlet temperatures of a cooling device or piece of computing hardware.

Hot and cold aisles—A layout of Data Center server rows in which inlets on the front of IT hardware face an aisle designated for delivering cool air, while the hardware's exhaust is vented into a different aisle.

POP (Point of Presence)—A facility containing servers, networking devices, and call aggregators that is an access point to the Internet.

PUE (Power Usage Effectiveness)—A metric for Data Center efficiency, calculated by dividing a facility's overall power draw by the amount of power used solely by the Data Center's IT equipment. The lower (closer to 1.0) a Data Center's PUE, the more of its power is used for computing.

Rack unit—A unit of measurement for the height of internal installable space within a server cabinet. One rack unit = 1.75 in. (4.45 cm). Abbreviated as U, as in a "1U server" or a "42U server cabinet."

Tiers—A classification system for server environments based on their physical infrastructure redundancy, developed by the Data Center industry group the Uptime Institute. A Tier I Data Center has non-redundant infrastructure and a single distribution path; a Tier II Data Center has redundant capacity components and a single distribution path. A Tier III Data Center has redundant capacity components and multiple, independent distribution paths. A Tier IV Data Center has multiple, independent, physically isolated capacity components and distribution paths.

UPS (Uninterruptible Power Supply)—A standby power supply used to keep Data Center computing equipment operating for a short period of time if primary (utility) power fails. Conventional UPS systems consist of batteries; others employ a spinning flywheel.

VESDA (Very Early Smoke Detection Array)—An air-sampling device that uses a laser to check for smoke particles.